THE RESTLESS WAVE

THE RESTLESS WAVE

My two lives with John Bellany

Helen Bellany

SANDSTONEPRESS
HIGHLAND | SCOTLAND

First published in Great Britain by
Sandstone Press Ltd
Dochcarty Road
Dingwall
Ross-shire
IV15 9UG
Scotland

www.sandstonepress.com

The publisher acknowledges subsidy from
Creative Scotland towards publication of this volume.

ISBN: 978-1-912240-02-9
ISBNe: 978-1-912240-05-0

Jacket and plate sections design by Gravemaker + Scott
Typeset by Iolaire Typography Ltd, Newtonmore
Printed and bound by CPI Group (UK) Ltd, Croydon, CR0 4YY

Dedicated to someone we never met
And about whom we know nothing.

———————

With my love and admiration
For Jonathan, Paul and Anya,
My beloved children,
Whose difficult journeys brought them
To a good destination.

———————

And of course, above all,
to John.
With the last beat of my heart
I'll be blessing you

CONTENTS

Contents

List of Illustrations

Black and white and colour plates

1. Helen Percy when six years old
2. 'The Big Three' John, Alan Bold and Sandy Moffatt 1963
3. John, Castle Terrace exhibition during the Edinburgh Festival 1963
4. John's portraits of himself and Helen that he exhibited at the Edinburgh Festival 1963
5. Helen at St Abb's, Berwickshire 1963
6. Helen and John's wedding in 1964
7. Helen on honeymoon in Dieppe 1964
8. Helen with Doubtfire's coat (oil on board 151 cm x 90) 1964
9. Sandy Moffat and John, outside the Royal Scottish Academy, Festival Exhibition, 1964
10. Self-portrait of John Bellany R.A. (oil on board 121 cm x 91 x 2.4 © The Artists Estate, Royal Academy of Arts, London. Photographer John Hammond) 1966
11. Kinlochbervie (oil on board 243.5 cm x 320) 1966
12. Helen with Jonathan, Paul and baby Anya 1970
13. Paul, Jonathan and Anya 1970
14. The Bellany family at Lurline Gardens, Battersea 1971
15. Paul and Jonathan with their father in Battersea Park
16. Catalogue portrait of John 1970s

John Bellany – a personal reflection

There's a painting which has hung in the General Assembly Room at the Royal Academy in London for the past two years which haunts me every time I see it. It is rendered in oil on board and shows a face full of life and character staring off to the right and into the distance from beneath a large brimmed black hat. Behind are high clouds and a handful of soaring seagulls distantly visible. The face itself is slightly smaller than life-size but feels larger, more monumental. It is framed by hair, sideburns into whiskers into a voluminous beard but one which is emphatically cropped along the bottom giving the image a harder edge than one might expect, which in turn is echoed by the way the shoulders and arms are organised, so that the torso becomes almost but not quite a perfect square. In addition, the figure is cropped just below the rib-cage by a gilded frame surrounded by a green mount– except it is all painted as if to suggest a window or mirror, framed within a frame, a painting as a portal into another world.

The painting is, of course, a self-portrait by John Bellany. It was made in 1966 sometime towards the end of his first year in London as a post-graduate student at the Royal College of Art. He was either just or not quite 24 years old and yet the painting suggests a man of talent and vision who has lived a bit, indeed considerably more than one score year and four. His face reads, as the painter Chuck Close once put it of a

Rembrandt self-portrait, 'like a road map of human experience' and reminds me of that wonderful story told of Kokoschka, one of John's many artist heroes. Apparently, on seeing a portrait the Viennese master had made, a particular sitter complained that 'it looks nothing like me'. 'It will in time' came the reply.

I can't know for certain that the young John Bellany was necessarily envisaging his older self but it seems a distinct possibility. He was immensely self-aware as an artist and haunted by human mortality. His Calvinist upbringing, alluded to by the crucifix than hangs around his neck in the self-portrait, contributed to this as did the precarious existence of the fishermen in the community he grew up in at Port Seton. But his art seemed to be a way both of reflecting on the inevitability of death and fronting up to it.

I only got to know John in the last twenty years of his life. I say only because it feels too short. It was, however, a privilege and a pleasure; an inspiration and an education. We met through broadcasting at which he was a natural. The man you heard ruminating on Picasso or Goya on Radio 4 was no different to the man he was on the street, in the studio, in the pub. He'd stopped drinking by that time but seemed to love the ambience of bars where we would sit and talk about the thing he loved most – painting. He knew I was callow and had little clue about the deeper issues of painterly processes and traditions, but he also knew I was curious and occasionally cocky and he somehow managed to imbue me with a sense of what mattered as well as gently challenging my taste and understanding. I remember having an argument about a particular contemporary painter and he finally cut across me and said, 'life's too short to bother with mediocrity Tim. Find what you really like and spend time really looking.'

The most memorable time I spent with John was in Amsterdam in early December 1991. We had gone there to see the great Rembrandt exhibition at the Rijksmuseum and recorded a walk through the galleries for Radio 4's then daily arts programme Kaleidoscope. I managed to find a copy of the programme recently and although the holy grail would be the unedited version of our conversation – well over an hour of conversation which the producer Jerome Weatherald still hopes to find one day – the seven minute broadcast version still brings me out in Bellany/Rembrandt inspired goosebumps.

Face to face with Rembrandt's paintings and drawings and etchings, John was overwhelmed and overwhelmingly brilliant. Much is made of his affinities with Beckman and also with German and Austrian Expressionism, justifiably so, but he seemed even more engaged with the great European tradition and came to life in a way that I've rarely encountered with anyone standing in an art museum or gallery, before or since. He was not interested in the sub-text of the exhibition, namely which works were by the master and which by the studio, as recently determined by the Rembrandt Research Project. He was interested in his perception of the master and his visible, tangible achievements. Was the very young Rembrandt supremely talented or just competent I remember asking him? He looked shocked. 'God no – this is no plodder trying to get his A-levels' he said, rather wilfully overstating my implied criticism, 'this is a child prodigy ... an artist whose stupendous eye and touch conveys the deepest sense of humanity and almost brings a tear to my eye.' He went on to speak of the tenderness and love with which the Dutch master depicted his ailing son Titus. He spoke of the magnificence of 'the easy bits ... he never eases off ... every inch of the painting matters, every inch gels'.

The great, late Rembrandt self-portrait which usually hangs at Kenwood House became my favourite painting from that day after John eulogised its 'compassion and humanity'. I asked him, impossibly but necessarily for our listeners, to try and summarise Rembrandt's genius. "It's not about words', he said, 'you have to look and absorb, think and feel. That is what he is asking us to do'. Finally, pausing for breath and looking again, John concluded: 'I feel so humbled ... like a pygmy looking at these things ... yet I also feel uplifted and inspired. It just makes me want to rush back to the studio and paint my heart out'.

The book you are about to read tells the story of a man who painted his heart out until he could seemingly paint no more.

And then he painted on until he really could paint no more. Carol Weight, one of John's tutors at the Royal College and the man who gave the Bellany self-portrait I have become so captivated by to the Royal Academy, said that John 'had tremendous roots' growing up on the East coast of Scotland. The historian and critic John McEwen began his masterful monograph with the line 'John Bellany has a strange a story to tell as any painter and his talent has the match of it' which is as true and compelling an opening to an art book as I have ever encountered. Other great art writers have told some of John's story – John Russell, Sandy Moffat, a fellow painter too, Alan Bold, a poet and close friend. But the picture feels profoundly incomplete without the story as told by the love of his life, his soul mate Helen. Of course, no account of a life lived is ever fully completed but like a great Bellany painting, a beezer as he would call them, the vitality, the life force that seems to tumble out of the frame as well as the vulnerability and profundity that underlies it, this is what Helen brings to the fore. He was a man of elemental force and vision and this is what is most powerfully conveyed in the pages that lie ahead.

Tim Marlow
London
2017

The Good Hope

Edinburgh, 1963

Taking up almost half of one vast wall in the mural room, was the biggest and most ambitious piece of work John Bellany had ever completed. Four panels of the highest and broadest hardboard available, banged together to comprise a surface 9ft tall by 16ft wide. It had been on the go for several weeks and at last it was finished. He couldn't wait to show it to me and I had to be there to see the final touches being made.

He signed his name, put his brushes down and stood back and looked at what he had done. This was a moment to be savoured.

We gazed at the massive painting together. His arm around my shoulder was trembling with excitement. He knew, by any standards, that it was a triumph. What he was always to call, when he was happy with a painting, *a beezer!*

Only a few weeks into our romance, we had already made a pact to spend the rest of our lives together. Our plan was simple. He was going to take on the world and I would go with him to do the same. It needed the two of us and so, as we admired the new masterpiece, it was in the knowledge that our future would be totally focused on nothing else, nothing less, than taking on the world. Together.

Standing high up on the slip, proud against the bravest bluest sky, towered a newly built boat. Not an ocean-going yacht. No, to him they were only toys of the rich. This was a magnificent seine netter, and ahead of it lay a heroic mission. A hunter-gatherer of commanding authority, singing out in brash assurance and steadfast resolution, it was ready to fish the deepest seas and reach for the far horizon. From the proud glory of the mast the voice is vibrant, drowning out the seabirds' call on the winds.

Rigging has been fixed, the wheelhouse made fast to the hull, and the helm awaits. Toilers are wearing sea boots in solidarity, others are bare-chested. There is urgency in heaving muscle and straining sinew, in the perpetual calling and laughing and repartee of this moment, of the pride and promise it holds.

All is well formed, well prepared.

The lifeboat and coble are up on deck so that however billowing the swell and ferocious the tide, there can be survival. The propeller is fixed and the rudder awaits the guiding hand.

There too, braided deep within the solid barque, is faith.

And there is love.

The launching will shortly take place, to a surge of celebration. The waters will rise up to embrace and grant buoyancy to the departure, and the great voyage, the future, will begin.

The chosen name, which comes from its own rich ancestry, and the numbers of the boat have been carefully and lovingly inscribed, leaving no doubt as to where the home ground lies, the pride in which will be its lodestar. The pride and love of home: the heartbeat that will unfailingly go with it, carrying it towards the far-flung destination and, in the end, see it safely back once more to cross the harbour bar.

It is the song of the beauty of a new morning, the beginning of a new life, an odyssey starting off in the brightest radiance of the day. Leaving shore, it will sail forward into realms that challenge and dare in waters rough and calm, that exact a heavy price whether in sun or rain or winds that whirl and blast and spoil. There will be days of triumph and days of despond. Days of delight will come, and days when the skies will turn dark and threaten, and death will be a taunting companion but the sun that disappears at will is bidden always to return and shine again. This voyage, as that of Ulysses, will be hazardous but the spirit of this new day, the memory of this exultant moment and the integrity of the boat will endure.

In time-honoured ritual, bowing to myth and omen, the restraints are being slackened and ribbons are now lifting on the wings of the breeze, streaming out, prayer flags fluttering into the brilliance of the day.

The Good Hope is leaving its berth, bidding farewell to the harbour of home and setting out into the open sea.

Taking on the world has begun!

CHAPTER 1

Leaving Sutherland

On a Sunday afternoon in October 1961, we joined the long queue of vehicles waiting our turn to board the car ferry at North Queensferry. There was no road bridge then but there was a sense of camaraderie among those anticipating the short voyage over the Firth of Forth, when we would be edged on to the boat with what seemed to be barely inches to spare between us and the dark lapping water. One false move by my father, Harold, and we were sure to be lost at sea. The escapade, like all similar breaks in routine, had put the boy with shining eyes back in my father's face. He relished adventure on any scale.

We had been travelling for well over five hours, the old road taking us from Golspie south over the Struie to Inverness then wending its way through the Cairngorms and all the villages en route: Aviemore. Blair Atholl. Pitlochry. Then Perth and on south again. Waiting for the ferry allowed us time to study the enormous structure of the Forth Rail Bridge. It was an impressive sight, especially when a steam train puffed its way high up across the span of the girders, and it was always part of the entertainment to try to identify the place at which the bridge was currently being spruced up with red oxide paint in the famously unending task.

But for me there was a momentous excitement to this day and an acute sense of apprehension. Although I hadn't given it much thought, it probably affected my father as much as it did me.

This was the day I had left home, said goodbye to everything I knew, to go out into the much wider world to start my own grown-up life. We were on the last lap of our journey now, our destination across the water in Edinburgh, where I was to enrol at the College of Art the next day.

My eighteen-year-old heart was beating fast.

Leaving home, I had known, was going to be an emotional experience. I was ready to go but I would be leaving a place where I knew everyone in the school and in the village and in the surrounding environment, and they all knew me. Such security would never be mine again. Now it was out into that world down south that I had always wondered about and daydreamed of since my first infant days at school looking away out over the sea towards the distant land masses on the horizon.

Of course, I would be coming back to Golspie, often and always, but it was unlikely that I would make my home there. I had a whole world to discover and many worlds within that one. But, like every other human being, all I had known throughout my early years I would carry within me.

From my earliest days, my father's pride and passion had taken us at every opportunity over all the single-track roads traversing the vast empty moorland and mountain landscape of our county of Sutherland. We followed every road and track round the rugged inlets and lochs and dramatic cliffs. We saw the awesome rise of ancient rock and the motionless falling of distant mountain waterfalls; long, deserted sandy beaches with their swell of aquamarine tides and dazzling white breakers, and far in the distance, island vistas through mists and rain and strokes of slanting sun across a timeless and silent land. We knew the mountains – Suilven, Canisp, Cul Mor, Cul Beag, Quinag, Ben Loyal, Ben Hope, Arkle, Stac Pollaidh, Foinaven ...From the west coast village of Lochinver to the reaches of Cape Wrath and along the north coast, Bettyhill to Melvich, the whole vast, deserted grandeur of Sutherland was what we were born into and what forged the spirit within us. We used to return down through the lonely wastes of the county by Strathnaver and the Kildonan Strath. Often we would follow the winding road

into Caithness and then pass Dunnet Head and John O'Groats, looking across to Orkney, before making for home down the east coast, following the cliffs from Wick by Latheron Wheel to the notorious Berriedale braes and Helmsdale until at last we saw 'the Mannie' in the distance once more, a gladdening reassurance, as night would be closing in, that we were home again.

Not until I had left home would I know anything of the notoriety of 'the Mannie', the first Duke of Sutherland, the person who was commemorated by the 100-ft-high statue that dominated the landscape and looked down from the summit of Ben Bhraggie over Golspie and his family seat, Dunrobin Castle, nearby. I remember no talk of the notorious Sutherland Clearances or of the ruthless, cold-blooded part he played in that not so distant story of the ancestors. It would, however, have been murmured among the old folk around the fireside, an inhumanity too shocking to be forgotten, an injustice too brutal to speak of. At school, as in the home, we were left in blissful ignorance of this period of our heritage. Later on in life, even as I became aware of our recent Sutherland history, it was something we were not encouraged to ask about for fear of being disrespectful towards the present Countess. In my early days therefore the statue was, to me and to most other young people, simply a symbol of home.

Because we lived in a remote area, as we became older, my brother Michael, my sister Joan and I would moan at the thought of mountains and rock and relentlessly more and more of the bleak dreary same. Please can we go and see some 'life', we would beg. Human life, not more golden eagles and red deer on the hill, leaping salmon and seals...The novelty of towns was what we ached to see and know about. The familiar, no matter how wonderful and full of beauty, had become monotonous to us, in the same way that a constant diet of the finest foods could dull the appetite of the most dedicated gourmet. We were now eager to see what else there was in the world.

All this, however, by the time of my departure from Sutherland, had become entrenched in me. I had been stealthily formed by all that my father had made me see. He had instilled in me a deep love and pride in all of it and this would form the heart of who I was, as it was of him. The power of home would always call me back.

'Don't you be coming back now with a fellow with long hair and a beard, mind!' they were calling after me, the warmth of the banter of the goodbyes long ringing in my ears as, across the hills in the distance, I saw the Mannie fade from view.

CHAPTER 2

Edinburgh College of Art

The first week at the art college in October 1961 was Freshers' Week. The whole of Edinburgh was taken over by student stunts and processions along Princes Street, and the university and all the other colleges, including the art college, were involved in the fun. I still bear the scar on my knee that I received when I was hauled onto the medical students' float and made to be their patient while they all too enthusiastically demonstrated their 'operating skills'.

Back at the college there was the Freshers' concert. It was held in one of the large studios. There was music, dancing, all sorts of revelry, but it was a play that I remember most vividly. It was a wild, orgiastic, anarchic charade. I would later find out that it had been devised by Alan Bold, a university student, and two of his friends. It was raucous and outrageous, involving scantily clad bodies on a bed. One of the main characters was crouched over a piano, thundering out crazy jazz. Over his jeans he wore up-over-the-knee fur leggings that looked like they had once been the arms of a fur coat, a large black hat, and from his waist, hanging from a rope, swung a great bone straight out of the butchers. The whole ensemble was topped off with an old fishing net adorning him from his hat right down to his boots.

The buzz of a strange new world thrilled me.

I had spent the last three school years following my passion for painting and had made up my mind that this was what I wanted to do. When I applied to Edinburgh College of Art it was recognised as being the best art school in Scotland at that time, so to be accepted to study there was a considerable achievement. I was solely interested in developing my skills in drawing and painting and being educated in the history of art, about which I knew little. My father used to proclaim Stubbs a great painter because to his mind no one could paint horses like he did. The only other person he rated as an artist was Winston Churchill. If I could paint as well as he did, then I could go no further. Of course, on special occasions while growing up we had had access to the great paintings in Dunrobin Castle. The Duke of Sutherland's collection contained Gainsborough, Van Dyck, Turner and Canaletto among others, but when you are young and with no guidance, little remains in memory except perhaps the elegance and grace of the grand people in the portraits which seemed so far away from my world.

What I had not bargained for at college was the amount of time we had to spend on other subjects during the two foundation years, such as graphic design, textiles, glass, calligraphy, sculpture and colour practice. My bête noir was design. I had not the mindset for such a discipline. I had not the neatness, the accuracy of calculation or the finesse required in presentation. To me, all those activities seemed to be concerned with getting things right, getting the right answer, and, although I was at that time ignorant about what art really was, I instinctively believed it wasn't about that.

What I did like, when it was later introduced to us, was life drawing, with the mysterious Mr Gold or the voluptuous and friendly Carol and solemn Mrs Nico among the models. The idea that Sean Connery had at one time worked as a model in the college was tantalizing. We were never so fortunate! However, in later years as a student I was asked to help sort through the college collection of drawings and saw him in many poses.

I liked costume drawing too, with the models dressed up in silks, satins and velvet, and the challenge of capturing the pose along with the textures of the fabrics. I loved all kinds of drawing, including antique drawing. The college was fortunate in owning a magnificent collection of antique casts, copies of the Elgin marbles, and one class a week was devoted to drawing them in the Sculpture Court. The other thing I looked forward to was painting. We would go to Lawson's, the wood merchant in the West Port, choose pieces of hardboard and after carrying them back to college, prepare white primed surfaces on which to paint. Canvas was not for us at that time: too pricey, too posh.

This must all sound very academic to modern-day art students. In the seventies, drawing classes in art schools were discontinued and many of the rigorous disciplines we had been taught were deemed obsolete. The death of painting was brashly declared, as would be, on the introduction of the e-reader in later years, the death of the book.

In the sixties, however, we were learning the craft of painting and drawing in many different media, giving us the means with which to express our ideas. The imagination, of course, the key element, is the only thing that cannot be taught or learned and it goes without saying that if there is no inner vision, there can be no work of art.

Today it is not necessary to have such skills to be acknowledged as an artist. Today it is all about the concept, the impact – immediacy of sensation catering for our minuscule attention spans – and in many cases the artist employs other people to create his ideas. It is creativity of a different nature, with its own place in the scheme of things. Although in vogue, it neither replaces nor invalidates what could be called traditional painting, which has centuries of history upholding it and, like books, will without doubt endure while the world continues to exist.

In that first year we were taken on field trips by one of the most enterprising of our tutors, John Busby. Health and Safety did not curtail our exploits, nor did student insurance enter into anyone's consideration. In the first week we were taken to the wildlife and bird sanctuary down the coast at Gullane. The idea was to record what we saw there, and back at college to show what we had done. I think most of us found it somewhat bewildering as we stumbled through the tufts of tough marram grass looking for something to draw. It was a freezing cold day with a biting wind and no seabirds on the wing. However, it was the first of several good days out and the start of many friendships.

Another time we were taken to the scrapyard at Burntisland, where the rusty metal carcasses of boats and industrial machinery were piled high. Some spectacular drawings resulted from our efforts. But the most memorable of all our trips out with John was when we visited Prestongrange coal mine. We were allowed to draw and then asked if any of us would like to go underground. The few of us who did got into a cage with our miners' helmets, and went down and down. At the bottom we followed our guide along dark, wet tunnels. We saw the bogies of coal arriving to be hoisted on to a belt and transported to the surface. We walked for miles to a coalface that was way out under the Firth of Forth and by the time we arrived at the seam the miners were currently working on, we had to slide on our stomachs like they did as they chipped out the coal. It was an unforgettable experience and gave us a small idea of the hardship and discomfort endured by miners in their ordinary working day. Every day in a lifetime of such days.

I had acquired some new clothes to begin college: tweed skirts and home-knitted jumpers and a Black Watch tartan dress that had been specially made. I had felt suitably equipped until I arrived in my new environment, when I soon felt as comfortable in this attire as probably many other fledgling students in equally uncool garb. By the end of the first term most of us were draped head to foot in black – big jumpers, skintight jeans, pointed winkle-picker shoes and boots, second-hand rags from the grimy second-hand shops to be found in the Grassmarket and the Cowgate. The ultimate source of our distinctive apparel was Madame Doubtfire's basement in the incongruously grand Royal Circus of the New Town where she would sit among the heaps of what might nowadays be called 'pre-loved' clothing in various stages of decomposition. Mrs Doubtfire was a shrewd, crabbit, elderly Aberdonian who kept a gimlet eye on her wares.

Permeated with the intoxicating smell of cat's piss that greeted you as you approached, her shop was not for the faint-hearted. 'Dinnae touch that pile,' she would bark. 'The cat's just hed kittens in there.' Her small scruffy terrier would follow you around, snapping at your heels as you tried to rummage through the great piles of clothing. The considerable challenge of the visit always paid off in the end, and we were always highly pleased with and proud of the unique items of clothing we came away with: moth-eaten furs, wartime leather coats, 'fully fashioned' fifties dresses, old cashmere and scratchy wool. We peered out from under thatches of hair we were desperately trying to grow long. All this was topped off with elaborate dangling earrings. Thank goodness I had sneaked off to Inverness the day after I had finished school and had my ears pierced – forbidden until then.

The social life of the college revolved around Clark's Bar across the road. The bevvy was beer, for everyone. It was the only thing we could afford. Most of us were innocents in the matter of drinking but worked hard at acclimatizing. Boozy nights made for many wretched mornings but it was all worth it. Drugs were not on our horizon. Our world went round quite adequately with alcohol.

The hot tickets in Edinburgh in those days were for the art college dances. Everyone wanted to be there. We had the best bands and the Sculpture Court was the best venue. Charlie McNair, Al Fairweather and Sandy Brown and the Clyde Valley Stompers, appeared among many others and on big occasions we were treated to the likes of Tubby Hayes and Johnny Dankworth. They were all great but I think my favourites were the West Indian Steel Band and the Temperance Seven, who were popular on TV then too. All of us girls used to drool over the delicious Paul MacDowell in his cool white suit and shoes to match as he whispered out his breathy delivery of 'Pasadena'. The feeling was entirely mutual as he softly sighed the words of 'You're driving me crazy'.

One of the highlights of that first term was when Kenny Ball came. I have a picture of my friends Irene Scott, Moira

Doherty and me making our way down through the dark streets of Tollcross on our way to the college for the occasion. Shifts were the apparel of the times and so we had kitted ourselves out in our own home-made versions, which we found surprisingly easy to make. We simply chose the jazziest fabric, the cheapest we could find, folded it over in half, cut a hole for the head and sewed up the sides leaving space for the arms and making sure that it was as skimpy as we could make it. No sewing machine was available, so it was all done by hand. The results delighted us and I can picture us shimmying along the road, carried away on our own enthusiastic rendering of 'Midnight in Moscow'.

We occasionally went to the University Union but we found their events generally unexciting and, in our haughty view, rather inferior to what we enjoyed at the Art College.

The term was rolling on towards Christmas and all the talk was of the Christmas Lunch and the Revel. At the beginning of December all extracurricular energies were concentrated on transforming the whole college according to a chosen theme. Elaborately painted paper adorned every wall, pillar and stairway. All the studios were to be taken over as dance floors, each with its own band or bar. Paper tunnels were constructed leading down to the canteen in the basement of the college and it was transformed from a pie, beans and chips comfort zone into a lurid depiction of the horrors of Hell. There were enormous papier mâché structures suspended from the ceiling above the Sculpture Court, the most memorable of which was a spectacular, gigantic fire-breathing dragon. How we got away with all of this is unfathomable. The regulations of the time demanded that the college was inspected for fire safety. It never failed to pass!

During the second last week of term came the Christmas Lunch. This was a kind of trial run for the Revel and I don't remember much, except that it all began in the canteen with a turkey lunch. Everyone was there, all students and staff. By the end of the afternoon, as the day darkened, by which time the Christmas lunch seemed to have wafted away on the mists of time, prone bodies were stumbled across on the floor in various studios, appearing as ghostly icebergs in hazy waters. Many were indeed unable to get themselves on to dry land until the next day. Staff or students, no one was immune. Those of us who were still reasonably mobile would follow the herd to the nearest party and then on to the next. No one could recall exactly what had happened, so it went down in history as a roaring success and that's how I think of it still. Wild and wonderful!

The climax of the whole year was, of course, the Revel. It was the Christmas Lunch to the power of zillions: there were fancy-dress costumes we had to make for ourselves, stunts that we enacted in the Sculpture Court, with people crowding in from all over Edinburgh if they were fortunate enough to either have been invited or have acquired a ticket . . .and the music! It was a bacchanal that didn't seem to end, certainly not until well into the next day at least. What could be remembered was sublime and what couldn't was probably for the best.

Then it was off to catch the train up north to Golspie for Christmas. This time I would be crossing the Forth Bridge in the steam train chugging slowly over the girders high above the Firth of Forth. It was the custom for good fortune, so they said, to throw coins out the window of the train while it was passing over the bridge so they would land in the waters below. I don't know a student who was in the happy position to be able to be so profligate, but many a coin was nevertheless thrown in order to uphold the superstition.

I loved the journey home and my excitement grew as the landscape became more and more familiar the further north we went. The train, keeping company with the old A9, dawdled on in wisps of billowing steam, stopping at all the little stations on the way. Random halts were a feature of these journeys north, as was the consequently prolonged contemplation of the bitter winter landscape. Weariness would set in but there was always something of beauty to see: the fading winter light streaking over frozen mountain sides, picking up the rust of dying bracken; the blackness of burnt heather and now and then the surprise of a luminous patch of tender green moss sheltering among the rocks; swathes of snowdrifts lingering in the deep corries of the hills and, in the valleys, the silver slash of a river gleaming its way through the deserted and frozen wilderness. For much of the journey was only that – deserted wild land claimed by the deer, foxes, birds of prey and other wildlife that roamed there. The melancholy beauty of that desolation was something which held a powerful, familiar attraction for me.

It always seemed to be a struggle for the engine to reach the Slochd summit and on the many occasions we travelled in deep snow there was a lengthy halt there as the driver contemplated the negotiation of sometimes impossible snowdrifts. Everyone seemed to hold their breath at this point until slowly we heaved forward, inch by inch, to finally gather speed and begin the long descent to Inverness. As we hurtled over the bleak moorland slope to our destination it was possible on a clear day to glimpse, over the Moray Firth and the hills in the distance, beyond the Black Isle and the Sutors of Cromarty, the Mannie. And this meant home!

Of course, the dying light of a December afternoon didn't afford me this little rush of comfort but I knew it was out there in the dark. I could see it in my mind's eye and knew we were getting near.

The shock of the icy cold as I alighted in Inverness brought me to my senses. With my heavy suitcase deposited in left luggage, the two-hour wait for the north train was spent wandering around the streets of Inverness. The festive atmosphere added to the excitement of going home. Not only that but I felt good about myself because I had coped with the challenge of leaving home, going to a place where I knew virtually no one, and where I had had to fend for myself in a world that was completely new. I had tackled all that was required of me at the art college and not only had I loved every moment but I had made good friends and a wide circle of acquaintances. Nothing remarkable about any of that. Most new students would have similar feelings at the end of their first term but it felt very good nevertheless.

The train drew out of Inverness station around five o'clock in the evening and ploughed on through the dark, clanking in to Beauly, Muir of Ord, Conon Bridge, Dingwall, along the shores of the Cromarty Firth to Invergordon and Tain, following the track by the edge of the Kyle of Sutherland to Ardgay, where the people travelling to Dornoch would be met. Over the moors to Lairg, where the mail car would be waiting to collect any passengers who were making for Lochinver and the west coast. Finally back down the Rogart glen and last stop, the Mound, before at last, two hours after we had left Inverness and almost eight hours from Edinburgh, the train steamed in to Golspie.

The euphoria of being home was sweet. The warmth and comfort and the special welcome cocooned me and I relished the treats prepared for me. Not even the prodigal son would have tasted anything as exquisite as my favourite bramble crumble my mother had made with the wild fruit she had gathered in the autumn for the purpose.

Christmas was the happy celebration with extended family and friends it had always been. It was good to be back sharing my bedroom once again with my sister Joan who wanted to hear all about my new life at art college while she told me about her days at school and what had been going on in the village. We laughed and talked well into the early hours, our bedroom light 'the only one blazing in the whole length of the dark village street', according to my father. Michael, four years older than me, was by now married and living in England and Joan, four years younger, was the last sibling at home. We had missed each other. We would always be close. She would in time go on to study in Aberdeen where she would marry and bring up her family. Back in the village it was also good to see again some of my former classmates and hear how they were getting on in Glasgow, Aberdeen or Dundee.

In the new year of 1962, back in Edinburgh, college life continued. Design projects, field trips with John Busby, evening classes when we could summon up the self-discipline to stay late, lectures in the history of art, lessons in how to lay a gesso ground by Jimmy Cumming (I wonder how many of us ever made use of such specialized information).

Socially, there were other treats in store. The Glasgow visit was an annual jaunt to Glasgow School of Art, and healthy rivalry meant that there was always an element of skulduggery planned. On one occasion the Edinburgh visitors had been herded into the Glasgow lecture theatre for the welcome reception when all of a sudden the doors flew open and in stormed the Glasgow students with a barrage of snowballs.

Revenge was sweet, of course, on the return visit. Memorably, a stilt race was organized for the two teams to do a lap of the RSA building at the Mound in Princes Street. The prize was a bottle of gin. Everything went to plan and at an appointed spot about halfway round, the leading Edinburgh students turned on those following, causing havoc and knocking rivals off their stilts, after which they pelted round to the finishing line, collected the prize and made off with it, with the Glasgow lot in hot pursuit. In order to put them off the scent the villains scampered up and round the castle rock, fuelled by the gin, of course.

Towards Easter there were the Border Raids where we set off in coaches to Galashiels, Melrose and Kelso. Fancy dress was the order of the day and the purpose was to raise money for charity. I remember woollen mills and rainy streets with icy blasts round every corner and of course the sanctuary we found in the pubs. On one occasion we seemed to end up at a coalmine at Newcraighall, just outside Edinburgh.

Not everything was frivolous. During my first term we had all been out marching for CND. We, and the rest of the world, had been paralysed with fear over the Cuban Missile Crisis and the imminent threat of nuclear attack by the USSR on the United States.

The end of the academic year came all too soon and we were busy preparing our work for assessment. By this time my friend Irene and I had moved into a bedsitter in Bruntsfield. We were at the top of a house full of students and I recall working through the night, fixing our drawings and completing the presentation of all our work. This was June and the light never really left the sky. In the early morning we took turns going down to a nearby bakery to buy hot morning rolls straight out of the oven before we struggled down to college with our portfolios.

Then it was time once again to get the train north. I was sad that the year had come to an end and that three whole months were to be spent away from my new life.

CHAPTER 3

Encounter

After all the rituals of the beginning of another year of academic life and the welcoming of the new students, our routine of classes continued in much the same vein as the year before.

The painting studios of Edinburgh College of Art are spacious, light-filled rooms on the first floor. Vast windows look out over the old rooftops and chimneys of the Grassmarket and directly on to the dramatic battlements of Edinburgh Castle. The light was ever-changing amid the continual drama of weather. Storm-lashed clouds would obliterate the sun, turning the castle rock to darkest black, then just as unpredictably would come the sudden return of the light. Seagulls would wail and cry as they were buffeted and lifted on the wind, or the mist would creep silently and surreptitiously round the rock so all that could be seen was a disembodied fortress rising out of the clouds. Our view was of the back of the castle. Beyond it was Princes Street and the New Town, the symmetrical layout of grand neoclassical residences built between the late eighteenth and the beginning of the nineteenth century. Around the great sandstone edifice of the art college ran the gunnels and alleyways of the West Port and the Grassmarket. This was where the sad and wretched hung out amid a pervading air of desperation, and dejected wraiths came and went among the shadows with their bottles of gin and meths. This was the haunt of art students too, where in the second-hand shops many bargain items of clothing could be purchased, and where we found inspiration for our work.

We also frequented the National Galleries of Scotland on the Mound, which housed the great European classical paintings of Titian, Tintoretto, Giorgione and many other masters of the Italian Renaissance. There were the landscapes of Van Ruisdael and Claude Lorrain, the elongated religious portraits of El Greco, the formal works of Poussin, leading up to the exotic mysteries of Gauguin. Ramsay and Raeburn told of the Scottish life and its people, and there were collections of drawings and sculpture available for our study.

Fairly recently, a gallery of modern art had been set up in Inverleith House in the Botanical Gardens and a growing collection of twentieth-century art amassed. We went there to see the changing exhibitions of contemporary painting and sculpture, some Scottish, among the international shows brought north to Edinburgh.

It was mainly in the annual exhibition of the Royal Scottish Academy and in the commercial galleries of Edinburgh that we saw the work of the Scottish school, many of whom were our tutors at the college.

One night during the last week of November, I was in evening class doing life drawing. Halfway through, the model had put on her dressing gown and gone off for her break, and all the students had vanished to the canteen as well. I decided to remain and continue drawing and was doing just this when I was surprised by someone approaching me. He had been taking part in the class too but I hadn't noticed him. He looked at my drawing and said he liked it. It was John Bellany from the year above me. I had never spoken to him but of course everyone knew of him. He had always been an interesting figure to me but he had a reputation for being a bit intimidating. It was common knowledge that he had almost been thrown out for his 'arrogant approach' to a design project. He had seemingly been asked to design an LP cover and what he produced was considered a step too far. On being summoned before an incandescent head of design and his staff, he pleaded incomprehension as to why his work had caused so much 'insult and disrespect'. It had to be

pointed out to him that it might just be that the record cover was rectangular and not square! This was deemed the height of insolence and he had been made to complete an assignment over the summer in order to be allowed to continue his studies. We thought this was hilarious cheek but were suitably warned about incurring the wrath of our tutors.

Alone in the studio we struck up a conversation. He had shown his work in several college exhibitions and it had bowled me over with its energy and exuberance. I particularly loved his drawings, which were extremely powerful. Probably we talked about our work, about where we came from and so on, but all too soon the model and other students came streaming back to resume the class. It ended about 9 p.m. and instead of getting the bus I decided to walk all the way home. By this time, I had changed addresses several times and was now renting a flat with Irene in Warriston Crescent, two miles away down at Canonmills.

I was walking with my feet not touching the ground. Something out of the blue had struck me, something totally unexpected and unlooked for had set me alight. I felt crazy with elation.

It was the conversation with John Bellany!

All I had known of him was that he was wild and outrageous and slightly scary. Somehow, however, in those few minutes of conversation, I had caught a fleeting glimpse of something else, which seemed to displace his surface bravado. I was intrigued by what I had encountered and was drawn to him. He hadn't asked me out and I had no expectations of that happening, but I was on fire with excitement. It wasn't just physical attraction, although that was definitely part of what I was feeling. There was something more intangible, overwhelming strong feeling of recognition, of connecting to something that was already a part of me, of some shared inner element for which there were no words.

On the Friday at the end of that week, I went with my friends to Clark's Bar after college. It was crowded with students, drinks were being ordered and the air was blue with smoke. Lo and behold, sitting at one of the tables was John with three friends all decked out in evening suits, pints in hand.

Seeing us arrive, he beckoned me across to their table and introduced me to Charlie Valentine, Shug Martin and Bill Watters. It was my first meeting with The Blue Bonnets, the dance band of which they were the four members. Charlie, Shug and Bill were all miners from Prestonpans and they mostly played at the miners' welfare clubs in their local area of East Lothian. Bill's brother, Big Rab, was also in Clark's that night. His job was to chauffeur the band and their instruments around the various gigs. Apparently John played the piano, Charlie and Bill the accordion and Shug the drums. John explained that they were on their way to play at Prestonpans Labour Club and had just called in to Clark's to warm up beforehand. When it was time for them to go, John asked me to go out with him.

We were to meet on Monday night after the antique drawing classes had finished at half past six. We would meet in the college entrance hall.

Over the weekend my excitement could hardly be contained. By the time the class ended on Monday night and I was putting my stuff away in my locker, I was convinced that he would not turn up. I couldn't believe he was serious about going out with me but as I rounded the corner of the Sculpture Court and came into the entrance hall with my friends, there he was, waiting for me. The date was 3 December 1962. I was nineteen and John twenty.

We headed out of the college past the fire station and down through Tollcross and on up to the Golf Tavern overlooking the Meadows at Bruntsfield.

We were not seen at college until a week later.

CHAPTER 4

In Another World

John had shared a studio with other students but by this time he had it more or less to himself. It was at the top of a tenement in Rose Street, the narrow street of seedy reputation and many pubs sandwiched between Princes Street and the elegance of George Street, right in the city centre. This is where we spent the week and where we would live together from then on.

The top flat of 150 Rose Street South Lane was a tiny four-roomed apartment with no heating, no gas, rudimentary electricity, no hot water, no bathroom only a lavatory with a small sink, one cold-water tap, very little furniture – except a couple of beds – and no kitchen.

The entrance from the street, the door of which lounged off its hinges, was adjacent to the side door of Ma Scott's Bar. Entering the stairwell, one was plunged into pitch darkness. Well-worn stone steps wound round almost in a spiral and as one climbed through the gloom, subterranean-like tunnels branched off to other dwellings. Finally, at the top were two doors at right angles close together, one belonging to a couple of artists and their baby and the other to John's studio.

John would not let me out of his sight and, although I couldn't wait to tell my friends and the whole world how happy I was, I did not protest. We were floating in orbit way off the Earth! We had everything you could possibly want and had no needs that weren't being gloriously met.

Exploring my new surroundings and wandering through the tiny rooms of the Rose Street studio, I strained through the small windows of the flat to catch a glimpse of what was going on around us down on the streets. All I could see were the old stone walls of the tenements. Only from one window could I see the South Lane running parallel to Rose Street and serving the back entrance to the businesses of Princes Street where occasionally there were signs of life. There were a few small deserted back yards bound by broken-down stone walls where a glimpse of unruly grass might catch the eye. The street door of 150 was separated by the lane from the Charlotte Chapel opposite, and several nights a week and at weekends the lanes echoed with the sounds of fervent devotion.

I remember eventually catching sight of the top branches of a tree stretching up to the sky from somewhere behind the Charlotte Chapel. It made me feel good to see something living that had been able to find sustenance in such unpromising surroundings. It became for me an emblem of optimism and a thing of beauty to look for among the roofs. I like to think it still grows there.

Our days passed getting to know each other. Where to begin? There was so much to talk about and to tell. We were hungry to know everything about each other's lives. The more we talked, the more similarities we found in our backgrounds and the more the differences intrigued.

He came from a fishing family on the Firth of Forth at Port Seton in East Lothian. The tradition went back in his family for generations, through his paternal grandparents in Port Seton and his maternal family in Eyemouth, further down the coast near Berwick on the border of Scotland and England. He had one sister, Margaret, who was five years younger than him and still at school in Prestonpans.

He told me about his schooldays and his friends there. He told me about his many cousins and relatives, and especially about his grandparents, his mother's parents, who were still alive and living in Eyemouth. He spoke warmly about his family and friends, and had obviously enjoyed the happy experience of a secure and loving childhood as I had in Golspie.

For all fishing communities, in those days especially, religion was the fulcrum. The fishermen and their families prayed for safety on the open seas, for guidance and a safe return to land. It was to God that they gave thanks for deliverance from the dangers of the deep and for the health and strength they needed to earn their precarious living. The power of the Almighty dominated their thoughts and, for nearly all of them, their lives revolved around the Church.

According to John there were thirteen churches and religious meeting places in Port Seton. John's family worshipped at the Church of Scotland Chalmer's Memorial Church, where he was required to attend morning and evening service and Bible class on a Sunday. Some of his relatives attended the Red Tile Meeting, where an even stricter sect of Brethren congregated and to which he would often accompany his uncle James.

John still lived at home and travelled in to college every day by bus. The studio, condemned as being uninhabitable, was rented for next to nothing on the proviso that no one lived there. It provided much-needed freedom for him to enjoy a student social life. Most weekends, however, he played in the band at weddings and social events in East Lothian. This, along with working in a fish-curing business on Saturdays, provided essential money to help fund his college course.

The anarchic and formidable figure I'd heard so much about was beginning to unravel. This person who attended church dutifully with his parents on a Sunday was the same figure I had first clapped eyes on cavorting at the Freshers' concert with his bone and fur leggings and his hat swathed under fishing net. This was the same person who helped to cheat the Glasgow students in the stilt race and who ran off with the bottle of gin. He was also the student nearly thrown out for the insolence of his record cover by the design team the previous year.

The wild man I had heard about was now becoming a multi-dimensional creature of endless colour, texture and form, and I wanted to know it all.

We spent our days cocooned together. We would draw each other and paint as we talked until the evening, when we would venture down to Rose Street and wander in and out of the pubs until we reached Milne's Bar at the corner of Hanover Street. There we could be sure of meeting up with Sandy Moffat, John's best friend at college, his other close friend, the poet Alan Bold, and also a group of people as varied as they were remarkable.

That first week, we went to see *Breakfast at Tiffany's* at the Cameo in Tollcross, and the theme tune never fails to draw me back to that euphoric madness of falling in love.

Just two weeks after we met, it was the end of term at college and the Christmas Lunch and preparations for the Revel were in full swing. It was a glorious finale which sent me on my homeward train journey north delirious with happiness. I couldn't wait to tell them all about my new boyfriend.

Yet my heart sank when I thought about it. There was so much that they probably would not want to know.

They would like the fact that John's family were church people. But the thought of their daughter gadding about and fraternizing with the drunken and disorderly of Edinburgh would alarm and horrify them, as would the fact that the man of her dreams was an unruly reprobate known for his fearless challenging of the college authorities. To know that she was sharing a bed and living with him in virtual slum conditions in a notoriously insalubrious area of the city just didn't bear thinking about and, to cap it all, he sported glorious hair down to his shoulders, just setting off nicely the glint of auburn in his beard.

The dreaded 'fellow with long hair and a beard'!

It had been agreed between us that, on our return to college, John and I would set up home permanently in the studio in Rose Street. This information, of course, had to be strictly off the record as far as our parents were concerned. While in our eyes we would be sharing a beautiful existence we wanted to proclaim to the world, to them it would bring mortal shame from which there could be no redemption. As Irene and I still rented the flat in Warriston Crescent, my contact address for my parents was secure, although ease of contact less so. I would owe Irene much for the loyalty she provided.

In my eyes, the duplicity was unnecessary and I did not enjoy it. What could be wrong with two people loving each other? I could not see the problem with it and I could not fathom the reason in ecumenical law that forbade it outside of marriage. I loved my family and wanted them to be happy for me but there was a long way to go on that road.

During our short time together, John and I had already decided that we wanted to spend our lives together. The future was brimming with promise and opportunity. What was in front of us we had no idea but we knew, even then, that it was all going to be phenomenal. Now that we were together the sky would be the limit. We were going to take on the world. We were going to have such a life!

It might appear that we had run quite far ahead of ourselves. After all, we had been going out together for less than two weeks before Christmas and this was the beginning of January. But we had no doubts; everything seemed right. Although we were new to each other, there was so much that seemed to ring with instinctual shared experience. In the swirl of parties that marked the beginning of the new term (and the bounty of our grants arriving), John asked me to marry him. We had barricaded ourselves into the bathroom of a student flat while a queue outside urgently banged on the door, desperate to get in. It was not perhaps the most romantic venue but our passion transcended all other considerations, especially the folk battering on the door! Right from the start we knew that we wanted to be together. That was all that mattered.

The first weekend of the new term in January 1963, I was to be taken to Port Seton to meet John's family. I was looking forward to this but also felt suitably nervous. I was sure that I would like them from what John had told me, and I was not disappointed.

CHAPTER 5

Port Seton

We caught the 129 bus from St Andrew Square after college on the Friday afternoon. The journey was all new to me, of course, and I grew to enjoy it and all that we could see en route as we wound down through Portobello, past the famous and popular outside swimming pool and the nearby power station, both of which would be controversially demolished later in the decade. On to Fisherrow, where John pointed out the harbour and fishing boats. The bus then ambled through Musselburgh with its racecourse and Luca's, the Italian ice cream shop. After this, the road curved round and into Prestonpans over a piece of land that had recently been reclaimed from the sea. At this point I realized I had been here before. On our right, there beside the brickworks, was Prestongrange coal mine and the tunnels I had visited running deep and far away beneath the sea and the landscape I was now looking at.

In the old centre of Prestonpans, John pointed out Harlow Hill that led to Preston Lodge, the school he used to cycle to every day. Approaching Port Seton, we saw a massive build-ing site under construction. This was to be the new Cockenzie Power Station. To me, the site resembled the Quatermass pit from the recent science fiction television production that had held everyone spellbound, and I followed keenly the ongoing work which progressed for several years until completion. The power station construction provided inspiration for us and many drawings were done of the tiny figures wrestling with metal rods, the industrial shapes, the machinery, the growing forms of glass and opaque interweave, the pattern of light and the whole hive of activity there.

For the local people who had seen the site transformed from seascape to modern industrial colossus it must have been daunting. The power station provided much-needed jobs but it dominated the landscape for miles around. Said to have a life span of twenty-five years it has only now ceased operations and been demolished fifty years on.

Forty-five minutes after leaving St Andrew Square in Edinburgh, we were making our way along Golf Drive to No. 20, the post-war council house in which John's family lived. Arriving there for the first time I immediately felt warmed in the comfort of their home. John's father, Dick, was a handsome man with dark hair and dark eyes who had left the sea a few years previously and now worked in the boatbuilding yard, Weatherhead's, at the west harbour in Cockenzie. He had a twinkle in his eye and his conversation was laced with humour. John's mother, Nancy, was a shy, quiet person. She had come to Port Seton from Eyemouth after she married and had a part-time job in a fish shop in Tranent. They lived and breathed the fishing and their lives revolved around the church. Dick was an elder and Nancy was involved in the Women's Guild. It had been said at college that John Bellany's mother was an office bearer in the Temperance Society, which everyone found amusing considering his wild behaviour. Whether this was true of his mother or not, there often is a sad irony to this kind of joke.

Margaret was sixteen and still in the maroon uniform of Preston Lodge. She was shy like her mother but had her father's striking dark eyes and colouring.

We were all a little self-conscious but quickly the atmosphere relaxed and their warm welcome soon made me feel at home. There was a bit of explaining to be done by John about his staying full-time in Edinburgh. I had to underline the fact that I was sharing a flat with Irene and John was camping out in his studio, which seemed to satisfy everyone in the meantime.

From then on, I looked forward to visiting them at weekends. We relished the home comforts of hot baths and the warmth of the coal fire spreading through the sitting room, the home baking and the fresh fish. The routine we established followed without much variation. Out with the band on Friday and Saturday nights, sometimes Sundays too, in which case we would stay Sunday night and catch the bus into Edinburgh in the morning in time for college.

The next weekend was the first of many when I found myself crammed into Big George's car along with the accordions and drums belonging to the Blue Bonnets. I was now a regular member. The instrument given to me was the maracas, and I was seated next to the piano, all but chained to the pianist. John would not let me out of his sight and he certainly did not trust any of the miners with the prize he had won.

The whole experience of the Blue Bonnets and their events was bizarre: rough and ready, but totally joyful. 'One singer, one song, please!' and up the performers came to drape themselves around the microphone and give it their best while John accompanied them on piano, frequently having to change key in an effort to keep in tune with the singer. There were drunken renditions of Frank Sinatra's 'My Way', a good sprinkling of well-loved Scottish airs, then an Elvis number and, gliding over the dance floor, the punters elbowed their way around to the strains of 'Some Enchanted Evening' and, 'If You Were The Only Girl In The World'. I remembered to play my maracas as the spirit took me.

The calling of the bingo session at the interval brought forth plates of mushy peas and gave the band a chance to drink the pints of beer that had been sent up for them by members of the audience and which lined up in a never-ending row on the piano. Supply far exceeded demand and, assiduous as the Bonnets were at knocking them back, there were still pints lined up on the piano waiting for them at the end of the night. The finishing touch to the evening was the bag of white pudding and chips from Stella's chip shop in Tranent as we headed home after midnight. Some of the time Big George was called out with his car on taxi duties, in which case our transport was Bill's van with a well and truly sozzled Bill driving. In the van, space was at a premium and it was a work of art to be able to fit the five of us inside plus the 'coffins', the large black boxes containing the accordions. Suffice to say that the journeys took lurching to new extremes. Mostly sheer luck got us home.

I don't know how the band felt about having to accommodate me on a regular basis but 'the lassie' was accepted apparently with good grace and there were no concessions made, to their enjoyment, except the odd reminder to watch the language, though the apologies were required too many times for anyone to keep them up. The talk in the band was of local gossip – who was having affairs with whom, who had had the 'polis' round, who had been done for drunk and disorderly, who was dead, out of work, injured in the mine, or having to get married – and there were heated discussions of the latest football games.

The venues the Blue Bonnets played included the Labour Club, Billy's Bar, the British Legion and other establishments in Prestonpans plus the Miners' Welfare Clubs at Macmerry and other places in the surrounding area. At many of these events differences of opinion invariably arose among the punters, resulting in a few punches being thrown now and then, but fights mainly featured during the weddings at which they played, usually between members of the two families concerned. It was the Wild West comes to the 'Pans.

In stark contrast to this, the Bonnets were also the regular entertainment at the Women's Guild Socials in the 'Pans. Their behaviour would then be as impeccable as that of their audience, who, all women of course, sedately danced with each other.

After the band sessions, we were deposited near Golf Drive. For obvious reasons there was always a bit of difficulty in getting the key to work in the door, which resulted in it usually being opened for us. John's parents were accustomed to this kind of thing. On one notorious occasion, before I came on the scene, his mother opened the door for him whereupon he swayed giddily and promptly fell backwards, feet in the air, into the hedge by the door. The shame of it mortified them. 'Get in here this minute!' A severe lecture was delivered to the miscreant, who went on to have absolutely no recall.

On the Sunday morning we put on our best clothes and walked in procession along Gosford Road to the Chalmer's Memorial Church – front seat in the balcony, Bibles at the ready and pandrops in the pockets. Through the nausea of the lingering hangover we were railed at and admonished by the fiery red-haired man of God, and with his warnings of eternal damnation and the Burning Fire ringing in our ears we made our way home to discuss the sermon, the minister and the congregation over lunch. What was happening at the harbour, who was the top fisher for the week, who had had a poor catch and so on were the subjects of enthusiastic conversation the whole weekend. John's cousin, also called John Bellany (Wee John), invariably visited at some point, bringing a 'fry' and details of his week at sea.

The Monday morning bus journey into Edinburgh was never as enjoyable as the outward one on the Friday. We always sat on the upper deck, trying to get the front seat and therefore the best view if possible, but without fail the air was blue with smoke, everyone coughing and spluttering. There were still in those days signs prominently displayed announcing that spitting was strictly prohibited on the bus. On rainy days the windows quickly steamed up to add to the discomfort. Add to this the large pieces of primed hardboard that John tried to smuggle on board. This was another reason why we aimed for the front seat on top, as, after the difficulty of negotiating the narrow stairs, there was more space. Many an oversize painting sailed into Edinburgh blocking out the whole top window view. How we got away with this on so many occasions I do not know. Of course, there were times when the conductor was an awkward b******, according to John, and we were refused point-blank. 'Yi neednae think yir comin' oan ma bus wi' that board! Dinnae argue wi' me, son! Thir's nae chance!' We then had to resign ourselves to waiting for the next bus in the hope that that conductor would be a bit more amenable.

CHAPTER 6

The Fishing

The wild social life we enjoyed was offset by serious and intense work. Painting to John was akin to breathing and while unbounded *joie de vivre* was in his blood the whole unwavering purpose of his life was to draw and paint. It came before everything. It always would.

Fishing was his world and at the age of four that is where he began. The curve of the bow, the angle of the stern, the position of the mast, the attitude of the wheelhouse, the shapes, the proportions, textures and colours of individual vessels – all was his business. He followed keenly the innovations that developed in the design of the boats from the introduction of radar to the different methods of fishing and the nets employed. He rejoiced in the improved working facilities for the crews as they developed but at the same time he lamented the change from the graceful line of the older boats. In the sixties, with the introduction of the whaleback, boats became more tub-like in appearance.

He knew all the local fishermen, some of whom, like his friend Bobo, had been in his class at school. He could tell from a dot on the horizon whose boat was approaching harbour. He had profound respect and admiration for all those who made their living in this precarious manner and his heart would swell with emotion as a boat made harbour with its catch. The excitement and drama of the catch being landed and the buzz of the fish market always stirred him.

In the names of the boats he found poetry. Many were of a biblical nature, many honoured skippers' wives and family members. Often the name would be passed down the family line as their boats were replaced by newer vessels.

His father's boat had been *The Queen of the Fleet*, his Eyemouth grandfather's was *The Margarets* and Wee John, his cousin, went on the *Bonaventure*. There were also *The Bounteous Sea, The Provide, The Day Spring, Fortunatus, Sweet Promise, Mizpah, Star of Bethlehem, The Milky Way, Stella Maris, The Star Divine, Bethel, The Good Hope, The Crystal Sea* . . .

The bynames in the fishing community also fascinated him. Cookies lived in Golf Drive too and was brother of Dadles. Heckle, Kill the Duck, Poultice, Tarry, Toshie and Wa Wa were among the names that regularly came up in conversation.

All of this was at the centre of his work. He drew incessantly wherever he went. The family marvelled at his efforts, including his father, who would, however, have no qualms about criticizing any defect he detected in the drawing of a winch or wheelhouse. 'That's no' how it gauns, min!' he would scornfully declare. Artistic licence was something that John never really applied to his fishing boats and just as well, as there would certainly have been no negotiation with his father on that issue.

It's reasonable to imagine that had he instead chosen to spend his life as a fisherman, eventually owning his own boat, family dreams would have been fulfilled. But if such ambitions had ever been entertained by his parents there was never, at any time, any evidence of them.

They were mildly bemused by what he did and the passion with which he did it. They never professed to understand his later work. They were modest, uncomplicated people who would not have enjoyed any attention that made them stand out from the crowd. They were, however, enormously proud of him.

This did not preclude a certain amount of teasing from his father, who delighted in bringing him back to earth on the occasions that John might just have been blowing his own trumpet! When he told them he had won a prize or some favourable criticism for his work, the retort from Dick would be, 'For a puckle auld rubbish like that?' John seldom failed to rise to the bait, which, of course, made it all the funnier.

He loved his father, though, and admired him for the outstanding sacrifice he had made when John was a small boy. Dick had agreed to leave the sea for the sake of Nancy, who, as the result of depression, had begun to find the worry of his dangerous occupation too stressful.

Fishing ran in Dick's blood and in that of his family down the generations. He had lived for and loved no other way of life. He had had his own boat, *The Queen of the Fleet*, and seafaring was all he knew, his whole world. After the crisis of Nancy's illness, however, he made the momentous decision that, for her sake, he would have to give up the life he loved at sea. Dick's mother was a Weatherhead and he turned to that side of the family, who found him work at their boatbuilding yard in the town. This provided him with a job ashore for the rest of his working life on labouring wages, all the while watching his contemporaries with their own boats prospering at sea.

The subsistence was hand to mouth and there was nothing extra, but there was never any outward sign of bitterness. According to him he had a happy family and his faith, and that was all he needed. Contentment was what he said he had and contentment was something he would many times advocate to John when his son was worked up about some issue or other. This, however, was not a concept we could embrace and such a sacrifice as he had made remained truly unimaginable to us.

Dick's hobby was making boats, fishing boats, in the bottle and he made them for all and sundry. Such was his skill at the intricate task that he would be asked to provide them for special occasions: for wedding presents, presentations and for the Gala Day. John was very proud of this. Over the years he loved to bring people down to Port Seton to meet his family and many of these visitors would in due course become the proud owners of one of these treasures.

CHAPTER 7

Eyemouth

John wanted me to meet all his family and friends and couldn't wait to take me to Eyemouth to meet his adored grandparents. There was no family car so we planned to go with their friends Anne and Robbie Jarron in the back of their fish van.

On the appointed Sunday, we all piled into the van. Robbie driving, Dick in the passenger seat, Robbie's wife, Anne, Nancy, Margaret, John and myself crammed in the back. There were no seats, only a cushion protecting our seized-up muscles from the bumpy road, and the inside of the van was all we could see. Humour was our only antidote to the spine-jolting, bone-crunching agony.

Home Street in Eyemouth is a street of fishermen's houses that runs up from the shore, built into a steep incline; No. 10, where Grandma and Grandpa lived, was at the top. We entered a small shadowy sitting room and found them sitting either side of the coal fire.

I recognized the sweet face I had seen in college drawing exhibitions. This was the adored Grandma whose likeness now hangs in the Scottish National Gallery of Modern Art. There are many tender portrayals of her sleeping, reading, knitting or just sitting. *The Bereaved One*, an oil of her reading her Bible after Grandpa's death, makes her look rather stern. I see this more as the earnestness of her prayer, as I never saw any trait in her that was not the essence of gentle loving kindness.

36

'grandpa'   Bellany '63

Grandpa's name was Alexander Maltman, and he was known to all as Sonny, or Sonny Matt. Grandma was Margaret but called Meg.

The talk was all of the fishing – the market, the catch, the skippers and crew, and, always of prime importance, the weather. They were in their eighties and Grandpa was, of course, retired but these lifelong issues were naturally still uppermost in his mind. The fire was stoked and Grandma busied herself making the lunch.

An oil portrait John had done when he was sixteen and still at school hung above the dining table in the room. It was of Grandpa sitting in an armchair. There were also family photos arranged about the room and, as in any family home, many objects of sentimental value on display.

Behind the living room there was a tiny kitchen with a Baby Belling for cooking on and a small sink. From the kitchen, the door to the yard opened adjacent to the outside lavatory. In the yard were the drying sheds for the nets and on the outside of the building was a wooden staircase up to the garret. From the top of those stairs one could look over the high walls of the yard on to the tombstones of the graveyard next door. John told me that when he was young and playing with his Eyemouth friends, if the ball landed in there no one wanted to go in and retrieve it. They were afraid of the ghosts that were waiting for them.

On the other side of the front door from the living room was the main bedroom and leading off that, towards the back, was another tiny room with just enough space for a double bed. Primitive conditions perhaps but as the memories come flooding back they are not of deprivation but of abundance, of everything that is good in life. As I did at Port Seton, I felt at home here with this family into which I had been so warmly welcomed.

After lunch and before the light began to fade, we went on the customary Sunday afternoon stroll round the harbour. Eyemouth is a naturally beautiful place. Sheltered by high sandstone cliffs and guarded by the treacherous Hurkurs, rocks like sharp teeth rising out of the waves, the harbour mouth stood at one end of a small sandy bay where on good days swimming

and family picnics were popular. Great skill and an obliging tide were needed to negotiate the Hurkurs but on top of that, in order to reach home safely, the boats had to cope with the perilously narrow harbour entrance that was to be widened in the future.

Overlooking the harbour, up on a grassy bank stood the imposing structure of Gunsgreen House designed by John Adam in 1753. The house had played many roles in the life of the town, including making a significant contribution to smuggling in years past. Now it was a boarding house where John's mother had worked as a young woman.

After a final cup of tea at Home Street, it was back into the van for the return journey to Port Seton. From now on we would visit Eyemouth regularly, travelling by the same means. It was always a bit of an adventure and never failed to be a special outing full of hilarity and good memories.

John had been bewitched by Eyemouth from his earliest days and the impact it made on him never diminished. The history and heritage of the place was in his blood and one of his most treasured possessions was *The Disaster Book*, a well-worn account of the Eyemouth disaster when in 1881, the year Sonny Matt had been born, a freak storm had suddenly blown up, drowning most of the adult male population as their boats attempted to reach harbour.

Whenever the chance arose, John would get Grandpa and Grandma to sit for him. They were endlessly patient but usually fell asleep before he was finished. Grandma would always have the same thing to say when she saw the resulting work: 'Oh, that's awfy fine, son.'

'Aye, verra guid,' would be Grandpa's retort.

If they were adored by John, he was truly adored in return.

CHAPTER 8

First Days

During that first term we lived together, we began to do something about the studio in Rose Street. Apart from Sandy, the other students that John had meant to be sharing the space with had never shown up, so we had taken on the rent ourselves: the princely sum of £2 per month. Of course, we were not supposed to be living there but no one came to check on what was happening, so we set about clearing the place up and covering some of the old crumbly walls with white paint. We went to the weekly Lane sales held in the Thistle Street Lanes to get second-hand furniture and various household items for next to nothing. Quite often articles that had not been sold could be acquired for nothing if we carried them away ourselves. We furnished much of the flat in this way, our *pièce de résistance* being an upright piano. Once it was installed with the help of obliging friends we immediately divested it of its front panel in order to expose the arrangement of strings and hammers, after which we painted it a bright red. John played by ear and could play anything and everything in the realms of jazz and popular music. After seeing the legendary jazz pianist once in Paris, he became the Thelonious Monk of every party.

We had in our circle of friends and acquaintances a number of plumbers, electricians and plasterers who helped us in our refurbishment of the studio. When we began to update the electric wiring, for example, there was never any problem acquiring the finest, most expensive copper cable for the purpose. This must have been pilfered from the current jobs on which our friends were employed. The others provided services in like manner. No money changed hands but in true gentlemen's honour the work was rewarded by a few pints and a small work of art from time to time.

Tam White was a stonemason by day. By night he was a jazz and blues singer who went on to make a distinguished place for himself in the jazz clubs both in Scotland and London. His glorious gravelly voice and the considerable success he also had acting in television drama and films like *Taggart* and *Braveheart* has ensured him a place in the cultural history of our times and, in no insignificant way, the story of our life together.

Arthur Sharp was an electrician who moved in the same circles as Tam. They could be described as being the top brass of a collection of disparate characters that palled about together. Those included wee Norrie Kippie, Ken Harold, lanky wide boy George Lees, Eric Cameron, or usually 'Big Eric', the first black man in Edinburgh (according to him), and Jackie D, a ferocious jazz fanatic.

Jackie saw everything out of the corner of his half-shut eyes and missed nothing. He had a permanent list of people who, in his opinion, were well deserving of a thrashing and he would systematically cross them off his list after they had been attended to.

You didn't have to do much to get on his list: any unfortunate individual simply enjoying a conversation just a decibel too loudly for Jackie's liking, or an unwary stranger caught looking fleetingly in his direction, or someone with the wrong accent, or someone who, heaven forbid, liked different music to him, were suitable candidates. Alongside his local well-established foes of old, anyone innocent and unaware could offend him. He was like a cheetah waiting to pounce. And you did not want to see him pouncing.

He, along with many of our friends, became a willing subject of John's portraits. There was never any fear that we could find ourselves on the list. Jackie was our friend and if you were a friend you were accorded undying loyalty. Had we had any enemies, which we hadn't, they would have automatically gone to the top of Jackie's list.

Anything he liked and thought you should like, Jackie shared with you. Anything he thought you should like, he would steal to order and present to you on a subsequent visit. Shoplifting was his forte and all you needed was to be among the privileged few, his inner circle, and you would be lavished with unsolicited gifts of food, alcohol, items of clothing, you name it, but mainly, his speciality, books and jazz records. As I remember, among the countless unsolicited gifts that came our way courtesy of Jackie's sleight-of-hand was *The Joy of Sex*, newly published and controversial at the time for its graphic illustrations the peculiar wholesomeness of which had about as much eroticism as a Church of Scotland magazine.

He would turn up at Rose Street out of the blue with the goods under his arm. While we played his latest Charlie Parker or Sonny Rollins we ate the pies he produced from up the sleeve of his coat and learned quite a lot from him along the way about musicians, known and obscure, and about the jazz scene, what was happening and where, along with gossip from the jazz record shops with whom he traded in his own light-fingered way.

He often turned up in the garb of a Catholic priest, dog collar and big black hat, his slit-like eyes glinting behind round wire-rimmed spectacles, *sans* lenses, above a luxuriant ginger beard that presided over his enveloping black coat. In a particularly frisky mood he would black out his two front teeth creating a gap-toothed grimace as the finishing touch.

A chorus of loud bird sounds announced his presence and the evening was generously punctuated by jokes and tricks and impersonations. In the street, often similarly attired, he would spot you from afar and on hearing the bird call you would look in vain until he revealed himself standing on his head in a doorway or dangling from a lamp post or jumping out of a dustbin. He always had some new conjuring tricks to try out on you and a new joke. Across the street as he departed he would inevitably shout 'List!' and then the name of the most recent unfortunate newly appointed to it.

Courtesy of our friends, we were able to install a small Baby Belling electric oven with two hotplates, and the kitchen almost began to be entitled to the name. The Belling and a table with a few odd chairs were the only thing kitchen-like about it, mind you. There was only cold water from the lavatory sink, and of course no fridge. The windowsill had to suffice. But any improvement pleased us.

We also managed to have a small water heater installed in the lavatory. It was virtually an electric kettle, as it could only heat up about a bowlful of water at a time, but to have hot water was sheer luxury. Thrilled by the new convenience we decided to go to town on the decoration of that smallest room.

John was at that time a great admirer of Alan Davie and his own work had recently gone through a period of Davie influence. Alan thus provided the inspiration for the theme and in no time at all the cistern and pipes were transformed by stripes of all colours, with black, predominantly snaky, shapes proliferating throughout. It was a riot of colour right up to the small skylight above and even the lavatory seat proclaimed its tribute to Alan.

Due to the lack of a bath or shower in the studio, we had become used to frequenting the public baths. It was quite a trail up to Infirmary Street but the hot baths were good and served the purpose sufficiently until we got to Port Seton at weekends. We were beginning to feel quite established in our new life together. Rose Street was becoming a proper home in our eyes. Any deficiencies in our little love nest were made good by the steady stream of new paintings that we displayed the minute they were completed. The long narrow corridor from the front door we had painted white and that is where we placed the full-sized portraits of the two of us, John's at the end of the corridor so you could see it as soon as the door was opened. These were six feet by four feet and painted, as was everything else then, on hardboard.

The third room was at first retained by Sandy, who brought his girlfriend there at weekends, and the fourth was our studio, where we worked in the evenings. In that room there was an old upholstered chest which had been there when the boys had taken on the rent of the studio. Where it had come from nobody knew. In it a French edition of a large collection of Old Master prints had been discovered. It contained the finest drawings of Leonardo, Michelangelo, Rembrandt, Durer, Delacroix and of all the greatest European artists since the Renaissance. Most were in pristine condition, and though some of the prints had been cut up and damaged the rest of them we used for our own study and display. It was a treasure trove of such magnitude that while retaining as many as we could use, we decided to bring the rest to college for the benefit of other students. This was as much for our own benefit too, as we offered the drawings to the college for a small price that we were subsequently grateful, and surprised, to receive.

Also in the studio were some small plaster casts. At a fair guess they had once belonged to the college collection but how they had arrived in the studio remains a mystery. The benevolence that we had displayed in selling the print collection to the college did not extend to returning the casts. We loved them too much and they looked too good on our walls. As mysteriously as they came into our possession, so in time, however, they disappeared.

This first term we lived together had more than its fair share of excitement and reward. Lady Luck generally seemed to be on our side. Our life together had started the way it would go on. Always something turning up. Doors were opening and vistas were broadening.

In the spring of 1963 when the new Forth Road Bridge was nearing completion, one of the Scottish newspapers, the *Daily Record*, announced a competition with prizes to be awarded for the best paintings produced in honour of the great event. Lots of students all over Scotland responded and submitted work. The prize money was generous and competitions of this nature were rare, so excitement was high.

John had been studying the work of the French painter

Fernand Léger. His own paintings were for a short time very much influenced by this hero, and the painting he submitted for the competition reflected this. It was an industrial work celebrating the construction of the bridge, executed very much in the tubular stylized manner of Leger. It brought him the third prize.

I remember the euphoria of the prize-giving and the photographs in the press. One hundred and fifty pounds was a colossal sum in those days. It bought quite a few celebratory pints for all and sundry but the rest was handed to his mother in order to help the family make ends meet.

The story goes that when John was a very little boy his father would take him by the hand down to the harbour to see the boats. Sometimes the fishermen would give him a threepenny bit or a sixpence which he immediately flung into the harbour! His attitude to money was thereby revealed at an early age.

At college, twenty-five-pound travelling scholarships were handed out to deserving students and they were to be utilized during the Easter break. We were excited when John was awarded one of these. He had made one previous trip to France with Alan Bold and Sandy in his first year and one to the London Galleries but other than that, he had not been very far afield. He used to say that the furthest he had travelled was on the summer outings provided by the local bus company when he was small. Blaikie's Mystery Tours, always popular, took the adventurous of Port Seton to the mystery destinations of villages in the neighbourhood, never further away than around fifteen miles.

The travelling scholarship meant we had to alter our plans for John's first trip to Golspie. I went home before him while he and Sandy, who had also been given a scholarship, went to Paris to see all the museums there. They were gone for a week and the second week John caught the train north.

CHAPTER 9

Mon Hélène à Moi

Just before John arrived in Golspie, I received a long letter, the envelope addressed to: 'Mon Hélène à Moi', care of my Golspie address. He had sent it from Paris, telling me, mostly in French, about the inspiring masterpieces he had seen and all the great things he had learned from them. It had all been written on a sheet of thick best-quality drawing paper that had lent itself so badly to his attempt to fold it and get it into an envelope that it was bursting out and had been lavishly taped up, leaving my name and address barely legible.

He described every detail of their days in Paris – the galleries and museums they were visiting, the paintings they saw, the effect of seeing such great masterpieces for the first time, the particular artists he was impressed with and the works that he found most inspiring. He was taking notes in a diary about everything he was seeing and explaining what he was learning. In spite of the rats (his lifelong major phobia) that were also resident in Hotel Nouvel and the lack of money, he was on top of the world and full of excitement. Both he and Sandy were captivated by the beauty of Paris and were making the most of every day, existing on the starving artists' classic diet of bread and cheese and vin rouge at La Palette in the evenings.

Apart from overflowing with the sheer exhilaration of all that he was seeing and experiencing in Paris, where we must go soon together, it was a letter full of love for me, full of longing to be

47

together again (*'je te manque de tout mon coeur'*) and optimism about the life we were going to have in the future that stretched out so gloriously before us, the life that was still so new after only a few shared weeks in the studio. No greater good thing could have ever happened in the world than our getting together and no more magnificent happiness could there ever be than what was lying before us in the time to come!

My heart was singing as I waited for him to arrive in Golspie to meet my family and friends. They would like him. They would love him as I did. They would love the centre of him. They would love his openness, his love for his family, his warmth, his sense of humour and his great spirit of *joie de vivre*, which I saw as corresponding to that of my father. I had already foreseen the joking and bonhomie they would share together. They would love his enthusiasm and interest in everything. They would love the whole of him as I did and I couldn't wait to revel in the happiness that would be all around us as he was introduced to the rest of the family and friends and people in the village.

For my part, I had realized the necessity of making concessions to Golspie style when I was there and considered myself suitably attired. We had also made careful preparations for John to fit in, agreeing that it was wise to cut several inches off his hair beforehand, just to be on the safe side, as he was anxious to make a good impression. Always sharply attentive to the sartorial aspect of his appearance and confident in his own distinct sense of style, he had selected his favourite black hat, his knee-length boots and the long black coat he'd just acquired from Doubtfire's so that he would look his best.

I was at the station in good time to meet him. The train was nearly half an hour late, but finally I saw the steam of the engine fluttering across the Culmaily fields. At last it lumbered into the station and there he was!

We had been apart for a whole week. What would he make of Golspie? What would Golspie make of him?

My eyes were shining in the glory of being with my handsome lover and I never doubted that the eyes of the village would see exactly what I saw.

CHAPTER 10

The Nameless Ones

On their new television sets from over the Atlantic came news of all sorts of degenerate goings-on, including strange quasi-religious sects. One in particular had seemingly lodged in the collective Golspie psyche and word went round that Helen Percy's fellow was one of them.

He was one of 'The Nameless Ones'.

There was a lot of staring and curtain-twitching as we went about. People went to the trouble of visiting my father's grocer's shop just to tell him how shocked they were that he was letting his daughter go around with 'someone like that'. One of the pillars of the community was the most vociferous. Words like 'depravity' and 'lawless' were being used.

Men in Golspie had short hair. Short was normal. Short meant neatly shaved all round the back of the head and mercilessly round the ears, allowing a modest flourish on top. As far as the Golspie ones were concerned, John's hair was not short and most definitely not normal. He had a beard. His clothes were not tweed jacket and lovat-green trousers. So they were odd. He was odd. He wore knee-length boots. Knee-length! His long coat was not what they wore in these northern parts. And then there was the black hat!

How did I know what was being said? My father told me when he got me on my own. Public approbation was very important to him and these kinds of comments were deeply disturbing. It just wouldn't do.

In a small village especially, there was no room for variance. Anyone who thought differently would find it difficult to integrate. You had to join them or forever be on the outer ring. This was village life, in any village. You bask in the love and care that is warmly given out but there is a price to pay. You are not just your parents' daughter but a daughter of the whole community and everybody has a say in how you conduct your life.

All this would cause endless hilarity back in Edinburgh but at the time I found it far from amusing. How dare they judge someone they had never even spoken to and about whom they knew nothing? I was embarrassed and shamed by the unjust and arrogant response from my own village into which I had been so proud to welcome John.

He rose magnificently to the occasion and my admiration for him soared. He demonstrated a maturity beyond his years, teaching me something then of the necessity of being able to see from the other person's perspective while also being able to sustain your own view. It was a lesson in magnanimity that to me showed John's stature in the face of such small-minded bigotry. He pointed out that people in Golspie were unused to seeing students in different garb and I should take that into consideration. They would get used to it and once they got to know him things would be fine. I was taken aback by his generosity of spirit, which, I have to say, for quite some time afterwards I was too wounded to share.

So we stayed on in Golspie, braving it out until it was time to go back to Edinburgh. We spent the days going off on our own, walking to Dunrobin Castle through the woods and along the shore, with the family dog, Chippie, always in attendance. We climbed Ben Bhraggie and took photos at the Mannie, gazing out over the Dornoch Firth to the Tarbat Ness lighthouse at Portmahomack and beyond to the smudges of the Banffshire coast on the horizon. We followed the rocky path under the viaduct and up the Big Burn to the waterfall. We walked for miles along the shore watching the seals and otters.

I could tell that, although they were uneasy about his appearance, Mum and Dad liked John, as I knew they would. We were allowed to borrow the car and went all over the place. I wanted to show him the beauty of Sutherland that I loved and knew so well, and he was completely overwhelmed, drawing everything he saw as we went along. In our drawing collection the inspiration of his first experience of that starkly dramatic landscape is evident right down to the decidedly Légeresque clouds in the sky.

Following the single-track roads across the lonely uninhabited heart of the county, we found ourselves gasping in awe at Suilven rising out of the heather as we approached Lochinver. Lochinver itself was a busy fishing harbour which John knew of and looked forward to seeing. As usual in a harbour he lost track of time and we spent ages looking at the boats and drawing them and watching the catch being landed. From there we travelled on up the precipitous narrow coast road from Drumbeg to Kylesku, where we took the ferry before going on to Scourie and Laxford Bridge.

Quinag, Arkle, Foinaven, Ben Stack – these mountains were thrilling for John to see. Every vista, loch and cliff brought forth the same exclamation of astonishment. I can hear him now. The sparkling water-logged moorland, the boulders strewn in centuries past over the bare rocky landscape, the wild sea spray, the deep corries running from the craggy summit of the mountains, the roaming herds of deer, the hovering birds of prey …The enveloping silence and the absolute timelessness of it all was so new to him. He was bereft of words to describe how he felt and I was glowing with pride in my home land. He had never seen anything like this before. As we rounded the road above Badcall and began our descent to Kinlochbervie he could not believe his eyes. There amid this ancient landscape of such spectacular beauty he had spied something that he was not expecting – another harbour sheltering among the rocks. This really was paradise!

At an early age, a lifelong love for all of Sutherland had been instilled in me, not only of its rocky coastline with the sandy beaches and mountains but also of its dramatic grandeur and stark emptiness. To share this with someone of like mind for the first time and see it afresh through his eyes was an invigorating revelation. It was the beginning of John's love affair with Sutherland and the north that endured for the rest of his life.

Kinlochbervie remained a favourite place forever after and a constant source of inspiration. Three years later, using the information provided by the innumerable drawings he did while in Sutherland, John painted *Kinlochbervie*, a large oil on two panels of hardboard – the largest pieces of hardboard he could obtain. This now hangs in the Scottish National Gallery of Modern Art in Edinburgh and is one of his best-known paintings.

We spent the days speaking of painting and great painters and what he had learned from his Paris trip. He was exhilarated by all he was now seeing in the wild grandeur of Sutherland and it filled his mind. Our days were good in spite of the negative reception given to us, the sting of which still lingered with me.

My beloved Auntie Mary, my mother Ella's sister, was always there to reassure the family in any crisis that everything would turn out well in the end. As usual she was a source of much-needed comfort as, in the middle of all the fuss, she declared in her quiet way that she could see that we were meant for each other. There was something deep, some affinity she could see between us, something that intuitively told her so.

CHAPTER 11

Days of ambition

Back in Edinburgh the days were lengthening and we had to begin preparing for the end-of-year assessment of our work. For me, this would mark the end of my foundation course and, happily, the end of design projects forever. The next two years would be filled with drawing and painting, and I looked forward to that.

The 18th June 1963 was John's twenty-first birthday, which we celebrated with a booze-up on the Saturday night in the studio with our friends, which included a takeaway from an old favourite, Spaghetti George's at Tollcross. Usually a coin was tossed to decide who the runner would be. It was quite a distance to Tollcross from Rose Street but by the time food came into our minds the person going was usually quite sloshed and went without complaint. Somehow, however, I don't remember John ever going!

George was Italian and his spaghetti was renowned all over Edinburgh; I'm sure for many people the taste has never been surpassed. He packed all the portions together in a large can the size of a five-litre paint tin and hopefully it would still be hot by the time it reached home. There was one memorable occasion when we must have left our eating arrangements a little too late because by the time he got back to the studio with it our friend had eaten nearly the whole lot. There was nothing for it but to fall into bed, our guests sleeping it off on the floor.

The Edinburgh Festival soon came around and, along with most art students, I had entered a couple of paintings into the Scotsman Steps student exhibition. A newspaper cutting survives of Sir William MacTaggart, who opened the exhibition, praising my efforts while John and I look on. Dizzy heights!

The highlight of our year was the exhibition, during the Festival, on the railings of Castle Terrace near the Usher Hall. John, Sandy and a few other students had exhibited there during the Festival of 1961 and had decided to repeat the performance, but this time only John and Sandy participated. They, like all students, painted on hardboard and they painted large. It was no mean feat therefore to transport a whole exhibition of framed paintings ranging in size upwards from 6ft x 4ft, first down the winding stairs of Rose Street, into a van and then to tie them up to the railings. The van belonged to a pub acquaintance who had negotiated his price in pints. When this had been achieved, they had been resigned to the prospect of repeating the procedure at the beginning and end of every day until help came in the shape of the Almighty when the minister of the Unitarian Church across the other side of Castle Terrace generously offered over-night storage facilities for the paintings in the vestibule of his church. This unexpected act of kindness was accepted gratefully by the two artists and saved them endless hard work over the three weeks of the Festival.

During the Festival, Edinburgh springs to life. Every corner, every dusty room has a part to play, even more so nowadays. The place buzzes with energy and the Castle Terrace exhibition was very much part of it all, attracting large audiences of people passing by – actors, musicians and performers from all over and latterly, people who had been alerted by the press to the phenomenon. Alec Guinness passed by daily and never failed to throw a coin into the piggy bank that waited on the small table nearby. A well-known Edinburgh tramp, passing by with his hats and bags and tattered shoes, always volunteered an offering for the benefit of the students. Buses coming to drop people at the Usher Hall or the Lyceum Theatre slowed down as they passed the scene which, along with Sandy and John's formidably attention-demanding exhibits, included the full-length life-size portraits of John and me that had been hanging in our narrow hall in Rose Street.

The idealism of those open-air exhibitions in which they were taking art to the people was all part of their mission to 'Take on the World'. This mission would fuel the whole of John's life. It would govern all his days, not only those of competition or exhibition but every working day of his life – and virtually all days of his life were working ones. This was the only way he could work and he could not tolerate any other kind of attitude to painting. It was his *raison d'être* to communicate and to make his voice heard.

He had begun with the harbour and its fishermen and their boats, the world of the fishing that was his birthright and his enduring passion and inspiration. To him it was the finest, most heart-stirring experience in the world to watch a boat from a speck on the horizon make its way into the safety of the harbour. He saw nothing quaint or pretty; what he saw was noble and heroic, on a par with Greek legend. Each boat had its own individual characteristics and each one spoke of toil, hardship, danger and courage, as well as of potential loss and disaster. The fishermen were warriors at the mercy of the natural elements. He saw and knew the core of what it was about from the inside and worked from there.

In his first two years at college he had absorbed the sound academic training provided, but at the same time had experimented with abstraction under the influence of the American Abstract Expressionist Jackson Pollock. He and Sandy had also learned about Alan Davie, who had been an Edinburgh College of Art student a decade previously and who had provided the inspiration for the decoration of the smallest room in our Rose Street flat.

Alan had eventually abandoned the academic style characteristic of the college and of Scottish painting in general and had begun to make a name for himself in the wider world with his abstract jazz-inspired work. He had moved on under his own steam and that is what John and Sandy were going to do too. By the summer of 1962 they had come to believe, however, that the abstract approach was not for them. They firmly believed that their work should speak of their own time but, contrary to the current vogue in the art of the sixties in which the wave of the new was largely turning away from the scholarship of the past, their work would be well grounded and informed by the great European masters from the Renaissance onwards

There was no turning away from the contemporary art scene. They were au fait with it all but were left largely unexcited by what they considered an empty, transatlantic trend. Back home they also deplored what they saw as the facile decoration predominant in Scottish painting at that time and shouted out against it. There had to be more to creativity than that. There had to be something in you that you wanted to say and it had to be something worth saying. It had to address not just those in the New Town drawing rooms for whom the fine arts in Scotland seemed to be a monopoly but to call out across the class divide. Following in the great European tradition they would use their distinctive voices and their own personal experience to speak of what it is to be human. The fundamental aim of the arts in general is to connect with and nourish the hearts and minds of humanity, to speak with everyone on a universal level. Their aspirations were no humbler than that.

Many artists, writers, musicians and those in other fields whose particular vision and passion command attention and respect, frequently like to attribute the source of their journey to an inspirational school teacher or influential figure in early life. In John's case it was a fortuitous encounter with two other students.

In his first year at college he had met Sandy and through him Alan Bold, a poet and student of English Literature at Edinburgh University. It was perfect timing. All three found they were on the same wavelength and formed a strong lifelong friendship, modestly calling themselves 'The Big Three'. Al was similarly fired up about poetry and literature and was extremely active at the university producing *The Gambit*, a literary student magazine, while also organising numerous cultural activities. A vigorous dynamic of cultural debate sprang up between all three. Their attitude was soon very much one of 'us and them' as they aligned themselves with the poet Hugh MacDiarmid and the great figures in the Scottish literary renaissance, as opposed to the French-influenced decorative school of current Scottish painting.

Those years of the 'Big Three' were exciting and empowering as each on his own and also together in solidarity found their feet on a path that would take them fearlessly into the future. Those astonishingly productive years formed the nurturing ground for each of them, hungry as they were for knowledge of the arts, politics and all that life had to offer. This was their intellectual awakening and John was ready for it. It was the start of a real and profound questioning of all things. Art college provided a thorough grounding in the practical application of painting, drawing, printing and sculpture but only a scattering of art history lectures. There was so much to explore, a lifetime's worth. The future suddenly had many possible dimensions and it was going to be up to them to find a way into them.

After he had arrived at college, John had enthusiastically taken advantage of all that the National Galleries had to offer and knew the collection intimately. Once I had joined him we went together to look at his favourite paintings. At that time he was obsessed with the Titians on loan to the National Gallery from the Duke of Sutherland. He pointed out the technique that Titian had used for the skin tones in his mighty figures and we gazed in awe at the power of the mythological compositions. He studied the old masters, especially 'my Italian ancestor', Giovanni Bellini, and worked out his own transcriptions of their works. Piero della Francesca inspired him in the same way and one of those early transcriptions that remains a favourite of mine is the rarely seen *Homage to Piero* and also a painting inspired by *The Agony in the Garden* by Bellini. Those transcriptions thrilled me most of all the work he was doing at that time. He was learning from the great painters of the Italian Renaissance and his appetite was insatiable. He was impatient with the staff at college and felt that they should feel the urgency that he did in all that there was to find out.

He became more politically educated but his work was not overtly motivated by politics. He had an unwavering loyalty to his origins and what his early beginnings had imbued in him but there was much he needed to discover in order to focus his vision. The quest was shared with Al and Sandy, and the learning curve that began with their friendship was dramatic. It was bigger than anything he learned at the college. They visited many exhibitions in London, they studied and learned from what they saw and from the books they read and the music they shared too. John was excited and stimulated, and this was manifested in his own work. Not for nothing did their brazen attitude towards the college authorities earn John and Sandy a reputation. Felix McCulloch, arts critic of the *Edinburgh Evening News*, wrote: '[George Bernard] Shaw used to be pestered by the dreaded Chesterbellock but the Edinburgh College of Art's current gadfly is the virile Bellanymoffat.'

They had begun to frequent the Rose Street pubs in their first college year, especially Milne's Bar, which was the drinking den and meeting place of the major poets and writers of the time. There they would meet up with Sydney Goodsir Smith, George Mackay Brown, Norman MacCaig, Robert Garioch, Edwin Morgan and Hugh MacDiarmid. Al had invited MacDiarmid to contribute an article to *Gambit* and a friendship had sprung up from that time. He would in later years write, along with his own powerful poetry, an impressive biography and several other publications related to the great poet.

Apart from MacDiarmid and the other major poets they met and mixed with in Milne's, Al, Sandy and John found an important mentor in the composer Ronald Stevenson, who had been Al's music teacher at school. Many trips out to his home, Townfoot House in West Linton, provided inspiration and encouragement they needed and relished. The sharing of ideas and the wide range of their discussions were brought to a thrilling finale by Ronald performing some of his latest works for piano, most memorably his well-known Passacaglia. These occasions generated a passion and energy that reinforced their approach to their work and affirmed them in the direction in which they were travelling.

John Tonge, author of a critique of Scottish art in the thirties, *The Arts of Scotland* (1938), and a personal friend of Colquhoun and MacBryde, was another important figure we encountered in Milne's. He was full of anecdotes of the painters of that time and became a steady and dedicated supporter of both Sandy and John.

There were penniless trips to London to visit museums and galleries and to study the work of their current heroes. Sleeping rough in shop doorways and the London parks was a small price to pay for the privilege of seeing such treasures. On the first trip to London in 1962 John, Sandy and Al found themselves sleeping in Green Park among the gigantic festive crowns, the like of which grace the Mall at times of Royal pageantry. They had no clear recollection of getting there but obviously stumbled on their perch after a night's boozing. On a different occasion their sleep was disturbed by a police constable who wanted them to move on from the benches in Trafalgar Square on which they had bedded down. On discovering that the three tramps were from Scotland and that one in particular hailed from Port Seton he relented. The PC came from Tranent, a few miles from Port Seton, so the boys were given his blessing and told to make themselves at home and he wished them the best night's sleep that Trafalgar Square could offer.

CHAPTER 12

Rose Street Life

After the excitement of the Festival, in September 1963 we decided to try our luck again in Golspie. The shock of 'The Nameless Ones' had worn off a bit but my parents still had to swallow hard not only over John's appearance but mine also. It would never fail to be a sore point. They and their friends had, however, fallen for John's charms and begun to enjoy him as I knew they would. The feelings were mutual. There was constant merriment and joking and my father liked nothing better than to slink off to the pub with John and join in the local camaraderie.

Back in Edinburgh once more, life resumed its pattern on Rose Street. This was the beginning of my third and John's final year. It was work hard and play hard once again.

As the bitter winter weather set in, we would find ourselves back staggering with enormous hardboard paintings of not inconsiderable weight up over Princes Street during the morning rush hour on our way to college. The gusts of wind would take the hardboard, twisting and bending it to a dangerous angle, and all but lift me off the ground. The fear was that the boards would snap in the gales, thus destroying the painting, or that we would be blown off course into the path of oncoming traffic, the former obviously the greater concern. Quite often the nudes which formed the subject matter of these paintings increased the amount of unwanted attention we attracted as we struggled up the road with them.

While planning improvements to the studio, John had one of his brainwaves. We would knock down a wall between two of the rooms. We had been assured by our friends in the building trade that it was not a supporting wall, so that was all we needed to know. It never dawned on us to ask permission from the landlord. We would be doing him a favour. We would be improving the property and thus enhancing its value. It was a dusty and noisy business but the mission was accomplished with the help of our friends who received the usual payment and we were delighted with the new open-plan arrangement.

The paintings were now back *in situ* after the Castle Terrace exhibition. One night as we were painting we heard the flap of the letterbox followed by a loud cry. Going to the door we just caught sight of someone disappearing down round the spiral of the stair. We realized that it was one of our neighbours who lived in the dark rabbit warren of rooms one floor beneath us. A couple of meths-drinkers lived there, one of whom we had gradually become acquainted with.

When one of the men died in his room downstairs, his friend had climbed up to our flat to ask if we might like some of the dead man's clothes now that he would no longer be needing them. Our visitor was probably not much older than his mid-forties but he had the appearance of someone much older. He was gaunt and withered, like someone who has lived underground, and his eyes had the characteristic red rims of meths-drinkers. John thanked him for his offer, which we declined, but he was agitated and begged us to go down with him to the room where his friend had died.

Downstairs we made our way along the unlit corridor, finding not only the lack of lighting but also the smell a considerable challenge. In the room, lit by a single light bulb, was a bed and a grimy mattress, a table and a wooden chair. On the table, stacked up as in a funfair, were countless empty tins of cocoa. Lying about among the detritus were items of soiled clothing from which our friend had obviously taken his pick and now he was fretting about what to do next. Whether there were others living there it was not clear but the scene was one that Samuel

Beckett could not have conjured up more truly – one of utter degradation and despair, a living hell inhabited by the poor wretches who had fallen into it.

Back in the studio we realized the cause of the sudden cry we had heard at our door. It dawned on us that our friend had looked through our letterbox and got the fright of his life on being confronted with the portrait of John looking straight back at him. Life-size, it was super real to his raddled mind. It was something that must have retained a scary fascination for him because thereafter we often heard the letterbox rattle and knew it was him.

Our Rose Street stair had a story to tell and its history surfaced from time to time. Men's voices could be heard shouting up from the lane after closing time.

'Moira! Moira! Moira Kerr, let me in! Moira!'

Apparently our flat and the adjoining one had been brothels in the past and when the police raided the premises the punters would try to escape through a secret panel between the two flats. It could not have been too far back in the past as, from time to time, men were still turning up hoping to get in.

By this time we had become fully integrated to the life of Rose Street and had become acquainted with the characters of the street. On our way out of an evening we would have a drink in Ma Scott's bar. Ma Scott herself seemed to have disappeared from the scene and just as well for us because she was notorious for turning away punters whom she judged to be undesirable. Scruffy-looking art students would not have stood a chance. Bert, the manager, was ex-army, a worthy successor to Ma Scott and ran the place accordingly. Long-haired, down-at-heel students were not his cup of tea either. He was in the business of attracting the public-school rugby crowd, a better class of gentlemen (and gradually their ladies, under sufferance). It took a while for us to feel welcome, and we were often thrown out for bringing with us too rowdy an entourage. However, one incident gave us the seal of approval. The risky business of the delivery to us of a painting could have gone either way as far as Bert was concerned but we were in luck. A large 6ft x 4ft life painting of the model, Carol, was being returned after an exhibition and the van had to unload in the lane just beside Scott's side door. Someone going into the bar spotted the great nude being manhandled across the road and the place emptied for a full view of proceedings. It was the talk of the bar for long to come. Any misgivings Bert had were simply overruled by the punters whose day had been made. We were ever after cause célèbre. There would often be offers to help on subsequent occasions of this nature. Our place in Ma Scott's was an uneasy honour. It was there, early one evening that November, that we first heard the news of President Kennedy's assassination.

We were too wrapped up in our life together to be governed by convention. No one who cared about that would visit Rose Street at that time, never mind live there. Mind you, potential saviours did come, in the shape of the Salvation Army. A small well-groomed lady used to frequent the pubs at weekends, her neat perm contained by her Army bonnet tied under the chin in a bow and her navy-blue uniform immaculate. She was friendly and good-natured and always brought her pet monkey with her. The punters didn't want to be saved but they were very fond of her and the monkey and generous with their donations to her box.

One of our windows looked out on to Rose Street South Lane and down on to a patch of rough grass and its surrounding wall. Whose wall was it? We didn't ask. Nobody seemed to care and so we assumed it was ours. Another Bellany brainwave was hatched. John would paint a mural on the longest wall that faced us. It was no sooner thought of than it was fait accompli. Rapidly the lumpy old stone wall was transformed by great splashes of colour. First it was painted in a couple of coats of heavy-duty outdoor paint to form a base, on which he painted a large portrait of me at one end and himself at the other. On these he superimposed geometric shapes of bright primary colours in true Léger mode. The centrepiece was the innards of our red piano, which had become surplus to requirements after we had knocked down the wall in the studio. There was nowhere now for it to stand. The strings and keys of the piano lent a dash of abstraction to the overall effect. The paint used was Woolworth's household gloss in a range of the brightest colours obtainable, contrasting slashes and patches of which intertwined throughout, uniting the two portraits and enhancing the focal point of the piano. We were pleased with the result and considered the environment vastly upgraded.

No one complained, but then it seemed to us that no one was particularly interested in the ongoings of Rose Street South Lane. A couple of people had seen John painting the wall from their windows and shouted encouragement. At least we took it to be encouragement. The greatest fan of 'The Wall' was the owner of a nearby Greek restaurant, who saw it as an asset and would direct his customers to his open windows to admire the view. When I visited more than forty years on, the little patch of grass remained uncared for and was totally sunk in dilapidation but, on pulling back the rogue elder bushes, it was a thrill to be able to identify one or two traces of the paint still visible.

CHAPTER 13

Escapades

There was no other way of living. John lived to paint and he painted big. There was something feeble, he believed, in painting on a small scale. This would be a lifelong issue for him. To pay for paintings (or anything else for that matter) to be transported was unthinkable, as the money just did not exist. There was only one thing for it. We had to do it ourselves, whatever difficulties were involved, and I was in it up to my neck. I was excused if there was anyone else around who could be drafted in to help and I could then make a hasty escape.

John's ambition was fed by a logic that was entirely his own. Social conventions were far down his list of priorities, especially if they got in the way of his plans coming to fruition. No offence or disrespect was intended and he was generally courteous. His orbit was just not cluttered up by such encumbrances, many of which he was genuinely ignorant of. His rectangular record cover design was no more than an early example of his unworldliness. The rectangle was a more congenial shape and aesthetics came well before any thought of function. He was completely taken aback by the furore it caused. It had to be spelled out to him that record covers were generally square not rectangular!

'Just go for it' was his policy. With luck on his side all went well but on some notorious occasions he found himself in big trouble. The case of the *Young Contemporaries* has become legendary.

The Young Contemporaries was the title given to a painting competition to be held in London and open to all British art students, notice of which was displayed in art schools throughout the UK. There were quite a few good painters in John's year and, with himself and Sandy the ringleaders as usual, a number of them agreed to give it a go. Entrance forms were completed and sent away. The college authorities were having nothing to do with this, so the arrangements were in the hands of the students. John was the self-appointed commander-in-chief, of course.

The work had to arrive at the YBA galleries in central London by an appointed date. Entries had been collected from each student in a van owned by a pub acquaintance and were due to arrive at Waverley Station the night before the admission date in good time to load on to the evening train to King's Cross.

The not entirely innocent plan was thought through in minute detail, with timing that would have done the Great Train Robbery proud. The idea was to get the loading done as speedily as possible without attracting too much attention from the station authorities. A lookout would be on the alert for this while a relay of about four students would do the loading. Once the guard's van had been located, the first part of the consignment was shiftily and speedily stacked on board before an approaching guardsman noticed the unusual activity.

'Wait a minute, sonny! What's going on here?'

The ensuing argument was well underway when all of a sudden the door of the guard's van was banged shut and the train slowly gathered pace as it set off on its way out of the station. The total number of paintings, most of which were very large, came to about sixty but only half of them had managed to get on the train. They were now speeding merrily off to London on their own with no authorization, no documentation of any kind and no one to deal with them on arrival at King's Cross. The other half were still in the van or half out of it in the process of being manhandled by the gang now stopped in their tracks.

The big guns were called in and the stationmaster, in full top hat and tails like the Fat Controller, proceeded to deal with the matter in hand.

John adopted the only tactics that would have occurred to him. Honest man-to-man talk. Earnestly he began to explain about the competition and how important was the noble cause of art and how the train was the only way they could get the work to London on time, etc., etc. He was always bewildered when people didn't see things his way if art, or rather the 'grandeur of art' (his favourite phrase), was the issue. But however much he tried to worm his way into a favourable position, this time it was clear his efforts were falling on deaf ears.

It was pointed out to him that what they were trying to sneak on to the guard's van was the equivalent of the contents of a small house, without any agreement from the railway authorities, not to mention payment. Of course this fell on equally deaf ears and it was total stalemate.

As a last resort, all John could think of was to summon Robin Philipson, head of painting at the college, who, he was sure, would explain to Top Hat and Co. the importance and necessity of what they were trying to do.

In due course Robin did arrive, all done up to the nines in dinner suit and bow tie as he had been interrupted at an important function. Somehow or other he achieved a truce. Probably the college had to fork out for the cost of the transport and there must have been a dressing-down waiting for the culprits, but it resulted in John and the rest of the gang being allowed to wait for the next train in a couple of hours' time, when they were given permission to load on the rest of the work and accompany it to London. I am not sure what happened at the London end but all the work arrived in time. John and Sandy both had the honour of having their work accepted for the final exhibition. A news cutting and photograph of the two of them at the time celebrates the event. It describes Sandy's entry as a political painting of a protest meeting and the title of John's was given as *Mon Hélène à Moi*. This was a portrait of me, an uncompromising 6ft x 4ft nude for which I had had to pose standing on a chaise longue in the studio. Hardly the easiest kind of thing to sneak on a train or anywhere else in those times.

Those were heady days. There always seemed to be something happening which inspired and encouraged us. Taking on the World had begun. There was no turning back. John's mission was going to be big and exciting, and it was going to be my mission too. My commitment to my own work was not strong enough. However much I loved drawing and painting, I lacked the drive and the ego that was required if I was ever to get anywhere. Thankfully I possessed the wisdom to recognize my limitations and my pride told me that if I couldn't be a great artist, I certainly didn't want to be one of the thousands of competent but mediocre ones. Also, in the face of such a towering presence as John's my efforts would be totally incongruous. There just wasn't room for more than one artist in our ménage. Or rather, one of the two used up all and more of the available space both physically and psychologically.

Up until then I, along with most students I knew, had avoided thoughts of how to survive in the future. There was never any talk of 'careers'. The only option would have been to go and train at Moray House to be art teachers and that was looked on as being The End of Everything – defeat. 'Those who can, paint; those who can't, teach,' was the saying. All we thought about was the day we were living and loving every moment of it, painting in our studios.

Preparing to spend my life 'Taking on the World' with John instead of trying to make out as a painter in my own right didn't, then or subsequently, feel like I was embarking on a course of self-sacrifice. We were consistently encountering people, in the arts and in all other dimensions, who inspired us. Our range of experience was widening our horizons. The whole world seemed to be opening up to delight and educate and nourish us. What my contribution to our lives in the future would be would emerge in its own time, of that I had no doubt. In the meantime I had a part to play. I was a fully qualified fellow traveller on the ultimate Blaikie's Mystery Tour that promised to provide a lifetime's adventure and the adventure of a lifetime. There were no guarantees that it would be an easy journey. We had no thoughts of material comfort, and wealth was not the goal, but glories there would be, of that we were sure. I was John's sounding board, his accomplice, and our hearts and minds were in harmony. Our song was one of optimism and fearlessness, and our journey was starting off on a path illuminated by a spirit and imagination that would never fail us.

CHAPTER 14

Taking on the World

There were obstacles in our way and one was my father's declaration that we could not get married until we had finished our student days, 'until you have stopped living off the state,' he said, referring to the meagre student grants we were receiving (a rare luxury nowadays). But John was hoping to be awarded a postgraduate year at Edinburgh and we didn't want to wait any longer. We were tired of the charade. Although I was over the age of consent, I wanted my parents to support my marriage and so, after a long battle, they relented and the wedding was set for 19 September 1964.

In the fifties and early sixties, birth control was a problem for women. John and I had managed somehow to avoid trouble so far but there was now talk of the Pill and I was keen to find out more. I had heard about a family planning clinic in Edinburgh, so I went along. To get any kind of contraceptive advice the proviso was that you had to provide proof that you were going to get married. I was informed that the receipt for a wedding ring or some part of a bridal outfit (with your own name on it, no cheating) had to be offered. If you could not come up with the required paperwork, you wouldn't get help.

The Edinburgh Mothers' Welfare with its discreet brass plaque was situated on Dean Terrace on the ground floor of a fine Georgian house. Inside the large reception room there were two queues of women. It was explained that one queue was for the married ladies and the other one was for the unmarried ones, with their compulsory paper proof of legitimacy. A great air of embarrassment pervaded the room, especially in the unmarried queue, and everyone spoke in hushed tones. The consultations with the elderly female doctors, for some reason, entailed physical examinations, which, I imagined, might negate the symbol of purity that the required wedding-veil receipt seemed to imply and this only added to the feeling of guilt surrounding the women's visits. For some reason I can't now recall, and in spite of the admittedly dubious paper work I had obtained, the outcome of my visit was that there would be no contraceptive pill provided for me.

The end of the academic year brought John's Diploma show. This included a 3ft x 4ft painting of two boats on a slip, the large life painting of Carol, one of our favourite models at college, and an arresting still life of the crucifixion of three fish. *The Boat Builders*, the colossal four-panelled painting of the building of The Good Hope which he had completed in the mural room, his most ambitious and most accomplished work to date, was the centrepiece. All his best drawings were presented on challenging red mounts but the power of his graphic work was such that he got away with it. The whole show was outstanding and of course to our great delight he won his postgraduate year. This meant that we would both still be students while I finished my fourth and final year.

During the Festival, there was to be another open-air exhibition by John and Sandy. This time they decided they needed a more prominent pitch and so the idea formed in their minds to ask permission to site it on the railings just outside their bête noir – the Royal Scottish Academy. It was right in the centre of the city and furthermore it provided just the cheeky stance from which to stage their dismissal of what went on inside the building.

As usual the works were large and some still bore the traces of Léger inspiration. The dark upright figures of *Three Fishermen* stood next to one of my favourites of those early years, a striking transcription of Bellini's *Agony in the Garden* (now lost). There was a painting of a group of young men reminiscent of the Beatles grouped around a large cannon, *Homage to Douanier Rousseau*; a sepia drawing on hardboard, *The Silver Darlings*; and a life-size self-portrait complete with Russian hat. They, along with Sandy's politically inspired works, had to be heaved across Princes Street every morning and, once *in situ*, called out in noisy proclamation to the crowds of Festival visitors and performers that summer.

Soon after the start of the exhibition John appointed himself to go across to the RSA and, bold as brass, ask if it was possible to store their paintings in the building, just as they had been allowed to do in the Unitarian Church on Castle Terrace. The attendant on duty walked across to inspect the work involved and took it upon himself to give his consent for them to be stored in the basement overnight for the duration of the Festival. This was an astonishing coup and they carefully played down the barefaced cheek of the situation as they hastened to accept. It was going to save them the hard work of struggling across Princes Street every morning and night to and from the basement of Milne's Bar, which had been kindly put at their disposal by Bob Watt, the manager.

They considered themselves well set up. They had the benefit of the pipe band that paraded daily along Princes Street, attracting crowds of tourists and playing out their finale just beside their exhibition pitch. Friends would pass the time of day with them, and the media, along with the Festival onlookers, loved them.

Things were going well for a few days until the RSA attendant came to inform them that his benevolence to the lads had landed him in such deep trouble that it might result in him losing his job. The powers that be were rightly incensed at the effrontery of the pair of upstarts, so the deal was off. After that, it was Bob Watt to the rescue again and back to dodging across Princes Street with the heavy loads, morning and night.

The exhibition, however, was a great success. It had been three weeks of hard graft with virtually no money at the end of

PARIS NOV '86
BELLANY.

it but they had achieved what they had set out to do. They had had their voices heard and made themselves known to a much wider audience and the constant attention from the newspapers and television ensured that their enterprise would go down in the annals of Edinburgh Festival history.

Following that triumph, on 19 September 1964 John and I were married in the little whitewashed St Andrew's Church in Golspie. It was a typical early autumn day of sunshine and a few light showers as we posed for photographs among the grave-stones in the churchyard. Yes, I expected that we would have sunshine and showers too in our life ahead, but I believed that we also had everything you could possibly need to withstand whatever came our way.

'Grant them the love that knows no ending whom thou for evermore dost join in one,' the hymn of our blessing implored. That was all we wanted and we never doubted that it would go with us forever.

'Grant them the joy that brightens earthly sorrow.' Yes, we would have all of that too.

In my memory it was a day of pure gold. We could not have asked for more. All the people we loved were there from both sides of the family. All the invited guests from Port Seton had made the long journey north. All our old family friends and relations were with us, as were friends from school and from the art college too.

On the arm of my proud and happy father I made my way to the church accompanied by Lachie Leitch, the renowned Golspie piper who played us out of the church as husband and wife. At the reception in the Burghfield Hotel in Dornoch, after the meal there was dancing to a local band and my cousin John Wiseman recorded the proceedings on cine film. This was a great joy in the future to my father, who liked nothing better than to play it over to anyone who cared to see it – running backwards, which he thought preferable and absolutely hilarious.

It was a true Highland village wedding and, as with all great days, over too soon. The sun was setting over the Kyle of Sutherland as we climbed aboard the evening train that would take us south to Inverness, and the strains of the Bonar Bridge pipe band came wafting across the stillness of the mirror-smooth waters as we took our leave.

Then we were off to France. We travelled across to Dieppe on the ferry from Newhaven, sailing into the harbour under the high white cliffs with the little church on the top, an image that would be imprinted forever in my memory.

In those days the harbour was busy with the daily fish market and the atmosphere was vibrant. We particularly enjoyed the idea that Dieppe was a place always popular with painters and liked to think of Delacroix, Pissarro, Modigliani, Gauguin, Monet and Braque, many Scottish and English painters and countless others working away there, revelling in all that we were now seeing. Like them, John always had his drawing book with him and never stopped working.

We took the coastal bus and found ourselves at Fécamp, another fishing paradise. From there we travelled along to Étretat and marvelled at the towering cliffs and the needle standing proud in the waves where it had broken away. We did not travel far and we were not very adventurous, always conscious that the money might run out, but what we saw inspired us.

Our aim was to get to Paris and this we did. I had been there once on a school trip but I longed to see it again – the galleries, the food, the *vin rouge*, the look of everything French and the sound of France and the romance of the Seine for young people at the start of their lives together. We did all the tourist things like climbing the Eiffel Tower, boating down the Seine at night, going in awe into the Cathedral of Nôtre Dame, sitting at the cafes on the boulevards. But we also spent hours in the Louvre looking at the Courbets, especially *Funeral at Ornans*, and all the other favourite paintings of Delacroix, Gericault and Rembrandt. At the Jeu de Paume we immersed ourselves in the Impressionists and Post-Impressionists, and in the Musée D'art Moderne we saw the painters of the school of Paris. In every gallery John would be taking notes and drawing. We strolled along by the bookstalls on the left bank of the Seine and took the Metro. All we did and all we saw was unforgettable and we vowed that we would do it all again, often.

We just managed to get home with the last of the money. My father had agreed to meet us in Edinburgh, his car stuffed with our wedding presents. He was speechless, as I had expected, when he saw where we were living.

The generosity in villages at times of weddings is legendary. We couldn't use most of the household stuff, so it had to be stored at Port Seton. But the electrical goods became very useful to us at the ends of terms. By that time we would have run out of money and so we would take a couple of travelling bags full of our shiny new presents to the pawn shop. The money we got for them kept us afloat until the grants came at the beginning of the next term, when we could go and retrieve our goods again. We always had an unused bagful ready for the purpose and had reason to be very glad of them.

CHAPTER 15

Postgraduate Year

John began his postgraduate year full of enthusiasm. He was given a room of his own in a large house in Inverleith Row newly taken over by the college. There he would be able to work without any interruption. His room was on the first floor and had a spectacular view of the Edinburgh skyline. There was the Castle on its rock commanding the incline of the High Street as it made its way down to Holyrood Palace at the bottom of the Royal Mile, the whole movement of which was punctuated by the spire of St Giles and the towers of the Assembly Halls. Then there were the skies and the sunsets. He quickly realized that if he was going to get any work done he would have to find something to block out the view. Muslin draped over the large windows was soon in place and work commenced. I believe that it was one of the most productive periods of his life. He came home in the evening tired out but aflame with what he had done during the day and full of ideas of what he would do next. He loved having a studio all to himself and couldn't wait to show me his new work at weekends. We shared a deep instinctual understanding of what he was trying to say and the nature of his visual language, and I was just as excited as he was.

It was in this postgraduate year that he painted *Allegory*, now in the collection of the Scottish National Gallery of Modern Art. This was John's Crucifixion scene played out with three giant fish on the stakes, an idea he developed from his diploma painting of the still life but on a much grander scale. He also painted *The Box Meeting*, based on the traditional event that had taken place annually for many generations at Cockenzie and Port Seton when the deeds of the boats were blessed and carried in their boxes in procession through the town, gifts having been distributed to those in need, after which the day ended in a wild celebration. This painting has rarely been exhibited.

Fishers in the Snow was also completed during this period, a mural that was acquired for Chesser House, the Edinburgh headquarters of the Ministry of Agriculture and Fisheries. All of these works were painted on hardboard and all on a large scale of approximately 10ft x 12ft. They were triumphant works by any standard. John was flying!

He had long ago decided that he was going to apply to the Royal College of Art in London for their postgraduate course. This would enable him to continue painting for another three years and would bring him into contact with the wider world of art. This had been our ambition for the last few years – so much for my father's idea that we should wait to get married when we were 'no longer living off the state'! John would, if he was successful in being accepted for the RCA, have been a student for eight years by the time he finished. This fact was subsequently pointed out by some members of his local authority on discussing his application for a further grant for the RCA course and nearly caused his request to be turned down. It was granted by a narrow margin.

In order to apply for the RCA, John had to have recommendations from the staff at the college. Willie Gillies refused to give his blessing as he reckoned that 'he doesn't need any more student days.' However, John went ahead and joined the other applicants in an entrance exam at the college in London that lasted for five days.

When the news came through that John's application had been successful, we were mad with excitement and celebrated in style. The news filtered through to the newspapers and he was invited for an interview on the early evening television news. For this we had to go through to the BBC in Glasgow and in the lift going up to the news studio we bumped into the burly actor who had played Oddjob in the latest Bond movie, *From Russia with Love*. He was dressed for his part and was carrying the deadly bowler hat.

Sometime in the autumn term, I discovered a flaw in my wedding ring. There was, to my horror, a fissure where it had probably been made smaller for me. This went about one third of the way through the ring. The fishing community was governed by superstition to a degree much more intense than in the population at large but certain similar observances were part of my upbringing as well and I was young and immature enough to still be fettered by them. My ring was solid and in no danger of breaking but it still had this fault line. I tried to banish the feeling that the flaw in my ring was a bad omen but it bothered me. There was nothing that I could do about it, however, as I always believed it was bad luck ever to take off your wedding ring, even to have it mended.

At the beginning of 1965, our landlord came to inform us that he needed the studio. We flattered ourselves that he had been so impressed with how we had developed it that he had decided he could, with a little more work, have it classified as residential accommodation. We were panic-stricken until he told us that he owned another property just along the road in Rose Street and we could move in there. We loved the studio and didn't want to leave it. We explained that we would be leaving Edinburgh in the October as we were going to London and asked if we could remain where we were until then, but nothing doing: he turned us down.

Our new flat was on the first floor above the Auld Hundred pub on the corner of Rose Street and Frederick Street. It comprised three rooms and there was a lavatory on the landing which we would share with the quiet couple who lived in the other half of the flat. It had more light and was more spacious but we never felt at home there the way we had done in 150 Rose Street South Lane above Ma Scott's.

The best feature of the new place was a fairly large sitting room overlooking Frederick Street, from the two windows of which you could look out over to the castle. One of the other rooms looking down on to Rose Street was a kitchen with a cooker and a sink. We had gone up in the world.

It was quite a task to transport our belongings from one place to the other and it was all done on foot, including the removal of the bed, table and chairs. Most of the effort was spent bringing our paintings and finding somewhere to store them. One end of the kitchen was allocated for that; we would use the large room as a studio/sitting room. After we had everything moved in, I went out for a couple of hours and when I returned John was full of excitement to show me what he had done.

The large room, which had been newly decorated in what we had decided was hideous floral wallpaper, had been transformed. The walls were now a vibrant burnt-orange colour and adorning them were John's newest large paintings. The *pièce de résistance* was the high ceiling which now was covered in true Sistine Chapel style with a wild Alan Davie design. As I returned to the flat, John was just adding the finishing touches and was delighted with what he had achieved. I couldn't believe he had done all this in such a short time.

'But, how ... ? Where did you ... ?'

'Never bother with questions,' he said. 'What do you think of it? Isn't it fantastic?'

Oh yes, it was fantastic and I loved the effect. My suspicions as to the speed of the transformation were, however, instantly confirmed by gently pulling out one of the paintings from the wall to find the flowery wallpaper intact behind the painting.

He had started on the ceiling and put all his energy into the Davie creation, as he had done with the outdoor mural on the Rose Street Lane wall. After that, he had hung his paintings and then the brainwave had occurred. The flowery wallpaper had to be eliminated, so a handy supply of burnt Sienna powder paint mixed with adhesive would just do the trick. In no time at all he had swished the powdery mixture round all the paintings, with extra daubs required for the more persistent gold foliage. Job done. The whole effect glowed with a sort of grandeur which we felt suitably reflected our aims and ambitions.

During the Easter holidays we hitchhiked to Belgium. We wanted to go to Ostend to see the Ensor Museum. Ensor had recently swum into John's field of vision and he longed to see his paintings face to face. James Ensor had grown up in a sea port and there was an instant identification with aspects of his life. Ensor was grounded in the European tradition but at the same time his voice was of his own day and spoke of a personal and entirely unique vision. The scale and monumentality of *Christ's Entry to Brussels* overwhelmed John and he could identify with the work in general as being that of a kindred spirit, someone from a modest background who had stayed true to himself throughout his life.

From Ostend we travelled to Antwerp to the Royal Museum of Fine Arts, with Rogier van der Weyden, Bosch, Breughel, Cranach, Van Eyck and Hans Memling among the European Masters in its collection. In Rubens' House we saw works of Van Dyck and Jacob Jordaens. Then it was on to Brussels and the Musée des Beaux Arts. All those great masterpieces we found in Belgium were food of the gods for John and, as usual, he recorded his impressions. To see such wonders for the first time with a hungry eye and open heart is an unforgettable moment. Those paintings were speaking to him and affirming for him the road he was taking. They were strengthening the foundations of creativity, from which he would craft his own voice, and all that we saw educated and inspired me too. Everywhere we went my learning was enhanced by seeing it with him.

We travelled home full of excitement. Paintings were already forming in his mind and I could not wait to see how he would use the information he had acquired on our trip. We were returning to our last term at the college, my diploma and his postgraduate show, and after the summer we would be going to London. As we had travelled on the way to Belgium so we travelled back, standing by the road hopefully and jumping in and out of high lorries until we arrived at Burnmouth on the Scottish borders. From Burnmouth we walked to Eyemouth and stayed with Grandma and Grandpa for a couple of days.

Walking back up the road from Eyemouth to the main east coast road to Edinburgh, I started lagging behind. I was feeling dizzy and couldn't wait to get a lift home.

CHAPTER 16

Arrivals and Departures

A couple of days later I emerged from my GP's surgery at Holy Corner and caught the bus into Princes Street. I looked at my fellow passengers sitting there concerned with their own thoughts. None of them knew! Twenty minutes previously I hadn't known either, or even suspected. Now I was bursting to tell them all and the world too.

I was going to have a baby.

I was incoherent with happiness as I tried to tell John. He was just as excited and he too wanted to tell the world.

Our baby was due to arrive in the middle of December. There was no thought of whether this would be convenient or whether we could afford to have a baby, or any concern about the practicalities. We were going to London in October and we did not yet have a place to live there, money would definitely be tight but there was a total lack of apprehension. We had our dreams to follow and everything else would fall into place as we went along. We were going to London and we would soon have a baby to share our adventure.

For now it was back to college and back to hard work. In June, along with the rest of my year, I was framing and hanging my diploma show. It was hard work and we were all full of anxiety. Suddenly this idyllic time at college was coming to an end. We had been privileged for four years to study, in this magnificent building, a subject we loved, among a family of student friends, and experience the *joie de vivre* of student life that we would never forget.

John was also putting the finishing touches to his work at Inverleith. For this final college show he exhibited the great *Allegory* triptych, along with the vast diptych *The Box Meeting*, the first of the three versions of the *Fishers in the Snow* and the arresting (8ft x 6ft) painting of *The Fish Gutter*. There was also a self-portrait that the college now owns and a 5ft x 3ft portrait of me. I am standing against a red background and proudly wearing a new (Doubtfire's) fur coat and thigh-length leather boots. It was an astonishing show by any standards but not least for a young man of twenty-two.

As a parting gift, the college had awarded John another travelling scholarship. This we would use to visit Amsterdam and the other major galleries in Holland. As my friend Irene had also been awarded a small scholarship, she was going to come with us. We flew out to Amsterdam from Southend in a tiny moth of a plane. I was about five months pregnant and had become accustomed to the little fluttery movements which on this short flight went into overdrive. It was the first time I had ever been in a plane.

When we arrived in central Amsterdam, we queued up to find somewhere to stay. It was very hot that summer in Holland and we seemed to walk for miles to get to the museums. We had to keep on the move in order to see all we wanted before the money ran out. Occasionally we splashed out and ate *nasi goreng* or *bami goreng* in a cheap Indonesian restaurant but mostly we bought *broodjes* and delicious chips in mayonnaise from street vendors. The small amount of money we had was conserved for getting to the museums.

We made the rounds of the Rijksmuseum, where the great Rembrandts overwhelmed us and bade us return again and again. We were mesmerized by the power of *The Night Watch*. To add to the moment, John came across a small etching that was still in the early stages of preparation with only the ground and rudimentary drawing laid down. On studying this work he maintained that he could detect elements of cubism, pure and unadorned. He was so excited by this print that he subsequently based an essay on the theory that, way before Picasso and Braque, the origins of cubism could be traced back to Rembrandt.

Before travelling round the Netherlands, we spent hours in the Stedelijk Museum and the Van Gogh Museum. Then we found ourselves lingering in a park full of contemporary sculpture in Leiden, in the Museum of Contemporary Art in The Hague, and in the modern city of Rotterdam, we gazed up at the sinuous form of the great Zadkine sculpture as it twisted its way skywards in eloquent and moving memorial to the city which was largely destroyed in the Second World War.

For John, who was relating what he was seeing to his own experience and his own rationale of what he expected art to provide, those were moments of affirmation. He had just started on his journey and on the search for his own path, and these were beacons guiding him forward and fulfilling the deep human need for reassurance and sense of direction. These early tentative steps of his were landing on fertile ground. Although these first encounters with such great artworks made a huge impression on our young minds, we were aware that there was still much concealed within them that would only be revealed in future engagement.

Of course, we were not going to leave Holland before checking out what was doing in the fishing communities. We found ourselves at Enkhuizen on the Zuiderzee and, looking around for somewhere to stay, near the harbour we discovered a tower on the waterway. This was the Drommedaris, a medieval tower and gateway which had begun to be used for cultural events and, to our delight, also offered cheap accommodation. We settled there for the last week of our trip.

John decided that as we were to stay here for a week he would get on with some oil painting, which he would do in our room. He found an art shop in the small town and just got going. Several paintings were completed but as they were not small we had to leave them at the Drommedaris, managing to sell one before we departed. However, many works were done on paper, several of which were made in triptych form. These we transported home in a bulging portfolio.

At his own request John was allowed to go off on a fishing boat into the Zuiderzee, on an all-night excursion. By his account he had to steer the boat at one point while the fishermen had some sleep but he still managed to do some drawing. While in Enkhuizen we found a small museum related to fishing on the Zuiderzee and before we left John presented some of his drawings to the collection.

We returned to Scotland just in time to organize the railings exhibition for the 1965 Festival. For the second year running it would be situated outside the Royal Scottish Academy. The previous Festival exhibition there had, like the 1963 Castle Terrace event, been a great success, and it was their aim to make this one even better. The arrangements were the same as before – storing the paintings in the basement of Milne's Bar and calling in as many friends as possible to do the transporting to and fro.

After the glory of the Festival exhibition, we went back to Golspie and immersed ourselves in the comfort of the family and the peace and solitude of Sutherland. We were going to depart for London in about three weeks' time but we still had not found anywhere to live. There was mounting anxiety in both our families, not only about that but also because no arrangements had been made for the birth of the baby. They could not believe how laid-back we were and, in retrospect, nor can I. Our naivety and optimism did not allow for any problems. John's place at the RCA was assured and we knew the direction we were taking, so everything else would fall into place as we went along. However, it was finally decided that I should come home for the birth to take place in Raigmore Hospital in Inverness, as was the custom for Golspie mothers.

At the end of September we packed up our possessions in Edinburgh, storing all we could at Port Seton in the attic, and the paintings, including many that had been in the Festival exhibition, in the garage in the back garden. We bequeathed our flat, complete with ceiling mural and roaring orange walls (now with large patches of flowery wallpaper), to friends. We had not found anywhere to store some of our paintings at the time of our departure and so left them in one of the rooms with a promise that we would have them moved as soon as we could. The solution to this problem was difficult to find and our time ran out. I don't know what happened to them but they were eventually disposed of and we never saw them again.

It was time for our farewell at Port Seton. John decided to honour his family in the finest forget-me-not gesture he believed it was possible to make. While his parents were out at work he insisted I help him carry the panels of *Allegory* in from the garage and after moving the china cabinet and the rest of the furniture out of the way, and removing the small painting of a boat that had previously graced the room, the huge panels were, with three-inch nails, hammered in position on to the main wall of the sitting room.

The mighty *Allegory* in all its glory covered the whole wall. The great crucified fish towered over the small room and John was glowing with pride, unable to wait for his parents' return. One of his greatest masterpieces for them to see in their living room every day! What a thrill they would get!

It was with regret that he had to put the china cabinet back in position, because it rather spoiled the effect by concealing part of the painting. However his mother was quite fond of her cabinet and he didn't think she would want it moved out of the way. He couldn't have been more correct.

After they got their breath back at the surprise awaiting them, they thanked us for our awfully kind idea. Yes, it was very fine. Then, after our fond farewells they waved us off as we made our way to the bus for Edinburgh. Margaret was going to accompany us to London so that I would not be on my own during the day while John attended college.

After waving us out of sight, his mum and dad closed the door and immediately went to work. By the time our bus was taking its departure from Port Seton they were struggling out to the garage with the gigantic and totally unwieldy masterpiece where, among the lawnmower and hedge clippers and array of old bikes and half-empty pots of paint, it would remain for about twenty years. All that remained of *Allegory* in the sitting room were the unsightly gashes made by the giant nails.

We, meanwhile, set off to our new life buoyed up on the big-hearted benevolence of our gesture, in blissful ignorance of the fate that had immediately befallen *Allegory*.

CHAPTER 17

London

We arrived during the first week of a sizzling hot October in 1965. It was like going off to a desert island – only essential items to be taken, with survival the criterion. We had a suitcase each, one of which was partially full of paints and brushes and sketchbooks. John had decided that the new life in London could not be contemplated without the large model fishing boat called 'the Margaret' that his father had made. My essential item was my sewing machine.

A watchful pigeon looking on from the top of Nelson's Column would have seen the taxi rattling through Trafalgar Square, on down the Mall towards Buckingham Palace with a large model boat, a sewing machine and three uneasy passengers, one almost seven months pregnant, all beginning to worry about the cost of the journey. We believed the driver realized we were new to the city and mightn't know our way around, so he could take the liberty of extending the journey into the sightseeing tour we feared he was treating us to, and this would be reflected in the fare. Should we remind him it was Earl's Court we wanted to go to? We did and he was going there. The quickest way.

We soon arrived at our destination. Warwick Road is one of the two major arteries through Earl's Court and as we stopped outside No. 9, cars and lorries were hurtling past as though in a race. The noise was like thunder echoing through a canyon. Everything was speeding and screeching and never stopping and seeming to get louder by the minute. We had to shout to each other to be heard. We had arrived in our new life.

Just two weeks before we left Edinburgh, we had bumped into a friend who was living in London and asked him if he could possibly find us somewhere to live. I am stunned by our nonchalance, but we were very glad to have somewhere to come to and now this was it. The landlord showed us up to the top of the four-storey house to our room at the back of the building. We were shown into a room with twin beds and a table and armchair. On unlocking the door we were almost knocked down by the smell. This came from the cheap green carpet that covered a bit of the floor. Someone had recently tried to clean off the stains and it was still wet. The room was stifling and the sun blasting in the window was intensifying the odour of the wet stains. As usual my first need was to see the view from the window and there it was – the back of a funeral parlour in the yard, in which a row of hearses was parked. We flung open the window in search of fresh air and a cloud of sunbathing blue bottles swarmed into the room.

It was decided that Margaret and I would occupy the beds and John would sleep in the armchair. It was so hot that none of us slept and soon it was time for John to set off for his first day at the RCA.

In the morning after he had left, Margaret and I were still in bed trying to rest when there was a rattling at the door and there was the landlord. He had unlocked the door with his key and was letting himself in to clean the room, he said. Alarmed, I thanked him but assured him that we did not need any cleaning that day. Oh, but it was part of his contract and one of the requirements of our agreement in renting the room was that we vacate the premises daily, only returning in the evening. I explained that my husband was at college during the day but as I was pregnant I would need to rest while he was out. He was adamant. He would be back, he said, and furthermore he drew our attention to the fact that there were three of us while the room was only meant for two. Totally against the rules. We would have to find somewhere else to live.

At a street cafe nearby, we watched the world whizz by and tried to make light of the situation. It was Margaret's first visit to London and she was intrigued by all there was to see. There were so many nationalities, modes of dress and languages surrounding us. My thoughts drifted to all those other lives that were passing us by, and wondering about them took the edge off the precariousness of our plight.

Of course there were no mobile phones, so we could not know how John was getting on until we saw him later. He always loved to tell me the details of what he had been doing if I hadn't been with him. He was a great raconteur and I loved to listen to his tales. He was well aware that after enjoying the elevated status he had won in Edinburgh, from now on in London he would be coming up against 'the big boys'. His sense of identity was rock solid, as was his belief in his work, but he would need all the resolution and single-mindedness he had shown up north to cope with the swirling currents of this much deeper pool.

The painting school of the Royal College of Art in those days was situated in Exhibition Road in South Kensington, opposite the Science Museum. The entrance was an arched doorway tucked in adjacent to the Victoria and Albert Museum. The new students came from all over the country. What concerned John was the working area he had been given. The same proportions as every other student, it was minuscule in relation to the size of his paintings. He just could not see how it was going to work for him. It was something he would have to deal with as soon as he could.

The most pressing problem was our accommodation. We decided that we would have to start looking immediately in the local newspapers to find somewhere else to go. In the windows of newsagents we found plenty of adverts for furnished flats to rent. The problem was the cost. Most of them were bedsitters but were still too expensive. Others brazenly stipulated, 'No coloureds', 'No pets', and, relevant to our own particular search, 'No children'. Our choice was severely limited but obviously not as limited as for some other people. What kind of place was this? What kind of people were those landlords?

Margaret and I left our room every morning in order to keep out of the way of the landlord and went in search of accommodation, staying out until John returned from college. On the Friday of that week we saw an advert for two rooms with a shared bathroom in a house in Putney. It was just possible for us financially but the drawback was that children were on no account welcome. As far as I was concerned, there was no point in even thinking about that one. But, oh no, John was adamant that we should give it a go and made an appointment to see it the next day. We had seen nothing else whatsoever, so we had nothing to lose in trying.

'Now, Helen, pull yourself up tall. Hold yourself in. A bit more! OK, right, now walk up and down so I can see. Once more! Keep holding yourself in! OK, stay like that.'

We had taken the tube to Putney Bridge. John was in full 'where there's a will' mode and had made up his mind that we were going to get the flat. I was quite large by then and although the weather was scorching he thought it best if I wore Margaret's long woollen cloak in order to camouflage my condition. Just around the corner from the address he stopped and stood back and again put me through my paces.

Napier Avenue is a comfortable middle-class residential road with pretty front window boxes. It was devoid of the speed and noise and anonymity of Earl's Court. I liked what I saw and arrived at No. 16 walking as tall as I could and holding myself in for all I was worth.

Despite their Scottish name, Mr and Mrs Gordon were Polish and wanted to know all about us. We explained about John being at the RCA and they told us about the accommodation they were offering. It was a very quiet house, they said, and all the other residents were elderly like themselves. We were taken to see the available rooms upstairs. The main one was fairly large because of its bay window, from which there was a good view of the street. It was furnished in heavy, highly polished, dark mahogany, including a bed. There was a very narrow small kitchen, off which there was a tiny box room.

While we were being shown around, John, I knew, would

be eyeing up the doorways, mentally working out whether he would be able to get 8ft x 6ft hardboard up the stairs and into the rooms. He would also be moving the furniture to one side and removing the dreary prints off the walls, arranging his working space and where he would hang his paintings. To me this felt like home sweet home compared to where we were in Earl's Court. It was a refuge. Oh, yes, please, we would like to have it.

The Gordons had liked the fact that we were Scottish but the real stroke of luck happened when I told them that I came from the far north, away beyond Inverness. Mr Gordon had served in the Polish forces that had been stationed near Inverness during the war. He was thrilled by this connection and went to find his old ordnance survey map of the north of Scotland so I could show him where I came from. We were in!

While Mr G was finding the map, Mrs G was fetching glasses and the sherry bottle to toast the transaction. I was feeling quite light-headed by this time with the effort demanded by my subterfuge.

'We must tell them, John!'

'Just wait until we have signed the agreement,' said he.

But my Sunday-school conscience would not be silenced. As the couple came happily back into the room I blurted out, 'We don't have children now but we are just about to have a baby!'

'A *baby!*'

I could just feel John's despair. 'That's that f****d up!' he would be thinking.

Mrs Gordon's protruding blue eyes turned on me like lasers. As I opened my cloak and breathed out, she sighed.

'Yes . . .I see.'

There was a lot of frantic talking over each other as they repeated that they needed to have a quiet house and we hastened to inform them that I would be going back to Scotland in six weeks' time to have the baby. After that, we said, we would find somewhere else. Just please could we stay there until then.

Please.

Because they liked us and I had a favoured homeland, they

kindly agreed to let us live there until the baby was born. They were sorry they could not have a baby in their house but until then we were welcome. As a goodwill gesture Mr Gordon gave me the map as a gift.

The house was silent and gloomy. Everything in it was highly polished, which did nothing to relieve the darkness. All the time we lived there we never saw another tenant but from the occasional sound of coughing we knew they were in their rooms.

I felt safe there, however. While John was at college I roamed around the area, a collection of residential roads grouped around the prestigious Hurlingham Club. I would go down to the river and over Putney Bridge to the High Street, and back home I sat and read in the bay window.

I was completely untroubled by thoughts that the baby might come early or that something might go wrong. Those weeks I was in London I saw no doctor and attended no clinic. In fact I had sought no antenatal care throughout the whole pregnancy. In those days there were no scans to detect any problems and less attention given to pregnant mothers. Due to the uncertainty of our whereabouts I also flew under the radar of the basic care provided and it didn't occur to me to seek it out.

That first weekend in Putney we decided we would celebrate the fact that it was Saturday night. We were also feeling relieved that we had found a sort of home. We trailed round to the nearest pub just beside Putney Bridge tube station and sat there, John with his pint, and orange juice for me. It obviously wasn't a Saturday-night pub. It was a weekday, lunchtime place. We sat on, desperately looking for any sign of life to come along. We began to reminisce about all our friends in Edinburgh, imagining them at that moment in Milne's Bar, and were seized by homesickness. It took a lot of getting used to the fact that after college was over, London students just made for home and home was in all the far-flung corners of the city. There would be no meeting place as in Edinburgh where you could be sure of finding a kindred spirit.

John soon found a source for the large hardboard he required. It was a wood yard conveniently situated round the corner.

His mental calculations had been very accurate and soon, to my increasing anxiety, he began to smuggle his 8ft x 6ft panels into our flat. Once they were installed, the large furniture would have to be moved over as silently as we could manage for them to be laid on the floor and primed with several coats of white paint before he could get going on them.

We went to elaborate lengths to avoid the Gordons getting into our room, because we knew if they could see what was happening we would be out on our ears. Our luck held much longer than it should have done but the day came, as it must, when they crossed the threshold to be confronted with the full 8ft x 6ft glory of *Two Fish Gutters* propped up against their giant wardrobe. Behind it there was a stack of assorted-sized work, including a couple of paintings of the Thames at Putney, portraits of me and of Grandma. To add insult to injury, their eyes could not fail to behold the array of boards in the process of being primed, the large pot of white paint resting on the numerous newspapers that covered their shiny polished floor.

John was the cleanest painter I have ever come across. He always used to claim that he could paint in a dinner suit and it was true; he never left any rogue traces of paint. There was not a mark on the floor or walls of the apartment but it was too much for the Gordons. They were good people who had been kind and did not deserve tenants like us.

One of the two fish gutters John had painted, he thought, looked like Auntie Mary. But if, indeed, any part of her benevolent spirit was in that painting she had lost her touch, because when the Gordons surveyed the scene they told us we must find somewhere else to live as soon as possible.

Margaret had gone home after staying a fortnight and we had now been at the Gordons' for about four weeks. I would be going back to Golspie shortly as there were only four weeks to go before the baby was expected. We began searching once again for accommodation, scouring the London newspapers and the newsagents' window adverts.

We went to look at several places, the most memorable of which was advertised as a flat in Shepherd's Bush. It was situated fairly near the Shepherd's Bush market on Uxbridge Road. What we found was a butcher's shop, below which we were taken to see two rooms with cement walls and no windows. The bathroom was an outside toilet. It was the stuff of horror movies and made me want to get on the first train back to Scotland.

John eventually found a place in Streatham. This was a small ground-floor flat in a newly refurbished Victorian house on a residential street. It had a small garden. Apart from being much further away from the RCA, it would be ideal. We said that we would take it and agreed to move in two days later. It was unfurnished but we considered that to be a short-term problem. We'd soon find the local junk shops. In fact we had seen some from the bus on our way there.

The next day we went looking for a bed that John was convinced he had seen. A long walk down an unending road, round another corner and another one and another one. By this time I had developed a constant nagging pain due to the position of the growing baby and I had to stop and rest on a low wall. John went on to find the shop with the bed outside. I sat on the wall for a long time waiting. Eventually I spotted him returning. He told me he hadn't found the shop and as my face fell in despair and exhaustion he laughed. Only joking! Not only had the bed been purchased, he triumphantly told me, but he had bought a chair too. A nursing chair!

I had been told by my mother that we would have to have a nursing chair for when the baby was born. We were not quite sure what kind of chair that was but I was under the impression it had to be quite low and comfortable and without arms.

We left the Gordons', with much regret expressed on both sides, and moved to Streatham the following day, where we found the bed and chair already delivered and waiting for us stacked outside the front door. There was no one around, as the upper floor was as yet unoccupied. We wandered through the small flat, John busy with his mental calculations and me with forming our nest. Was I seeing a small child playing there in the garden with me keeping watch? Were there good people living upstairs? Could I imagine us being there for some time to come?

The bed was dragged inside and eventually put together. The nursing chair was high backed with wooden slats and narrow wooden arms. It reminded me of the old rustic chair my Granda used to sit in as he read his newspaper. When I sat in it, my feet dangled off the floor but once John had sawed the legs down a bit it would be the last word in comfort – well, maybe something like that! Fifty years on it remains part of our lives, still with the slight wobble in its uneven legs.

That night neither of us slept a wink. We had tried to make ourselves cosy with our bed and chair and the model boat displayed on the mantelpiece but I was concerned about all the things we would have to buy. The floorboards were bare; we had no furniture. We had not kept anything from Edinburgh, as the cost of transporting things to London would have been out of our reach. I knew that our money was severely limited. John, of course, was probably more preoccupied with the practicalities of his painting facilities in the flat than anything else. If he had other worries he had probably consigned them to the 'something will turn up' box.

After a sleepless night we discussed the problem of money. The flat was going to cost us a whole £10 per week, on top of which were John's fares to South Ken, and no matter how we added everything up there was no way we were going to be able to cope. We were both sure that something would turn up and the future would be fine but now was the problem. We just couldn't see how we could afford the flat. We made the decision to move out when daylight came and hoped that the landlord would return our deposit. We tried to console ourselves that it was too far away from the college and well, maybe, I thought, it wasn't right for us. Or rather, too deadeningly right. Not conducive to the creative spirit.

So we set off for Clapham.

Jack and Margaret Murray had been students with us in Edinburgh. They had a little girl, already shared their flat with Margaret's sister and her husband but still had an unfurnished room that they did not use. To our astonished relief we could have it. There was room in the inn. Oh, blessings on their heads!

The room that became ours had large French windows looking out on to the garden and the trees beyond. I enjoyed the privacy it gave us and it was a sanctuary for which we were very grateful. I was there for about three weeks before I took the train north from Euston and in that time I felt the comfort of friends around me while John was at college during the day. Our room was big enough for him to paint in and there would be room for our baby too until we found a place of our own.

CHAPTER 18

Highland Happiness

Because we were so far north from the hospital, it was customary then for Golspie mothers to be admitted to Raigmore Hospital in Inverness one week before the due birth date. I was, accordingly, taken down to Inverness at the end of the first week of December. John was going to join us as soon as the baby was born or the term finished, whichever came first.

Raigmore, in those days, consisted of a group of long Nissen huts that served as the wards. The maternity ward of about ten beds was at the end of a long corridor of polished linoleum, on one side of which were a number of single rooms. To my delight I was given one of those. I could mix with the other mothers and retreat to my own room when I wanted. This proved to be a great benefit. It was a long wait. During that time there was a lot to occupy me. The other mothers were endlessly entertaining – the older ones on their sixth birth, seasoned to the whole performance; the large lady who had had no idea she was pregnant until the week previously and due to give birth the same day as me; and the tinker girl of about seventeen who, they said, wasn't very clear as to how or from where her baby would emerge. The ward was a source of education, leaving the young ones like her and me in no doubt whatsoever as to what we were in for.

John called me regularly on the phone at the end of the corridor and told me what was happening in London. Sandy had been down and they had gone to see the Royal Shakespeare production of the Marat Sade directed by Peter Brook and starring Glenda Jackson, Timothy West, Ian Richardson and Patrick Magee. It was one of the most potent pieces of theatre he had ever seen. But it was the Beckmann exhibition at the Tate that had totally energized and inspired him, and whose power left a profound impression. At college he was getting to know the staff and his way around and couldn't wait to talk to me about it all. I couldn't wait until he was up in Scotland with me too. We were both becoming excited.

Mum and Dad travelled down to see me twice a week when the shop was closed. The December weather began to deteriorate and the roads became hazardous. Even by the shortest route over the Struie the journey then took about two hours each way. In ice and snow it would be slower still. The days passed and the birth date came and went. A few days after the baby was due, John arrived to see me on his way to Golspie. He caused a huge stir, with the mothers peeping out of the ward to catch a sight of him in his long coat, big black hat and knee-length boots. The Nameless One walked again! But I was so glad to see him even for the short time he had before he caught the train north.

I had been in the hospital for two weeks before I went into labour. Then as things progressed in the slow way of first births, day turned into night before I was eventually taken to the delivery room. I remember very little after that. I was so full of pethidine it seemed as if I was in a funfair hall of mirrors with the sound muffled and distorted to match. I have just a vague memory of strenuous activity and the first tentative sounds of a new life beginning before everything faded into deep sleep.

They must have told me it was a little boy and I must have registered my relief and happiness that he was safely here but I have no recall of any of that. He was born in the early hours of 22 December, after which he was taken to the nursery and me back to my room on the ward.

About four hours later the lights were all suddenly turned on and the hospital day began with a brutal start as usual. It was an effort to pull myself round until something knocking at the edges brought me into the reality of the morning with a jolt. My heart began to beat wildly …*yes!* It dawned on me in a tidal wave of excitement that I had had a baby.

'Yes,' the nurse said as she took my temperature, 'you've had a baby boy. He will be brought in beside you soon.'

There are no words to describe how I felt. Where do you find the words for an event of such magnitude? Elements of mine had entwined with John's, along with strands of all those ancestors coming alive once more within a tiny being who was totally unique.

Then came the sound of baby cots being wheeled along the corridor and there he was.

I was speechless. He was lying on his side wrapped up tightly in a blanket, with only his little head visible. He was fast asleep. His pink cheeks in sleep squashed his little mouth so it looked like that of a baby bird. His small downy head and the look of peace on his beautiful face filled my heart with an overpowering love that would never leave me.

I lay gazing and gazing down into the cot, entranced. Who will you be? What kind of person will you grow up to be? Will I be able to be a good enough mother? And John a good father? Will we be able to keep you safe and guide you towards a fulfilled and happy life? I felt sure of all the positive things that would be his in the new life that he was now beginning with John and me. And I wished for all of that. He was just a few hours old and I wished for all the blessings in the world for him.

I lay there watching him sleeping, my heart aching with love. Eventually a nurse came into my room to do something and she said, 'You can lift him up and cuddle him if you want to!'

There were also so many orders to obey that it had not dawned on me that I would be allowed to lift him while he was sleeping. It had been enough, more than enough, to just look at him, to absorb his extraordinary presence. But of course I could hold him. He was my baby, and I was his mother. When he opened his eyes, he would see me for the first time and he would *know* I was his mother. He would get to know the sound of my voice and he would find comfort in the warmth of my body.

He slept on in my arms. We were fused together in blissful harmony.

In Golspie they had known he was on his way that night and had been ringing the hospital for news. At two o'clock in the morning family and friends all over Scotland were being informed, whether they liked it or not, that John was a daddy and we had a son called Jonathan. I was told that they were already on the early morning train and would be here in time for visiting in the afternoon. It could not come soon enough. I couldn't wait to see John's face as he held his little son. Mum was coming with him.

John was euphoric. Jonathan was a masterpiece we had created together and he wanted to shout out the news to the whole world. Which is what he did. Letters were written and notices posted in the *Northern Times* and the *Scotsman* and the *Berwickshire News* and the *Haddington Courier*, and everyone had to be rung up and informed.

It was dark when they reluctantly left to catch the five o'clock train for the two-hour journey back north. I had to remain in Raigmore for another few days for no other reason than that was how they did things then and therefore I would have to spend Christmas in the hospital, making my stay there three weeks in total.

While I longed to go home to Golspie with Jonathan, the atmosphere of Christmas began to pervade the wards and corridors of Raigmore. Decorations were strung up and sprigs of holly perched over doorways and pictures. Carol singers arrived to wander through the wards, the echoes of those beautiful old melodies lingering in a faint whisper as they moved further into the heart of the hospital. On Christmas morning as I rose to attend to Jonathan I opened the door to my room to find a small gift, wrapped in Christmas paper, lying on the floor outside. A pair of tiny hand-knitted baby socks. All the babies had been given them.

There was also a concerted effort to bring some Christmas cheer to the patients and we all enjoyed some kind of Christmas dinner with paper hats. While I had been giving birth some of the other women had been busy too. The young tinker girl had had a son and apparently he was to be called Elvis Presley Terry Dene Williamson.

The weather was at its worst, with snow and blizzards and icy gales. The roads were treacherous and the Struie was closed but they all made the prolonged journey to see us on Christmas Day.

Finally back in Golspie, I was sitting one morning breastfeeding Jonathan, as John quietly concentrated on the drawing he was doing of us. The door opened and the spell was broken. In came the doctor on his rounds. He stopped dead in his tracks and for a couple of minutes he glared at John. Sternly he enquired if all was well and after examining Jonathan he stalked out.

I only remember this incident as it was so totally in contrast to the warm and happy atmosphere surrounding us all at that time. It was difficult to understand. In those days a father was *persona non grata* as far as the births of his children were concerned and mothers had to be very circumspect in breastfeeding, but for an intimate and loving family scene such as this to be frowned on was beyond me to comprehend. It turned out that this doctor who had so conscientiously and kindly looked after me during a serious illness four years earlier was the same person who had made his disapproval most forcibly known to my father when John first arrived in Golspie. But despite his disapprobation, the tender drawing capturing a classic moment of family intimacy was completed once the doctor had gone and many years later would be displayed in John's retrospective of 1986 at the Scottish National Gallery of Modern Art in Edinburgh.

CHAPTER 19

Royal College of Art

While I was in Scotland, the staff at the RCA, realising that John couldn't work in a small space, were at their wits' end as to what to do with him. Carel Weight, his professor, who was a constant support throughout all his Royal College days, contrived eventually to find him a place to paint in a property the college owned at 19 Cromwell Road. There in the basement, without the benefit of heating of any kind, John gladly set to work. It was freezing cold but he hit on the brainwave of what he called his Steptoe (fingerless) gloves, which, along with his long black coat and scarf, took the edge off the icy conditions. My stay in Golspie had been prolonged by several weeks as Jonathan needed to return to Raigmore for a small operation to correct a minor digestive problem. Once I was reassured that he was fully recovered I longed to join John in London. As soon as I got there he took me to visit his new studio to show me what he had been doing. He loved working there, he told me, because he was more or less left on his own, with Carel Weight, Peter Blake, Leonard Rosoman and others calling in to see him now and again. They didn't stay long, he said, because it was too cold!

In the first term a project had been set for the students. The subject was the Science Museum. John produced a large work, the main feature of which was the staircase with people ascending and descending flanked by machines on both sides. The image of crowds of people in a small space, in response to the impact of the crowded city, appeared in several of his works around this time.

One of the paintings he was most proud to show me was *Star of Bethlehem* which is now in the collection of the Tate Gallery. This was one of the first of his paintings in which the figures on the deck of a fishing boat stand mute but confrontational, staring out at the viewer and appearing isolated from each other as they jointly engage in their harvesting of the sea. Like them he was, at this time, standing resolute and determined in his confrontation with the London world of art in which he now found himself. Like them he was undeterred in his harvesting of the knowledge that was now being made available to him while he followed his own personal vision.

Through the General Studies Course he came into contact with a wide range of composers, painters, poets, writers and scientists. He would come home and tell me about lectures by the scientist who had discovered black holes or the man who had devised and built the hovercraft or the talk they had been given by Thea Musgrave, the composer. Iris Murdoch was on the list of future speakers. He found it invigorating to be in the presence of people who had steadfastly followed their own vision and found fulfilment.

He had always been a reader but now he was engaged in serious critical study. He devoured all the major texts on art criticism from Herbert Read, Fry and Ruskin to more contemporary writers such as John Berger. He and Sandy corresponded about the books they were reading. *The Necessity of Art* by Ernst Fischer and *Permanent Red* by Berger were their Bibles at that time.

We also took advantage of being in the metropolis to visit all the exhibitions, from the museum shows of great masters to those of the contemporary work of Europe and the USA. He had been to see the great Beckmann exhibition at the Tate. This had been a major moment for him. Beckmann, it seemed to him, was able to combine in perfect balance the issues essential, in his opinion, to a work of art – the balance of form with content.

It was work that spoke of its own time in a language entirely passionate and unique and infused with poetry, a language with which he could identify. All creative people have heroes to whom they pay homage, who are sources of inspiration and who act as guiding stars. John had many giants he looked up to, including Titian, Tintoretto, Bellini, Rembrandt, Grunewald, Picasso, Léger, Ensor and now Max Beckmann.

In the summer term Peter de Francia began his lectures on the history of art, which John found informative and in tune with his own philosophy. He made friends with many luminaries of the London art scene. Sandy was also part of everything and many hours were spent together in spirited discussion in which, from time to time, Alan Bold was also included.

By this time John had begun to organize a student's club at the college similar to the one he'd started at Edinburgh. The sole purpose of this was to provide an opportunity for students to show their work in the college and have feedback. He was thrilled when Berger, the invited critic, chose his work, *Three Fishers*, for this ultimate accolade and a friendship was born. It was from that point that John felt he was beginning to make some kind of mark. His work went totally against the grain of the current Pop Art fashion and it took courage to keep on track in the face of such strong opposition. His courage and commitment were never in doubt but he had during that first year become disheartened at times that there was no kindred spirit among the students with whom to share his views and enthusiasms. This recognition by someone he so highly respected was the encouragement he craved.

The first academic year in London came to a close with John feeling more established. It was still slow going as far as social contact with the students was concerned and we still missed Edinburgh and our friends there. When the term ended, we decided to return to Edinburgh for the summer holiday. Friends had a room available in their rented flat in Fettes Row and John found a job as a lifeguard at Drumsheugh swimming pool in Stockbridge, an experience that resulted in many powerful paintings and hilarious anecdotes.

Of course John was painting every day and during that summer at Fettes Row he completed several large works. There had been early discussion between Sandy and himself about the possibility of putting on another Festival exhibition but Sandy was by now working full-time in a factory with little time to paint and it was going to be too difficult.

At the end of the summer John left me in Golspie to go and begin his second year in London. His intention was to find us a flat of our own. We had loved our room at the Murrays'. In the spring, life came back to the garden, filling it with a fresh green light from the tall leafy lime trees. Jonathan would fall asleep as the sounds of Julian Bream's guitar and Bach's *Goldberg Variations* wafted in on the fumes of oil paint. Jonathan's easy-going nature meant that he happily took to the life we offered him and, just as we had blissfully anticipated, there were no difficulties that I remember. John expressed to all and sundry our happiness and parental pride. But we now needed more space.

Our new home was a flat at the top of 361 Queenstown Road adjacent to Battersea Park. We shared it with Ben Johnson, another student in John's year. We had one bed-sitting room plus a tiny box room for Jonathan to sleep in. The communal bathroom situated on the middle floor of the house would be shared with Ben and the other five tenants in the house. John was delighted with what he had found for us and it sounded good to me. It was just across Chelsea Bridge and so much nearer to the college in South Kensington.

I immediately felt at home there. The house wasn't remarkable in any way. Our room was very small, with just enough space for our bed, a couple of chairs and shelves in the alcoves that accommodated our books and our Dansette record player. Again this is where we ate, slept, spent the day and where John would paint out of college hours. In spite of the lack of space he really preferred to paint at home. There was just room for Jonathan's cot in his little room. The cooker and sink on the landing served as the shared kitchen. To reach our part of the house we had to use the staircase that we shared with the girls who lived downstairs. None of the accommodation was self-contained. Some of the girls were civil servants and they were young and unattached. There was an easy atmosphere about the place and we all got on well.

Queenstown Road is part of a major route crossing the Thames over Chelsea Bridge on the way up to Clapham Common. The 137 bus used to stop at our door and could take us all the way up to Chelsea, then on to Hyde Park and Oxford Circus. There was always something to see from our windows – the surge of people getting on and off the buses, the trees beyond St Stephen's Church on the corner of the roundabout at the entrance to Battersea Park and the pale rusty gas towers rising and falling against the backdrop of what was to become our new icon of home, Battersea Power Station. It was five minutes' walk to Chelsea Bridge and the River Thames, across to Sloane Square and King's Road, then, in the sixties, the hub of the universe. It was also within walking distance of the Tate.

Battersea Park was full of interesting corners. It would never be able to compete with the fields and hills and shorelines of my own Golspie childhood or John's at Port Seton but we would come to see it as our first, and more or less only, garden in which our children played and grew up. There was the lake with its rowing boats and islands and the Barbara Hepworth sculpture in dialogue with the Henry Moore on the opposite bank; the little children's play area and sandpit and the One O'Clock Club. There was the famous funfair with the helter-skelter and big dipper and the ghost train. There was the children's farm, which provided the only opportunity for some city children to see newborn lambs and foals and calves. There were the tennis courts, football pitches and running track and the wild areas of woodland. Broad carriageways followed the circumference of the park and there was a row of red and white striped kiosks selling sweets and souvenirs. There was the line of cherry trees that went diagonally across half of the park where, in April, luxuriant blossom hung over the path in heavy clumps of pink and white. And there was the fragrance of the secluded Old English rose garden with its ponds of water lilies and goldfish and extravagant beds of roses and multicoloured summer flowers among the boxwood. Then there was the great river, swirling on down under the bridges, Battersea and Albert, and on past Chelsea, bearing an assortment of barges and other craft towards Westminster and the City and eventually on out to the Thames Estuary. Across the water we looked on to the Royal Hospital and the fine buildings of Chelsea.

After dusk the river shimmered with light from the floodlit bridges, and the mighty chimneys of the power station would loom out of the darkness as the trains rattled by on their way in to Victoria. The territorial rights we established over those landmarks in 1966 endured for all the years we lived in London. Their power never diminished and, emotionally, they belong to us as much today as they did then.

As soon as we had arrived from Scotland that October, we went to Cromwell Road to see John's latest work, *Kinlochbervie*, the large two-panel painting inspired by the remote Sutherland harbour I had taken him to on his first visit to Golspie in 1963. I remember the excitement I felt in seeing those paintings begin to take shape. There had been such concentration and deliberation called on in their making. He made small preparatory drawings of the work he was about to do. He studied the techniques employed by his heroes of the past and brought them to play in what he was currently working on. After completion in 1966 *Kinlochbervie* was transported, over the years, from pillar to post, stored in many unsuitable places, hung on walls wherever John was living and, finally, ended up in the Scottish National Gallery of Modern Art in Edinburgh.

Our lives settled into a pattern. When John came back from college we discussed over the evening meal how his work was going. He told me about the lectures he had been attending, every detail of his day, and I loved to listen. We had always done this from the early days and we had talked over everything from the soapbox orators of Milne's Bar to the Marxism/nationalism of MacDiarmid, and now the views of the new acquaintances he was making. We had begun to feel more at home in London but feelings of isolation persisted and we still hankered after the social warmth of Edinburgh. Walking across Chelsea Bridge we often wistfully caught sight of the intercity coaches setting off for Edinburgh and suffered pangs of homesickness.

Sandy often came to London and John welcomed the hours of talk with him. Everything from the current exhibitions to the latest trends were up for critical debate. The good and the bad were clearly delineated; the latter condemned in no uncertain terms. One word said it all – John's usual unequivocal denunciation: *trash!*

Some of our other friends from Edinburgh, musician Tam White, with Arthur Sharp and some of their entourage arrived in London around that time. Tam was now focusing on obtaining a record contract and Arthur was acting as his manager. They hit King's Road with a bang and John gladly joined in – and every now and then so did I when babysitters were available. Through De Francia and his partner Joanna Drew, John had been able to meet a succession of prominent painters, writers and other creative people. This had an important stimulating effect on him. Al was involved in poetry readings and other literary events in London. He provided other intellectual outlets for both Sandy and John and through him they were introduced to contemporary poets. At other times, after working intensely all day at the college the rekindled camaraderie with Tam and Arthur and their friends provided the light relief and the fun and games we had been missing since we arrived in London.

CHAPTER 20

Halle and East Germany

In the early summer of 1967 the Scottish Composers' Guild had been invited by the East German government to attend the Handel Festival in Halle. As there was not much enthusiasm from the members of the Guild for the visit, Ronald Stevenson invited Sandy, Al and John to go in their places. They were informed that they would be in East Germany for one week, which in the end turned into two.

It was a fully programmed cultural trip in which formality and humourlessness were punctuated by farcical and hilarious interludes. Their first day in Halle saw Sandy and John marched off for compulsory haircuts, their decadent sixties locks shorn to comply with East German standards of conformity. My father would surely have been in full agreement but nevertheless horrified to find that his views in this instance accorded with those of communists – and communists from behind the Iron Curtain at that! While they were having their hair cut John and Sandy happened to look up to see a bust of Karl Marx sporting a full flowing mane. Their protestations in view of this fell on stony ground. Al had no need of such attention. He didn't bear the nickname 'Bullet' for no reason.

Apart from the musical events in Halle, Handel's birthplace, they were taken to meet prominent East German painters including Willi Sitte and Werner Tübke. They would meet Bertolt Brecht's widow Helene Weigel and they were looked after by the English composer Alan Bush, who generously made sure that they didn't go short of East German currency while they were there.

They were provided with a guide, a young music student who accompanied them everywhere. His name was Hans-Dieter Schöne, and he now holds a prestigious position as a respected master of organ music in Dresden. He was there when John celebrated his twenty-fifth birthday at a performance of *The Threepenny Opera* by Bertolt Brecht at the East Berlin theatre of the Berliner Ensemble. He also accompanied them to Leipzig and also to Dresden where they saw for themselves the devastation of that beautiful city. Most memorably he took them to visit the remains of the Buchenwald concentration camp.

Hell was not a new concept in John's mind. It had been introduced to him at a young age at church and Sunday school, and its very real existence had always been a steady fixture in his nightmares. What he learned at Buchenwald, however, provided concrete proof of a darkness which was impossible to comprehend: a living hell perpetrated on human beings by other human beings. A hell that was not confined to that place beyond the grave but which existed in the everyday lives of innocent people.

The impact of Buchenwald was seminal in the subsequent development of his work. The values we had both been taught in childhood probably could not be bettered as guidelines for living but now there were big questions revolving around the issues of Good and Evil, Sin and Redemption. There was so much that could never be resolved. Love God? Fear God? How could you do both? We had been taught to fear bad things. God, they told us, was good. Love and fear were contradictory energies. What John had seen and learned at Buchenwald gave legitimacy to our doubts and he was reeling from the impact. His paintings became darker, preoccupied with death and sin and the consequences that led to Hell. Whatever you did, there seemed to be no escape. There could be no benevolent God who would look after us for the rest of our lives. There had been no such rock for the innocent victims of the concentration camps. The deal offered by our Protestant indoctrination of goodness irrevocably leading to benign reward now seemed a mirage. How could we be sure of anything any more? It was a long while before John regained his equilibrium after the East German trip.

Nothing and no one could ever destroy the *joie de vivre* that was the essence of his being or blot out his amiable personality. Intellectual development in his early student days had led him to question and reject the literal dogma he had been fed by the Church but its ethical guidelines had always provided the infrastructure of his life. After Buchenwald, however, the core of his inner world was destroyed. In the depths of the nights he was tormented with the hell and damnation he had always feared since boyhood and to which, he never doubted, in the end, he would be consigned. The Burning Fire was always smouldering in a corner of his mind. The dichotomy of the sacred and the profane, love and compassion, sin and damnation informed his daily existence and the discourse of his life's work. Though it seemed less powerful in daylight this was a torment that would grow and in the end dominate his hours of darkness.

At the end of his second year, after he returned from East Germany, he was awarded a scholarship from the RCA, which he decided to use to visit Spain. The intention was to get to Madrid to see the work of Goya and Velázquez in the Prado. We were all going to go: John, Jonathan and me. We could take advantage of student train fares and after changing in Paris we managed to pay for one sleeping berth for the three of us to get to Barcelona. This was August and it was hot. There were four berths in our compartment, all fully occupied, ours more than most as we had our baby with us. It was a long journey and we were glad to get to our destination. As usual, when we got there we queued up to find cheap accommodation and spent a few days seeing all that the city had to offer. It was all Gaudi, Picasso and strolling down the Ramblas.

We decided to seek somewhere a little cooler and moved to Villanueva i la Geltrú further down the coast. This was the first time that either of us had experienced Mediterranean heat and the sensation of burning sands under our feet. It was also the first time we had seen or tasted such sumptuous food and fruit, which bore no resemblance to what was then available back home.

We had our return tickets to London but barely enough money to survive on. We counted it all out and realized that there was only enough for one return fare to Madrid. Obviously the important thing was for John to get to the Prado. The only way he could do that was if he travelled overnight there and back, as there was no money for accommodation. Jonathan and I would stay in Villanueva until he returned.

He got his ticket to Madrid and had settled down to watch the countryside flash by when a rail inspector arrived to look at the tickets. Apparently, although he had paid the full amount for Madrid, the ticket with which he had been issued would only take him as far as the next town. Panic set in as he tried to explain. If he was put off at the next stop he would be stranded, as he had no other money. A priest travelling in his compartment saved his bacon by convincing the inspector that an error had been made at the ticket office in Villanueva and he was allowed to continue to Madrid.

Seeing Goya was another key event in his working life. The visceral images of the Spanish master had a great deal to offer John in his own efforts to express his horror at what he now believed humanity was capable of. Back in London he painted a series of harrowing works based on the nightmare of the concentration camp, the major one of which bore the title *Pourquoi?*

CHAPTER 21

The End of Student Days

October 1967 saw the start of John's final year at the RCA. Our social life had improved marginally and occasionally when one of the other girls in our house could babysit we attended college events where bands like the Rolling Stones performed. The sixties were now in full swing and the RCA was the place to be. Mary Quant and Twiggy were newly famous and, for women, Biba, Bus Stop and Kensington Market were the places to frequent. In Biba, you could find within the mystic gloom of the purple lamplight marabou and feather boas, and clothes in the gorgeous aubergine and plum colours of the era. In the patchouli and cannabis vapours of Kensington Market you could pick up exotic ethnic jewellery, embroidered Indian dresses and vintage sunglasses and gloves and shawls and hats – all the hippy stuff you could want.

By this time Ben and his girlfriend had moved out of Queenstown Road and their room became our sitting room. We acquired a piano which, of course, was immediately relieved of its front cover and painted red. I was pregnant again and, as before, the lack of money did nothing to dampen our excitement. This baby would be born in August after John had graduated, when Jonathan was two and a half. We had no idea how we would eventually make a living, but we spent little time worrying about it. Something would turn up.

In June 1968 John graduated from the RCA with first-class

honours, and winning the Burston award. Robin Philipson and Willie Gillies took us out to dinner and immediately offered John a job back at Edinburgh College of Art. This he readily accepted.

I was, however, very uneasy about John going back to Edinburgh. It felt wrong. I told him of my fears. Instinctively, it felt like giving up and it seemed contrary to the direction in which I believed he had to go. Taking on the World indicated to me the opposite direction – forwards not backwards. This was in no sense a turning away from Scotland. Our love for Scotland was the core of our being and our pride in our roots was unassailable. It was instead the fear of the comfortable armchair. John thrived on challenge, so I was afraid that if he went back he would just run himself into a cul-de-sac. It would be a disaster. His voice and vision were strong and would flourish wherever he lived. Also, wasn't there a noble tradition of émigré painters, poets and musicians throughout time whose work not only remained true to their own spirit but also quite clearly derived a power and eloquence from the objectivity afforded by distance?

It was a wonderful offer in the material sense. We would be able to live above the breadline at last. We would have comfortable and spacious accommodation both for living and for studio facilities, and we could provide a better childhood for our children. We would have all the things we lacked in London. I did not dare to dwell on such tempting notions. Instead I urged him to change his mind and decline their offer. We were strong. Good things would lie ahead. We would be OK.

There was nothing else on the horizon as far as income was concerned. I had no idea how we would survive but such was my optimism and faith in his talent that this issue worried me far less than the danger of succumbing to the lure of easy comforts. John finally agreed and wrote to express his gratitude for their kind offer and to tell them that, on reflection, he had decided to remain in London after all.

Was this a good decision? Well, to use one of his favourite statements — time would tell.

Very occasionally he sold a small painting and we had to hope for more of these sales. We were desperate for money. It was not pride that prevented him from applying for some kind of social security; it was our sheer ignorance that such help might be available to us. We were so naïve about everyday things it is a miracle we survived anywhere, far less in a city such as London. We were possessed by the belief that nothing could go wrong, and our view of the future made no allowance for problems. It would all turn out well at the end of the day.

We were now looking forward to the birth of our second baby and had arranged for my sister, Joan, to come and look after Jonathan while I was in hospital. John had kept in touch with some of his friends from the RCA and, Joan being with me for company, I was perfectly happy for him to go out with them from time to time in the evenings. He would, however, soon test my patience to its limits.

CHAPTER 22

A New Bellany Boy

I was a week overdue when, one night, John didn't return home
until dawn. The story he attempted to give me, if only I would
give him a chance and hear him out, involved an RCA student
and her nervous breakdown ... I was stunned.

Then, a couple of hours after he returned home, I felt the first
signs of labour starting at last. I had no option but to deposit
my anger with John in another place for the time being. I needed
all my concentration and equanimity to ensure our baby would
arrive safely. I would let nothing spoil the event. A necessary
truce was called.

It was a fiercely hot day. John set about painting a family
portrait of me sitting in the wooden nursing chair bursting out
of my floral dress, Jonathan playing in a long wooden boat that
John's father had made as a cradle for him when he was born,
and John standing behind us. A plastic parrot suspended above
our heads completed the picture. The painting is now in the collection of the Perth Museum in Scotland. This all took place in
our small sitting room at the top of the house. All the windows
were fully opened in search of cool breezes which brought with
them the deafening sounds of the London traffic. Turns were
taken by John and Joan throughout the day to go for ice cream
from the kiosk down below and we turned our radio up to listen
to the current hits of the sixties.

It was late at night when the ambulance came for me and

by then things were moving fast. We arrived at St Thomas's quite quickly but there was a delay in being admitted. Then the paramedic came back to tell us St Thomas's was full that night and they were trying to find somewhere else for me to go. Deep breaths! Eventually we found ourselves queuing up with other ambulances at the entrance to the General Lying in Hospital for Gentlewomen near Waterloo, an old dusty building I had never noticed before but which seemingly was still used as an overflow annexe for St Thomas's.

I had wanted John to be with me at the birth and although he had agreed to be present I was never convinced that he was really enthusiastic. I believe he was forever grateful that, in the commotion, events overtook us and the drama was all over and done with before he got to see me. I didn't mind – we were both so entranced with our new little boy that nothing else mattered.

Paul was born, healthy and beautiful, in the early hours of 21 August 1968. Again, I was entranced by this new little person who would be part of our lives forever. Your heart swells with the promise of all the love you have to give your baby. He arrived with his little face squashed up in a don't-muck-around-with-me expression. Or was it a taking-on-the-world intimation? Probably the latter, inherited directly from his father.

Early the next morning I woke to the sound of tinkling water. I was in a bed in the corner of the ward on the first floor looking down onto the roundabout at the Lambeth end of Westminster Bridge across the Thames from Big Ben and the Palace of Westminster. The traffic had barely begun and the soothing sounds of water were coming from a small fountain across the road outside County Hall. There was something good about that unlikely sound. I liked the omen for my baby, for all of us.

As usual the hospital ward provided diversion from one's own circumstances. The other new mothers were South Londoners and full of vitality. But amid the repartee of who fancied this or that doctor and the bawdiness of their efforts to attract the fancied one's attention, the reality of their lives was brought to bear on everyone who cared to listen. The film *Cathy Come Home* had recently caused a sensation with its portrayal of the plight of homeless families, and one particularly attractive blonde woman turned out to be a veritable Cathy. She had just given birth to her third child but when her husband came to take her home it appeared they had just been evicted and where they were going to be put up was uncertain. The fact that they had a newborn baby only made their situation more desperate.

Throughout all those years in Edinburgh and in London I never felt anything other than extremely privileged and rich in all the things that mattered. Devoid of material ambition we were full of anticipation and optimism about our future. To witness people in such desperate circumstances only underlined the feeling as we luxuriated in the happiness in bringing our new baby home. It was all happening in our two and a half rooms – John, me, baby Paul, Jonathan, Joan, oil painting, new tricycle, eating, sleeping, cooking, crying, laughing – but we wanted for nothing. At weekends we joined the crowds in the park and once home again we watched other tired families with fractious children waiting below for the bus to get home after a day at the funfair.

The bonus of living in a community is in the scenarios we invent for the diverse characters we encounter. Queenstown Road was our theatre. We watched the amorous middle-aged couple across the street whom we assumed to be newly married, and further down that side of the street there was the abode of the 'Samuel Beckets'. They lived in a flat with supremely filthy curtains that never opened. The whole place had a dilapidated, condemned appearance that made me shudder at the thought of the interior. Out of this home an immaculately dressed jaunty couple set forth every night for, we imagined, the pub: he in a tweed coat and bookie's hat and she resplendent in her best leopard-skin coat, her hair a breathtaking shade of orange. We devised endless names and narratives for them and all the other people we saw. London was a melting pot full of dramas being played out simultaneously with our own and I spent a lot of time imagining the lives of others. I loved the cosmopolitan flavour of London and the idea of other worlds impinging on my own.

In the autumn of 1968 John took up Robin Philipson's offer to show his work in Edinburgh and so in the Sculpture Court at Edinburgh College of Art he arranged an exhibition of the paintings from his RCA graduation show plus some of the others he had painted during our three years in London.

This was an impressive body of work and he was boosted by its success. Among them were *Kinlochbervie*; *Star of Bethlehem*; *The Fright*; portraits of the extraordinary RCA model Antoinette, with her mass of wild auburn hair; and of another RCA favourite of his, an old man, an amateur astronomer, who modelled for *The Old Astronomer*; and *The Wedding Breakfast* based on Alan Bold's riotous wedding. Also for the first time he exhibited *My Grandmother*, which now hangs in the Scottish National Gallery of Modern Art. The Edinburgh City Art Centre bought *The Sea People* and offered him an exhibition in the near future in their then premises in the newly refurbished Royal High School on Calton Hill.

The only other promising event was an exhibition at the Trafford Gallery in Mount Street, Mayfair, at the end of 1968, which did not really come to much in the end. Such was our financial desperation that John did eventually go to the employment office on Battersea Park Road but all they had on their books was a few hours a week in charge of the waltzer at Battersea Fun Fair. He decided to keep looking!

During the last term at the RCA John had been among three students who were invited to do one day's teaching a week at St Martins College of Art in central London. This gave him an insight into the practicalities of teaching art students and through the contact in art schools his circle of acquaintances began to grow larger. Also during the last year at the RCA he had been commissioned to paint a portrait of Mr Andrew Davis, who had recently devised the graphic innovation, Letraset, and had set up a company marketing it. Their conversation throughout the sittings had been enjoyable. They had talked about John's prospects after he graduated and suspecting money was in short supply, Mr Davis asked John if he would give him weekly lessons in painting. This friendship was something John valued and enjoyed, and Mr Davis's kindness saw us through a very sticky patch.

Storage of the paintings was always a problem and for this, throughout all John's years in London, we had to rely on the goodwill of many people. The mostly large paintings were moved from pillar to post and kept in all sorts of unsuitable places. Mike Tracey and his wife Frankie had been students at Edinburgh and after they arrived in London were a constant support. Mike was always drafted in, along with other endlessly accommodating friends, to help in moving them from place to place until John made the acquaintance of Alan, a lovely man who for years transported the paintings to and from exhibitions in his rickety old lorry. At the end of the exhibitions, when he came to remove the unsold paintings, which was usually all of them, he would say resignedly, 'Nothing sold, John? Oh well, never mind. Back to the same place? OK. Just pay me next time.'

Many things were paid for at that time in pints but when some money did come his way John always made it good with Alan. He was always generous; he appreciated it in others and honoured it in turn. What he had, he shared. If he had nothing, well, there would be next time. That applied to food and day-to-day household expenses too.

We never knew Alan's surname but he was like part of the family. He must have had some problem with his feet as he always walked on his heels with the uppers of his tattered shoes flapping. He was eternally good-natured and forthright. He could detect any form of pomposity at a glance and deal with it in an appropriately witty manner. He was deeply loyal to John, never hesitating to offer advice and guidance, or a telling off, as he saw the need, particularly when things really did go wrong for us. He lived just off Clapham High Street in a tiny flat above the garage in which he kept his van, the source of his livelihood. We eventually lost touch with him but I hope that in the future he found more lucrative work than with penniless artists.

At the end of the summer John managed to find a job: one day a week at Brighton College of Art. But this meagre employment only lasted one term. A new head of department was appointed who subsequently chose his own staff and the rule was last in, first out.

CHAPTER 23

Albert Palace Mansions

Through a mutual friend we met George Rosie, the Scottish writer and journalist, and his wife Liz. They had two boys of similar ages to ours. We lived on the corner of Lurline Gardens and they lived on the ground floor of a Victorian mansion block on that street. It was through visiting them that we became aware that there was an empty flat in the same block and we decided to try to rent it. There followed a long-drawn-out process of negotiation with a tricky private landlord who one minute agreed we could have the flat only to change her mind the next. It was off, then on, several times before we finally moved in to 63 Albert Palace Mansions, Lurline Gardens, SW11 in January 1969.

We had been happy living on Queenstown Road with the girls in the house but over the previous few months our landlord had disappeared. No one knew to whom we should pay rent, so none of us paid any. It was fine for a while but we were all becoming a bit uneasy about the situation, as had we been asked to pay the back rent we would have been in trouble. Apart from that we were in dire need of space.

Although the rooms in the new place were modest in size, we were thrilled as, compared with what we had been used to, the flat seemed so spacious. It was on the first floor and comprised a sitting room with small balcony, a dining room with a tiny kitchen squeezed into an alcove, two bedrooms and a bathroom. The smallest bedroom and kitchen dining room were at the back

122

and were decidedly gloomy, as Albert Palace Mansions backed on to the grander mansion blocks of Prince of Wales Drive that overlooked Battersea Park. The largest room would be John's studio and we would make the dining room our sitting room.

The first thing that happened was that we were burgled. It was barely worth the effort, as we really had nothing worth stealing. At that time we had hardly any furniture at all and the place was largely empty. Sandy, who was down for the weekend, came off worst as his camera was stolen, while we suffered the loss of my sewing machine and our precious Dansette record player. The nursing chair with the wonky legs had not appealed to them. Nor had the model boat or any of the paintings.

John customized his studio by covering the windows with opaque white paper – for better light diffusion and to prevent distraction from outside. Around the frieze he painted in indelible blue ink his favourite MacDiarmid quotation:

And let the lesson be –
To be yersel
Ye needna fash gin
It's to be ocht else.
'Tae be yersel and tae mak' that worth bein'
Nae harder task tae mortals has been gi'en.

Those words may still be coming through the subsequent layers of decoration, as when I eventually decided that I didn't want to live with the noble sentiment any more and tried to smarten the room up, they just could not be eradicated! They kept emerging no matter how many coats of paint were applied.

In that room John painted the great triptych *Homage to John Knox*, one of his key works, now in the Kunstmuseum, Trondheim, Norway. This painting, without doubt, was the essence of John's inner turmoil. The irrepressible fun-loving joviality that was a very real and large part of who he was competed for supremacy with the fear of death and the sure promise of Hell beyond, that featured regularly in his nightmares.

In *Homage to John Knox* the black cloud of doom permeates

all of life. Marriage is a burden in its union of damned souls. He is sinking in the depths of temptation and sin, and the black bat and carrion crows have got him stunned in their talons. The man of God rants on and on from the Bible proclaiming deepest damnation with no hope of salvation. It epitomizes his worst nightmare.

The further his road was taking him from the innocent days of youth, the blacker and more threatening were the nightmares and terrors of death that tormented him. In later years he would many times paint the image of a Janus head and that too, of course, was a self-portrait and an indication of how he lived his life. In the daylight hours it was easy to enjoy, with gusto, what life brought his way but in the depths of night he was power-less to prevent his gaze turning in the direction of his deepest terrors. He would often wake screaming and fighting against some unseen threat.

After we moved in to the mansions we decided that we had to retrieve our piano from Queenstown Road. It was quite daunt-ing to think of getting it down the narrow stairs and along the road. One boozy night after a good few beers, when all men turn into what they think they are or want to be, John and Johnny Williams, an Edinburgh friend, decided the time was right and they were suitably fit for the job. It was thus sometime after midnight that a great rumbling was heard coming along the street. People were opening their windows and complaining about the disturbance, which at that time of night was deafen-ing. Nothing would stop them, however, as they were having such a laugh.

Now and then the rumbling stopped and we would hear the clear notes of John's resounding rendition of the national anthem until their procession came to a satisfactory end with the red piano safely installed in battered glory in the studio.

The noise was replicated a few weeks later by the thundering din of Concorde as it passed over Lurline Gardens on its first flight over London, when everyone rushed to their windows in alarm at what sounded like impending disaster.

CHAPTER 24

First Flickerings

A few months after Paul was born, John heard there was work going in a commercial glass-painting studio in Fulham. It was piecework, so the more you did, the more money you got. He hated having to do something like that but he soon found himself working as many hours as he could, after which he would come home and paint. It was a hand-to-mouth existence but life was OK. We now had more friends with whom we socialized. John went out with some of his pals and always had hilarious tales to tell on his return.

I loved my life with the children. I had no desire to do anything other than be at home and look after them. Those years I considered a gift that would last but a short time in which I could watch them acquire language, movement, thought, imagination and social integration and all things necessary to becoming complete human beings. My contentment was fortunate as, lack of money notwithstanding, John would have been firmly against the idea of my working. This arose from his extreme possessiveness, a deeply established trait. He was and had always been suspicious of any interest, even normal social interest, that was paid to me. It was so ridiculous that I chose to ignore it when it surfaced but it was always there and did not get better or go away. As there were never any grounds for this paranoia, ignoring it was the only way to deal with it.

Up until the sixties, once married, a woman generally had

to give up her job and any decisions about her life had to be officially sanctioned by a man – husband, father or any male figure who was seen to have automatic authority over her. Although the vote had been won in the early part of the century and women had more than capably filled the places in men's occupations during their absence in the world wars, once peace was secured the place for women had been decreed to be very firmly back in the home. But now change was coming at last. The second wave of the women's movement was gathering pace and the excitement of what they were trying to achieve was empowering. Albert Palace Mansions became a hotbed of women at the forefront of the feminist movement, with many political meetings and discussions taking place in one or other flat. The fight to win freedom of choice for women was a colossal battle. Many of the equal opportunities we take for granted nowadays would not have come our way without the energy and determination of people like the women who lived around us in the Mansions.

The positive concept of being a full-time mother, however, became a casualty. When one was asked about one's occupation, it began to feel shameful to admit that you stayed at home to be with your children. While I wholeheartedly supported the efforts of my neighbours and friends in the women's movement, I could not escape the feeling that someone like me might be perceived as not living up to the efforts being made on my behalf. This made me feel uncomfortable, if not actually guilty, but I knew I was not ready to take advantage of those benefits. Not yet.

In the summer of 1969 came the first moon landing. We were going to watch on television the landing of the craft and Neil Armstrong taking his first steps on the surface of the moon. There was a popular belief that the whole thing was staged, just a sham, and John professed to go along with that view. We had to stay up until the early hours of the morning to witness the great moment on black-and-white TV and it was thrilling – for both of us. We were on tenterhooks to see what would happen to the astronauts. Would they disappear in some kind of explosion? It was extraordinary to see them eventually bouncing about safely on the lunar landscape. There had been a steady build-up to this achievement with the US and Russia neck and neck in the race. The first man to orbit the earth was Yuri Gagarin, and there was great celebration when the first woman, also Russian, had done the same thing. That was Valentina Tereshkova and when Alan and Alice Bold's daughter was born she was named Valentina in her honour. What more inspiring name could she have?

I felt fortunate too. We had everything we wanted, a continual stream of paintings on the walls, drawings, books, music, time and space for John to paint and time to enjoy our two little boys. The studio was our priority and I had to make sure the boys did not manage to get in unsupervised among the paint. On a notable occasion my failure to do this resulted in one particular masterpiece being anointed with experimental daubs put there by busy little hands. Another time, a pot of blue gloss household paint went flying down from the balcony splashing a particularly smartly dressed lady passing on her way up to town for the afternoon. The slash of cobalt blue was still visible on the pavement many years later.

For over a year we mainly scraped by on the earnings from the glass painting. As it was easy money John began to go at weekends as well. Sundays had up until then been a day we both looked forward to when we took the children for a walk in Battersea Park. It was a time of intimacy that enabled us to share everything that had happened during the week, and talk about his painting, the people we had met, family matters, our hopes and fears, everything sublime and mundane while at the same time we took delight in our boys. It was what might now be called our 'quality time'.

Now that he was working at the glass studio he had to hurry. I walked with him and the children across the park to Albert Bridge and watched him disappear over to Chelsea on the other side of the Thames on his way to the glass studio, the children waving to him until he was out of sight.

That image – seeing him walk away from us – filled me with

melancholy. As I made my way back home along the river and through the park, passing other families having 'quality time', I tried to throw off this vague sadness. The weekends had always been ours together until now. John was out quite a lot in the evenings during the week but when we were together we were close and united as we had always been. I was quite happy that he went to meet our friends, most of whom I liked. Now and then, when we could find a babysitter, I went with him.

This feeling I had seeing him walk away from me was the first intimation of change. It was the first glimmering of loneliness with all its flickering doubt and insecurity.

Just before he graduated from the RCA John had met William Crozier, who would become his close friend and comrade in art. Bill Crozier was a painter who claimed both Irish and Scottish descent as it suited his purpose. He was twelve years older than John and came to London at the end of the fifties, where he hung around with the painters Robert Colquhoun, Robert MacBryde and their circle in Soho. He was a lifelong romancer in a class of his own. With him nothing was ever quite as it seemed. If solid ground beneath your feet was what you were after, Bill was not your man. He was, however, destined to become one of John's best buddies for many years to come. This led to John eventually obtaining a teaching job at Winchester College of Art when Bill became Head of Painting there.

Things were looking up for us, financially, at last.

Chapter 25

Longing

At Winchester John found a group of likeminded friends. He immediately fitted in and enjoyed teaching. He loved the repartee and the camaraderie of artists he respected and took to the social life surrounding them with enthusiasm. Sometimes he did not make it back on the last train and stayed overnight. Once in a blue moon he rang me to say he had been offered a lift home in someone's car but they were all drunk. This worried me so I gave him the answer he wanted. Stay in Winchester. Don't risk the drunken driver. It was a gift to our destruction.

Sometimes they all came back to London to attend a private view, then in the late hours he came home bringing with him someone who needed a bed for the night. John Bratby was a frequent lodger who bedded down on our couch in boozy oblivion.

Our existence was still hand to mouth. One occasion I remember clearly John had no money in his pockets when he left in the morning but he made a promise of his early return that evening, bringing the food for our dinner. Eleven thirty came and went. I went to bed and tried to get to sleep but I was so mad at him it was impossible. He was, by this time, out such a lot that I could not bear the sound of taxis. There were so many that were not bringing him home, and listening for him made me tense and kept me far from sleep.

At about a quarter to midnight, I hear the key in the door. In

130

he comes. He has obviously decided to try the 'everything in the garden's lovely' tactic.

'I'm home!' he shouts merrily. 'I'll just bring the food. Won't be a minute!' The lack of response from me tells him he is in trouble, so, optimistically, he whistles a tune as he clatters about with the frying pan.

I lie in frozen hostility, all energy concentrated on my fury.

Food! He thinks that'll do it, does he?

He eventually appears with a tray bearing a plate groaning with food, napkin folded, glass of something to drink, the whole ensemble topped off with a single rose in a see-through plastic cylinder, the kind that are handed out in third-rate restaurants. 'I'll just get mine,' says he jauntily, returning quickly to the kitchen before I can say anything.

I look at the contents of my plate. An omelette – ah, but no ordinary omelette! One with, for those times, a wacky variety of unlikely ingredients, indeed anything and everything he could find in the rather expensive (according to the packaging) twenty-four-hour supermarket he had come across in Chelsea on his way home. Cheese, yes, but also banana, ham, tomatoes, gherkins, sausages, peas, tinned mandarin oranges (the current novelty), beetroot ... All that could be speedily removed from a packet or tin, no expense spared.

I was so mad at him I did not want to speak and certainly didn't want to show any interest in his offering. I was also gasping with hunger. I just had to eat. He was hardly daring to look at me or indeed breathe as he too began eating.

Despite myself, I couldn't still the urge to laugh at this absurd concoction and his guileless attempt to placate me. As he saw the corners of my mouth beginning to twitch he couldn't believe his luck. He had got off with it! What he subsequently called his 'Rolling Pin Omelette' had done the trick.

We went to sleep, a truce called yet again.

Another memorable self-preservation wheeze was when he arrived home in the small hours with a 'present' for me. This was a large birdcage from which two sullen and completely silent sparrows (or so they seemed to me) glared with beady eyes.

'Lovebirds,' he told me. 'With a beautiful song!'

Seeing birds or animals in cages made me uncomfortable and those birds were so miserable and lifeless I could not bear to look at them. Singing, if they ever knew how, was obviously the last thing on their minds. They stayed with us for a while but they seemed so unhappy that I eventually took them to a pet shop and asked them to keep them alongside their other birds.

Waiting for John became a way of life and it was wearing me down. It had begun gradually, starting around the time Paul was born. At first it did not upset me but eventually when the ratio of his late nights increased I realized I wasn't enjoying life the same. I was missing him. There were the inevitable rows and sincere promises. He would be home early tomorrow. Promise. Tomorrow would come but at dead of night I was listening for taxis again. Again and again. And again I began to wonder which tomorrow the promise had been for. It never seemed to be my tomorrow.

This continued for a considerable time. When we were together, life went on in its usual harmonious way, and this quelled any suspicion that something was wrong between us. So when I began to spend more and more evenings alone waiting for him I never doubted the strength of our marriage; I doubted myself. Had he really said he'd be home that night or hadn't he? Had I just imagined it? I must have been wrong.

By this time we had begun to have serious rows about it. He could see how upset I was and he protested that he did care about how I felt, and of course he would not do it again. I did not expect or ask him to stay in with me all the time. I was quite happy for him to join in the social life of his colleagues. Creativity needs endless space. I understood that and I did not need him with me all the time. I needed space too. I just wanted some of his time. I was lonely for him.

Every evening I put the children to bed optimistically and pottered about, listening to a play on the radio or reading, trying to pretend to myself that I was not waiting. There were things I was longing to tell him – who had called, news from home or friends, something I had read or heard on the radio and always the endless funny things the children had said or done that day. Every time I heard a taxi I was at the window with my heart surging only for it to fall time and time again. I knew he would come. I knew he would come right up until he finally didn't come, by which time I was beside myself.

Of course there are much worse things than loneliness. For someone like myself who enjoys solitude (knowing the option of company is also available) why did it wear me down so badly? Loneliness is not solitude, not simply about being alone. An ache starts and the more relentless it becomes, the more it slowly turns into torment.

I told myself that on the other side of the world, in those very years, the Chinese Cultural Revolution was being played out. *That* was where you would find torment, torture, both mental and physical. What I was experiencing was just a day-to-day occurrence in contemporary life – simply a troubled relationship the like of which millions of people have to cope with.

Grow up, for goodness' sake. Just get on with it.

But I couldn't.

I longed for him to come home. I was lonely just for him. He was part of me, my deepest friend. I missed him to talk with and laugh with, share the children with and breathe the same air with.

If things had been bad when we did spend time together it would have been indisputable that we were in trouble but at those times we slotted back automatically into the warm and loving relationship we were used to. Then we had lots to talk about, to discuss, reason and dispute, fall out, fall in again. We laughed and joked together, enjoying the children, and he was painting – the whole spectrum of normal married life was ours. The evenings he was with me I went to sleep with a blissful sense of relief and the reassurance that all was truly well with us after all. But the following night I was doubting my sanity again, because I had ended up waiting for him in the early hours. It was the contradiction in this, the swinging from a normal loving life to bleak loneliness that broke me. Eventually I began to distrust my own judgement.

He most definitely wanted me and the children and our home – me and the children *in* our home. He never wanted our marriage to break up. Right from the beginning he had always been fiercely possessive and still was. He was always suspicious (to the point of embarrassment) of any man showing polite social interest in me. That would never change throughout his whole life whether we were together or apart.

The Winchester days, although disastrous for our marriage, were good in terms of John's career. While he taught there he also had painting space and used his own studio when he was at home too. He had already begun to have solo exhibitions and this gathered pace rapidly. His teaching time gradually increased to the maximum of three days part-time, following the tradition of teachers being required to be working painters. Part-time, of course, meant term time only. No money throughout the holidays or for days off sick. He still went to the glass-painting studio the rest of the time.

In the new year of 1970, I found I was pregnant again. I was assured that everything would be good from now on and I had to believe it. I so wanted to. But could he be the person we needed him to be?

After a brief period of respite the call of the wild took him away again. He couldn't keep a balance. It was all or nothing, and it seemed we were on the nothing side of things. Once again I found myself sinking. I wanted to run away from this despair but I couldn't see how to escape it. I was so weary of being miserable. I found myself questioning everything I did, said and thought. I had to judge and justify all of what I was, to myself. After that I was at a loss.

London was the City of Mahagonny. He just wanted to be out to revel in it all. He also wanted us there in the background while he enjoyed total freedom. He was always truly sorry when I was upset, but it was quite clearly a price he was prepared to pay. There was no other conclusion to make. He just wanted it all. On his terms.

That was the sole reason for the break-up of our marriage. It was as little and as much as that. The deal offered too little for me. I was broken by loneliness. I couldn't bear it any longer.

I decided to leave London for a while to see if that would help. My family at the other end of the country knew nothing about my problems. They adored John and he adored them in return. If I did not tell them they might never have to know and thus never suffer the distress such news would bring them. I did not want them to know any of it.

I could not believe that we couldn't sort things out. I never lost the belief that what we had between us was fundamentally good. Something so deep and right just could not fade away. That is what my instinct told me.

I decided to go to Port Seton. These good people did not deserve to be burdened with my unhappiness but I reckoned that if anything could help, it had to be his own family. Yet there was nothing they could say that would influence him; he had long outgrown their reach. My only hope was that from the loving fold of his family, the source of the idyllic childhood he cherished in memory, would come a reminder of what he himself had in the life we had made together in London, that same priceless thing he was now trampling all over.

He later travelled up to Port Seton to reassure his family with profuse denials and promises, and after a couple of weeks we returned to London to make a new start. I was then four months pregnant.

CHAPTER 26

Halima and Our Baby Girl

An exhibition at Winchester School of Art had been in the planning and I went there with John to the opening in June. This was when John first met Halima Nalecz. She showed Bill Crozier's work at her gallery, The Drian, on Porchester Place at Marble Arch in London and now offered John an exhibition on the strength of what she saw at Winchester. This was exciting for us, a major step forward, and Halima joined the band of unforgettable people in our lives.

Halima was Polish. She was a very attractive lady in her fifties with an aristocratic family background and a fascinating history. John always enjoyed telling people she was a Polish princess. Whatever her status, she certainly ranked high in our esteem.

She had opened the gallery in 1957, showing the cream of the contemporary art world at that time, including Henry Moore, Ben Nicholson, Victor Pasmore and Barbara Hepworth. She now also showed continental artists, especially painters from her beloved Poland. She was an accomplished painter in her own right and was well respected in the London art world. She was forthright in dealing with her artists and very energetic in promoting them. She could always manage to outwit any of their egotistic manipulations and kept a firm motherly eye on everything they were up to, retaining a fierce loyalty to them all. They loved and respected her in return.

Halima's private views were legendary. The days of preparation always found her keyed up and then once everything had been placed and hung, the sumptuous arrangement of flowers was delivered and displayed to advantage, the liveried doorman with his white gloves would be positioned to welcome the loyal band of patrons and invited guests, and there was Halima, decked out in her silver fox stole and full-length gown – every inch the beautiful princess in charge of proceedings.

'My darlinks, this is a very great artist! You must come and see ...'

This was the first of many annual exhibitions John had at the Drian. Alan drove his rickety old lorry up the narrow street and the doors were flung open. Halima gasped at the size of the paintings being shuffled in by Alan and John but in they kept coming. 'Don't worry, dear John, we shall find a place for them.' And she did.

The walls of the Drian were themselves a considerable challenge. There were pipes and cupboards and radiators and unexpected alcoves camouflaged with drapes of hessian, and it was a feat of ingenuity to cover so little space with so much. Of course, anyone who has dealt with John and his work will know that size was not the only challenge. Without fail he would insist that the exhibition had to include his very latest 'beezer'. It would always be 'the best thing I have ever painted!' There was thus the wet-paint factor to contend with and the often predictable repercussions.

The most notorious wet-paint occasion was a disaster at one of the Drian private views. Not only Halima but many of her important guests and collectors came dressed in lavish finery. One such lady sat down to have a conversation with John about a potential purchase only for her fine mink coat to graze the surface of that exhibition's beezer – to indelible damage. Halima was as devastated as the owner of the mink was incandescent and it was a problem that did not go away in a hurry. The sale, needless to say, went no further.

At the end of the exhibitions Alan and John loaded all the work back onto the lorry. If sales had not been good, and they never were, Halima bought something out of the generosity of her heart. She had all the costs of the show to pay for – catalogue, publicity, invitations, liveried doorman, food and wine – but she didn't want to see John go home disheartened and she was concerned for us, his family.

That September Jonathan, still only four and a half, went to school for the first time. Chesterton Primary was just off Battersea Park Road on the edge of the new Doddington Estate.

Since we first arrived in Battersea, in the name of slum clearance a massive demolition of the friendly terraced back streets had taken place and now, where families had sat on their doorsteps gossiping and watching the children play, high-rise blocks of flats stood in their place. Optimistic and shiny, these were glass, steel and concrete boxes reaching up to the sky. However, within a few years, graffiti, boarded-up windows and broken and filthy lifts declared the abject failure of the project. Worse, the warm spirit of working community life was lost forever. Desperation, alienation and crime seeded themselves there instead.

The little primary school, however, like most resources for small children, was a happy place, and Jonathan soon settled in. It took me rather longer to feel good about his start in life, compared to my own childhood of safety and freedom.

Back in the General Lying-In Hospital for Gentlewomen our surprise and joy were supreme when a baby girl was born on the warm sunny morning of 30 September 1970. Her beautiful face! Here was my little soulmate who, along with her brothers, John and I would love forever. But with this new baby there would be the added happiness, for her and me, of having all the ways of girls and women to share together. I felt close to John too. He had been brave in supporting me through the birth and afterwards, when he returned home that day, he told everyone he had been walking on air.

Anya's birth had to be registered within six weeks and on the last day John set off to the register office. On the way there he had one of his 'brainwave' moments and when he came back home he told me all about it. He had left home with the

1. Helen Percy when six years old.

2. 'The Big Three' John, Alan Bold and Sandy Moffatt, 1963.

3. John, Castle Terrace
exhibition during the
Edinburgh Festival, 1963.

5. Helen
at St Abb's,
Berwickshire, 1963.

4. John's portraits of himself
and Helen that he exhibited at
the Edinburgh Festival, 1963.

6. Helen and John's
wedding, 1964.

7. Helen on
honeymoon
in Dieppe, 1964.

8. Helen with
Doubtfire's coat
(oil on board
151 × 90 cm),
1964.

9. Sandy Moffat and John, outside the Royal Scottish Academy, Festival Exhibition, 1964.

10. Self-portrait of John Bellany R.A. (oil on board 121 × 91 × 2.4 cm,
© The Artists Estate, Royal Academy of Arts, London.
Photo: John Hammond), 1966

11. Kinlochbervie (oil on board 243.5 × 320 cm), 1966.

12. Helen with
Jonathan, Paul and
baby Anya, 1970.

13. Paul, Jonathan and Anya, 1970.

14. The Bellany family at Lurline Gardens, Battersea, 1971.

15. Paul and Jonathan with their father
in Battersea Park.

16. Catalogue portrait of John, 1970s.

17. Bellany family,
1973.

18. Celtic Sacrifice
(oil on canvas
180 × 161 cm),
1973.

19. Juliet Gray.

20. John and Juliet's wedding, 1979.

21. Juliet (oil on canvas 194 × 124 cm), 1979.

22. Paul (oil on canvas 172.5 × 122 cm), 1982.

23. Windmill
Drive, Clapham
Common, London.

24. Paul and
Jonathan, 1982.

25. Jonathan (watercolour 76.2 × 55.9 cm)
Exhibited at the National Portrait Gallery, 1986.

agreement that the baby's name was to be Anya Kirsten Bellany. The Russian name, Anya, and Kirsten, an old Scottish name, had appealed to us. But then the brainwave struck.

John arrived home with the certificate proclaiming the birth of Anya Seton Bellany. He claimed that he suddenly thought of adding 'Seton', thankfully without the 'Port', as a tribute to his birthplace. Thoroughly pleased with himself, he asked me what I thought. Well, what was there to say? As Anya grew up, much as she was fond of Port Seton, she took a decidedly dim view of 'Seton' as a girl's name and refused to acknowledge it. But it was too late. A sudden brainwave had ensured that it was forever part of her official name.

CHAPTER 27

Battersea High St

Life was cramped in the flat but eventually in the spring of 1971 John was given the opportunity to rent a space with another artist twenty minutes' walk away, in a dilapidated house in Battersea High Street. Norman Ackroyd had the top floor and John the middle one, the ground floor being the premises of Eric Paul, a tailor. Battersea High Street was still a traditional south London street of pubs and pie and eel shops and with a market running its length every Saturday. The house was condemned property, not fit for human habitation, and so in a bad state of repair. But because the minimal rent reflected this it was possible for us to afford it.

To all intents and purposes it was a move in the right direction. It would mean that we could now emerge out of the darkness of the back of the flat in Albert Palace Mansions and live in the bright bigger room at the front, where we would all benefit from less claustrophobic living conditions, John above all. He would now have quiet uninterrupted studio space.

One morning at the beginning of June 1971 someone knocked at our door. She introduced herself as Penny Barham and told me that she had just moved in to the flat next door. She asked if she could use our phone and thrust a tiny baby into my arms. He was beautiful and nestled in to the warmth of me. She said he was three weeks old, his name was Joe and she could not cope any longer. She needed to ring the hospital and have herself readmitted. She promptly completed her call and, taking her baby, thanked me and vanished. I did not see her again for about six months but that was the dramatic beginning of one of my most enduring and mutually supportive friendships, with her and her two boys who became best friends of our children.

For the first few months or so after Anya arrived there had been a respite from my fears about our marriage. John still went out and he invariably brought home a variety of characters from the spree at all hours of the day or night. In general, I did not mind people coming home with him, as it was preferable to always being left on my own. With some notable exceptions I liked his friends. But the situation soon deteriorated, with him staying out, and though I was preoccupied with the children it came to the point when I could no longer hide from the reality that my marriage was falling apart.

Things came to a head one night after I had been waiting as usual for John to come home. When he failed to turn up by eleven, I cracked up. I suddenly grabbed a pot of white emulsion paint and flung it at one of his latest masterpieces.

I was a crazy, sobbing wreck. How *could* he do this to me? Over and over and over again. He was bringing me to the very edge of madness. The rational answer, of course, was to have thrown the paint ages ago and walked away then. Other people might have done that but it was the last thing I wanted. I wanted *him* and the relationship with him that I knew was good. We loved and needed each other. The rows we had over his neglect of me and the children were always quickly made up and sorted out, and we eventually resumed the warmth and closeness we had always shared. Life was good again. But in no time at all it would start all over again. London dazzled John and, in his mother's words, he always got 'carried away' – a boy in the toyshop who wanted everything at once.

That night, after I had thrown the paint, I was beside myself. I knew I couldn't stay within those four walls any longer. It was approaching midnight when I wakened my little children, put their coats on over their pyjamas and headed to the Queen's Road overground railway station. The heartrending image of

Anya in her buggy, sucking her fingers, with Jonathan and Paul holding on each side and my urging them to walk as fast as they were able so we could catch the last train to Denmark Hill, is one I have tried to eradicate from my memory ever since.

'Where are we going, Mummy?'

'Why?'

We were heading off to Camberwell, to Liz and George Rosie's house. I had phoned to ask if we could come. I was at the end of my tether. I needed refuge from myself, if nothing else. In my bag I carried the bottle of red wine I had begun to drink. Only a few stragglers were around at that time of night but George was at Denmark Hill to meet us and take us safely to their house where we stayed the night. The next day I was shocked and frightened by what I had done. I wanted to cancel it out, wave the magic wand and be back with John, happy again.

We did manage to sort things out between us once more and went on to prepare for the approaching Christmas. The previous Christmases we had spent in Golspie to be with Mum and Dad but we had decided in 1973 to stay in London. That Christmas Day we walked from Lurline Gardens up Queenstown Road to our friends Johnny and Sandra Williams's house in Clapham with Jonathan and Paul holding John's hands and me pushing Anya in the buggy. From the houses as we passed came the sound of the current popular song of that Christmas, wishing us Merry Christmas and telling us the future was just beginning. The future, a new future and one I never wanted to be mine was, in fact, about to begin. I had decided that it was going to be our last Christmas together. I could not go on any longer the way it was.

My father had recently retired. He had sold his business in Golspie and my parents had moved to another house in the village. His never-forgotten plan to take my mother travelling was well underway, with a detailed itinerary spanning Africa, India and finally Australia. But Fate had different plans for him and their trip of a lifetime faded like a dream. About this time the cancer that had lain dormant in his body made its presence known. In 1971 the trauma of operations, recoveries, relapses, increasing pain and the steady weakening and withering of this once vibrant human being began. That was the reason we had not gone to Golspie to spend Christmas, my father's last. I had not the spirit needed to see my dying father. John and Dad, who shared a mutual bond of such warm affection, would never see each other again.

John maintained that separation was unnecessary, the last thing he wanted. I heard promises over and over again that his days would, from now on, include me and the children far more but I had heard all this before and it no longer meant anything. The minimum demands we put on his time were still too much for him. While he maintained his constant and extreme possessiveness over me he was not able to give more than a few snatched moments of his presence to me or the children.

He never offered anything in his defence and so from the little I was given in explanation the only conclusion I could draw was that, much as he might have wanted us, we would have to be there in the background making no claims on his attention, while he went on enjoying complete freedom as usual. There was no intention to hurt me and he had no antagonism towards me. There was never any major falling out or, worse, indifference between us. The only issue we had was his neglect. He still professed his love for us but he just couldn't cope with the obligations that came with love.

I knew breaking up would bring me nothing but misery. I did not want anyone else. I did not want another life, only the one I had, back the way it had been before, but I felt I was being systematically destroyed. Things could not go on that way; I had to change something in order to survive. But to end my marriage to John was the last thing in the world I wanted to do.

A few days after New Year 1974, in the evening after the children were in bed, I told him I had finally decided to leave London and take the children to live in Edinburgh, as I had often threatened to do. He was utterly shocked. How could I seriously think of going so far away and taking the children away from him? After much distress and discussion he agreed that, if I really meant it, he would rather go and live in the Battersea

High Street studio for a trial separation so that the children and I could remain nearby in the flat.

We are both upset. We say to each other perhaps a period apart will fix things. He decides to go that night rather than prolong the agony and so he gets a few things together and I hear him closing the door as he leaves, his footsteps fading as he descends the stairs. The outer door below clangs shut as it always does.

Is there really such a thing as a broken heart? I feel it so acutely as I write. It is painful even forty years on.

I am back there in the sitting room of our flat. I am slumped on the couch we had acquired from a skip. It looked good covered with the old patchwork bedspread my grandma had knitted for me when I was little. Calling out from the white walls are some of the paintings John has recently completed, including *Lobster Fetish*, and most notable among them the great glowing *Celtic Sacrifice*, with images that disturb and mock, that whisper of scenarios of intrigue and betrayal, and in some of which my presence is a haunting question mark. Powerful paintings of melancholy beauty.

Every other available space on the walls is covered with photos of the family, drawings by the children, postcards of paintings and other miscellaneous mementos. There is a tailor's dummy adorned with vintage clothing, old jewellery and feather boas. The alcoves are crammed with overburdened bookshelves and the windowsills are a profusion of plants, and then there's the MacDiarmid slogan scrawled tauntingly along the frieze – 'Tae be yersel' and tae mak that worth bein' ...

It is winter and the doors to the balcony are sealed and padded with cushions to keep the draught out. Apart from the old couch our furniture mainly comprises cushions on the floor. The gas fire from which we derived our only heating gives me nightmares even yet when I think of the compromise it must have been to our safety.

A knock at the door. He has forgotten his key to the studio. In he comes. We don't look at each other. We can't. He takes it off the hook and is gone.

There are no words to describe that evening, or the next morning, or the many other relentless hours, days, months that lie ahead. Only grief howling inside me.

The cry of the seventies was, 'Marriage is meaningless, unrealistic and unreasonable. Why should two people have to spend the whole of their lives together? Divorce is ten a penny and that is what happens. What is so special about your story?' The answer is, of course, nothing at all. Like birth and death, the breakdown in relationships happens day in, day out and the agony, although fashioned to individual circumstances, is ordinary, banal. Unbearable, but ordinary. Afterwards you are left to deal with the death of your future and nearly everything you hold dear. Like any death it promises to hold its sting forever and from its bereavement you can see no escape.

At first, I said nothing to the children. Jonathan was fairly used to John not being there. Paul and Anya hadn't noticed his absence at all. By the end of the week, however, Jonathan, who was eight now, was asking for an explanation.

In contrast to the fifties, children were at last being credited with feelings and the intelligence to understand according to their developmental stage and so, as gently as possible, I told Jonathan that John and I were now going to live apart because we would be happier that way but that he and his brother and sister would see him as much as ever at weekends or even more often than before. He did not like the sound of any of what I told him, so I did not dwell on it. When he could absorb it, he insisted that it was not that we would be happier living separately but that it would make it easier for his daddy to get on with his painting. He could not tolerate the idea that we would be happier apart. It was too hurtful to think that way and of course it was untrue for all of us.

How do you make such changes feel good for vulnerable children who need and want the exact opposite of what is happening? How can you begin to reassure and comfort them when you yourself are howling inside like a wounded animal?

CHAPTER 28

Fracture

I was tortured by thoughts about our changed future. Days to come would be days in which he would not know where I was, if I was safe or well or happy. Worse than that, the day would come when I would have faded from his mind and would no longer be important enough for him to care anything at all about.

Of course I was not just sad. I was angry with him and he was by now angry with me. He thought I was changing under the influence of the friends who lived in the Mansions around us, many of whom were journalists and leading lights in the feminist movement that was surging ahead at that time.

No self-respecting woman could fail to respond to the changes that were being fought for and implemented by these women. They were making history by winning for all of us the freedom, power and opportunity to realize lives of achievement and fulfilment on our own terms, unfettered by the traditional restrictions devised and imposed on us by men. Why should we not be excited and enthusiastic about anticipating the benefits such hard-won change would bring? The whole mood of the times had shifted and women everywhere had woken up and were supporting the efforts that were being made to change their lives for the better.

These were inspiring times and the empowerment won for women then is well established in the daily life of the twenty-first century. However, John's accusation that I was being 'led astray' by these pioneering women would have amused them highly, I am sure, as I must have seemed, from their perspective, such a non-starter. While I applauded their intentions and efforts, far from acting under their influence I was a pathetic failure at fighting for anything. I was no more able to live up to their ideals then than the two 'lovebirds' John had brought home in a cage had been able to sing. All the rights being won for me so valiantly could not help meet any of my needs at that time.

His inability to credit me with my own will and intelligence was John's problem and self-delusion. The compromise I had endured in terms of my own happiness and peace of mind had gone on far too long and the decision he had forced me to make, to break up with him, was no one's but my own.

We had decided that the children would spend Saturday nights with him in the studio. Then he would bring them home Sunday teatime and when they were in bed the two of us would have dinner together. The only good thing about this arrangement was that John and the children would see each other much more than they used to when we lived together. The studio, however, had no hot water, no heating, no cooking facilities, no proper bathroom, only a toilet. Mice rattled around in the walls. It was a dump. But that was secondary in the scheme of things. Hygiene and comfort are never the concern of children. They were just happy to be with John. At first they thought it was fun to be sleeping in a strange place, away from their usual routine.

Dinner together after the children had gone to bed, however, was generally a disaster. For some reason we were unable to hear what the other was trying to say. It was like being in soundproof glass boxes, each of us mouthing words that could not reach the other. I needed to know the other side of the story – the issues he had about our marriage. No matter how often I begged him to tell me there was nothing forthcoming. All he wanted, he would keep repeating, was for me, his soulmate, to be there in the home supporting him in the whole purpose of his life, his painting. That is what he needed. He, of course, promised to neglect us less and include us more. Surely I understood that this was how artists lived? Had he not noticed that during all those years that is exactly what I had been doing? I did not want anything other than to savour the precious early years of our children and feel involved in his work. My curiosity about the world, I knew, would, in time lead me to pursue my own special interests but no matter what I occupied myself with in the future, I would always, my whole life long, continue to be that vital support to him. My belief in his work was every bit as strong as his own. All I wanted was some kind of balance between the social and the personal: a better deal for myself.

I didn't bother to remind him that I was the one who had discouraged him from opting for a life of cosy security, a more conventional life, and had done so purely in the interests of his creative spirit and inspiration, persuading him to turn down the job he had initially so readily accepted back in Edinburgh and which would have given us a much better quality of life. I had never sought the comfort of material possessions, the evidence borne out, surely, by my indifference to their absence from our day-to-day life. We had always shared the same priorities. My belief in the need for any serious artist to seek out the challenges involved in trying to create something of value, to have ready access to unlimited unbroken time that was vital to creative work and to familiarize himself with the environment in which art flourished, was never in question. What was good for his work was good for him and good for me. His painting was our life. His and mine. Apart from that I had more than enough to occupy my time in those years and I was totally fulfilled by home and children.

I was fully aware of the artist's adversary – the pram in the hall – the hazards to creativity posed by family life, and there was no issue about accepting our secondary place in regard to his painting. I never at any time sensed that he found the presence of the children to be frustrating or detrimental to his work at home and if that had been the case he most certainly would have told me. I thought I had asked little of him and I believed he had all the freedom he needed.

Ironically, throughout his whole life John was offered studios, larger and with plenty of storage space, which he turned down in favour of one within his home. He always preferred to be working in the domestic environment. In one previous instance, long before we split up, he actually took up the offer of a large studio near to the Battersea helicopter pad but didn't like its isolation and continued to paint at home. There was never any inkling that our place in his life was a threat to him as far as his work was concerned. All I wanted, and needed, was for that part of his life that belonged to me and to our three children not to be squeezed out of existence. But for all his promises, I knew that while he wanted us there in the background for when he needed us, he simply wanted to be free to do exactly what he wanted regardless of anyone else.

At any time I could have asked him to move back and to try again and he would have done so gladly. But promises had been made and broken so often that I knew it would be a waste of time. I never, for a moment, throughout all the years, no matter how he would try to act otherwise, believed that he no longer remembered the love and the close bond we shared. I always knew he did and he always knew I remembered it. The trouble was that at that time there was so much on offer in life away from the home. It was a constant party where all his chosen friends, most of whom were not encumbered by families, shared the same hedonistic priorities.

After our Sunday evening dinner, when it was time for him to go, there were tears again, and the agony was stirred up every week until we were forced to admit that the dinner idea had to stop.

Around the time we parted, a film was being made about John by W. Gordon Smith for BBC Scotland's *Scope* series. I did not see this excellent film for probably a couple of years but in it John is his usual articulate self. He is sure of who he is, where he is going and clear about the values that underpin his work. There he is in full bravado, in the pub at Battersea High Street as usual among his cronies. It is all very jovial. While Gordon poses searching and direct questions, John replies ably. He seems full of confidence and buoyed up by the alcohol-fuelled camaraderie around him which helps to conceal from the outer world the trauma of that time.

Eventually I realised I had to get organized. Our finances had always been haphazard to say the least, largely but not entirely because of lack of money. I never again wanted visits from bailiffs for rent arrears. It would have been interesting to see what they would have confiscated from our poor pickings in order to recoup the debt! We got off with stern warnings on those occasions, when we managed, by borrowing from friends, to scrape together the money only just in time. Then there was the day our bank manager turned up at the door to talk to us about the lack of response to his letters about our overdraft, which had by then risen to the sum of three or four pounds. Usually when bills arrived they were left lying on the floor unopened, making their way under the bed to be attended to 'soon', 'later', 'next Thursday', or never.

John was nothing if not generous and I knew he would give us money when he could but I needed to know where I stood and was urged to apply to social services to see how they could help me. I hated all of this and I had to drag myself to the offices to be told that if I was to be eligible for an allowance I had to obtain a separation order from the court.

John and I had decided that a trial separation was as much as we wanted to do, both of us holding out hope for a reconciliation. Going to court had never entered our heads and was the last thing I wanted to do. It could only make matters worse and make things more final. However, I had to make sure I had money regularly to support us, as John's good intentions sometimes took a bit of time to materialize.

CHAPTER 29

Lavender Hill

'Date of birth?

Date of husband's birth?

Date of marriage?

How many children?'

I answered in whispers and each time my voice wobbled more and the pauses became more drawn out.

'Date of birth of each child?

Your first child? Jonathan, is it?

His full name?

His date of birth?'

Silence.

I tried to answer but no sound came.

Again. A softer tone of voice nudging me for the date of birth. All the poor man wanted was to get his form completed as quickly as possible. His next appointment would be following shortly.

'Jonathan's date of birth?

The date he was born?'

No response.

(Kindly tone of voice) 'Do you remember the day he was born?'

'Do I remember the day he was born? Do I *remember* that day?'

That was it. The floodgates opened and I was carried away on a wave of grief.

I did not want any of this. Could I not pull the time back and bring with it the happiness we had once had? The fun, the laughing, the joking, the sharing and the planning, the sheer optimism and sense of purpose? 'The love that knows no ending' that we sang about on our wedding day. Could we not get it back, even yet?

I was sitting in a side office of Wandsworth Social Services adjacent to the Lavender Hill Court at Clapham Junction while being taken through the relevant questionnaire. The information provided by my answers was essential for the instigation of the court order. But I was now a weeping wreck. I wished I were a million miles away.

I was advised to get a solicitor. It was necessary for the court proceedings. One of my neighbours recommended a friend, a rather prominent feminist lawyer who specialized in helping women. It was the same again with her. I found the whole process unbearable. Legal procedure all sounded vindictive to me and I was not interested in any of that. But I needed steady maintenance until I could fend for myself and I reluctantly accepted that this could only be arranged through the courts. While I appreciated the privilege of having such a top-level lawyer I was not decisive enough for her and my tearful responses exasperated her to the point that she told me I should go away and work out if I really wanted a separation. She could have helped me if I was angry and ready to rip John to bits. But I had no fight in me. I was just a waste of her and everyone's time.

Penny and her partner, Peter Sainsbury, were part of a circle of friends who propped me up and held me still while my world spun out of control around me. All of them wore themselves out trying to keep my head above water. They did what they could to encourage me to open doors to a future I could not bear to face. Their patience was never-ending with my pathetic fragility. Crucially for me, none of them criticized John in any way, in my presence at least. While I could rage against him myself, I could not bear anyone else to criticize him.

When I was on my own, the children at nursery or school, I spent much of my time lying curled up on the floor in front of the gas fire, devoid of motivation and immersed in bleak thoughts. I was not frightened of the future. I had no fear of bringing the children through this time. We had always been a close-knit little group. It was just that the part of me that was not the children had been torn out, leaving a brutal wound. In time, of course, wounds generally heal and other things grow in abandoned places. My problem was that I didn't want anything to grow in that place. I did not want a future without John.

How could my feminist friends help the likes of me? I was hopeless. Why did I find it so heartbreakingly painful to break up with someone who had treated me and the children so callously?

John drew people to him and was popular with a large circle of friends. He was amusing and lovable. He could also be impulsive, formidable and overpowering. He was passionate about his work, passionate and informed in the whole field of art. At times intimidating but overall great fun to spend time with, he was distinctively his own person. I loved all of that. But it was the glimpse of something within his inner self I had caught sight of in the few moments we spoke together that very first time so many years ago, something he emitted unconsciously and without any artifice, before we had even got to know each other, that had been the lightning flash. And forever more, whatever life with him brought my way, beneath all the blarney and bravado and all the rest, I knew that what I had seen that night was still in the heart of him and, like the MacDiarmid words on our walls, it would never fade away.

As long as we lived, that was beneath everything.

At Easter 1974 John took the children to Port Seton for the holidays. It was the first time they had been away from me and it was a black time. Jonathan was eight, Paul, five and Anya, three. The day they left I went to my friend Sandra's for lunch, returning home with my feet hardly touching the ground after a generous glass or two of wine, no buggy to push, no little hands holding on. The flat was silent. I was an echoing drum, emptiness clanging inside me.

CHAPTER 30

Separate Roads

The court hearings regarding the separation order and arrangements for the children began and the rift between John and me inevitably increased. When we had to appear in court, he glared at me. It was unpleasant and neither of us wanted to be there but I had no choice. He said he would give me money for the maintenance of the children and therefore court involvement was totally unnecessary. I was just being vindictive. Although it was a small amount of money, I had to be sure I would have it regularly in order to be able to manage. As it was, there were many times I had to attend the social services offices near Battersea Bridge only to be told that for one reason or another the money was not available.

If the payment did not come in, I had no money. To a faceless bureaucracy this meant nothing and there was no one person who could tell me when or if it would arrive, so I often returned across Battersea Park in tears.

During the summer holidays a friend offered me the opportunity to go and stay with the children in her house in the Cotswolds. We shared a few days with her and her family and when they went on holiday we were there on our own for a couple of weeks. It was a beautiful place, a cottage out on its own among the fields and woods at Througham, near Stroud, and it provided blissful sanctuary. I felt a million miles away from London and all our problems. The children loved all they

154

saw around us: the wild flowers, waving corn, sun and green shadows. No clamour of the city or its relentless bombardment of noise and neon light. For me, real life was suspended.

I had asked John to come and be with us for a few days. Maybe he too would feel our problems could be sorted in this place. We spent a few days together but the rift had become too deep. We were in those glass boxes all over again. We tried but we could not reach each other. The trust was gone.

My father was in serious decline, considerably weakened by his latest treatment. In early October I made the journey north to see him. When things had become critical, he had been taken south to Woodend Hospital in Aberdeen.

At his bedside, death was overshadowing us all. He was lying motionless, his skin pale and clammy, his breathing difficult and, when he was able to open his fading eyes, he could only whisper a word at a time.

'John?' His veiled eyes anxiously searched my face.

I told him that everything was going to come right between us. Everything, I lied, was going to be good.

As I was taken to the evening train to return to London I knew I would never see him again. A few days after I returned home, on 16 October 1974, my father died. I went back to Golspie on my own. John and my friends took care of the children while I was gone. It would always be a major regret for John that he did not come with me to the funeral. I knew though that his thoughts were with us and that his deep affection for my father would remain special to him.

My father, Harold Percy, in spite of his surname, was a Sutherland boy through and through with a proud Sutherland ancestry. His mother, Eliza Sutherland, had been one of a group of young village girls sponsored by the philanthropic Duchess Millicent and taken to London where employment was found for them. We have photographs of Eliza when she was a model of fine clothes in the store, D H Evans, on Oxford Street, and where she met her husband, Horace Percy, a tailor from an austere Victorian Doncaster family of tailors. It has to be assumed that the marriage had broken down as there was never any explanation given to Harold and his elder sister, Norma, why they returned with their mother to live in the village with their grandparents when they were still very young. Harold saw his father one final time when at the age of nine he was summoned to England and made to recite the Lord's Prayer at his deathbed.

My mother would now be alone, as all of us, her children, were away 'down south'. The children and I came up to be with her that Christmas and we shared our grief. It was a thought to get on the train back to London to a life which held out no welcome and bore no enticement. The threads had to be picked up, however, and we were soon hurrying along to school in the dark wintry mornings having to shout to be heard above the noise of the Battersea traffic. Paul had now been at school for a couple of years. He was the one to dawdle along peering into hedges and gardens looking for something to interest him, a snail or the fragment of a bird's egg. We walked along with some of the other mothers and children in the street and the camaraderie which was repeated at the end of the school day was one of the better things about our lives then.

CHAPTER 31

New Directions

As the shockwaves of marriage breakdown gradually began to subside, I set about trying to work out what I could do to support myself and the children. I wanted to get out of the benefit system. It was a vital source of support, an essential safeguard available to all those in need and I was glad of it at the time, but to be dependent on it for an extended period would do nothing to help me feel good about myself.

The most obvious thing for me was to use the qualifications I already had and train to be an art teacher, an occupation that would be easy to fit around the needs of the children. Apart from that benefit, being a teacher did not appeal to me in the slightest, but I applied all the same for the one-year course at Goldsmiths College and began shortly after Anya started school in the autumn of 1975.

The Goldsmiths course offered a second option – art therapy. I signed up and was soon visiting a variety of establishments where art was used in this way and found that I could tune in to the needs of those who found solace or stimulation in creativity. This seemed to be a more useful and fulfilling occupation than trying to help pupils who, apart from the small minority, treated the art room as a place to let off steam.

Later on in the course, all who had opted for art therapy were allocated to different placements – special schools catering for people who suffered from a range of mental health disabilities, psychiatric hospitals, residential homes and so on.

My tutor decided that as a 'mature student' of thirty-two, I would be able to cope with their most demanding placement – the psychiatric wing of Holloway Prison. Flattered by her confidence in me I set out with a younger student to visit the North London women's prison.

The Victorian building was in the early stages of being rebuilt. One of the original wings still intact was the one in which we would be working. To get to the psychiatric wing we had to pass the small building that had housed the suffragettes at the beginning of the twentieth century. It was a solemn moment when we were shown the tiny cells in which they had maintained their hunger strike.

A succession of gates were then unlocked and locked, unlocked, locked, unlocked, locked until we found ourselves deep inside the centre of what seemed like an underground bunker. Each door we passed through intensified my claustrophobia and induced a feeling of being buried alive. Inside the unit there were areas designated for those inmates suffering from a range of psychiatric disabilities, the very last one being for those women displaying the most disturbed or violent behaviour. It was here that we would work.

It was a small room with four cells on each side and a tennis table in the middle. This table was used not only for games but also as a dining table at meal times and for education, craft and other recreational activities.

We were greeted with varying degrees of curiosity, hostility and indifference by the women held there. Everyone watched each other and waited, the prison officers being extra vigilant for any sign of disturbance.

Art? Here? Were we really expected to find enthusiasm or even compliance for such an activity in these circumstances? Had I been one of the women who was secured in there, would I have felt good about being asked to join in with the activities on offer? I doubt it. The presumption of people from the perceived 'normal' life outside to believe that they had something to offer, along with a right to intrude upon lives so disturbed and so damaged by that same world, could only, in my view, engender animosity and anger.

We decided to lay out the paper and other materials on the table and we started drawing. No one volunteered. A radio quietly playing pop music softened the constant eruption of angry exchanges between the more volatile women and gradually one or two of the others came up to talk.

It was soon time to pack up, as the lunch was approaching through the succession of locked doors. We were still sitting at the table waiting to be escorted out of the unit when a plate of boiling soup came flying past our heads. One of the women who had spent the morning standing silent and motionless had aimed her soup at one of the others and all hell broke loose. She was manhandled out of the room to one of the special padded cells with much shouting and colourful language coming from all involved. This, our first morning, was just a normal working day in the bedlam of life in such places.

I had been reading R.D. Laing. He was the cult psychiatrist of those times whose viewpoint revolved around the notion that psychiatry was a tool for social control rather than sanctuary, containment rather than recuperation. He questioned the definition of madness and sanity and proposed that madness, as diagnosed, in fact usually involved some degree of rationality, whereas real madness lay in so-called 'normal' behaviour. It was an interesting thesis and, although Laing was eventually more or less discredited, it is not difficult to encounter aspects of his theory which resonate with contemporary life. I was fascinated by the workings of the mind and most of my reading was centred on Freud, Jung and many other contemporary thinkers. The more I read, the deeper became the realization that the way through such hazardous depths took many turnings.

For my final thesis of the year's course at Goldsmiths I used my observations from working at Holloway and in the interests of research I decided that I would have to visit all the other London penal establishments.

It was while I was being shown round the education department of Wormwood Scrubs that I was told the position of art therapist was shortly coming available. My course at Goldsmiths was at its end. The idea of working in prison education was not appealing but I was becoming anxious about finding employment, so as this appointment would come under adult education, and therefore better rates of pay, I decided to apply.

At the end of June 1976 I was called for an interview with the education officer at the Scrubs. I was asked to attend at 4.30 p.m., just before evening classes began. It was a lovely summer evening and I was feeling very hopeful that my financial prospects were about to take a turn for the better. However, on the way there I had something else to do first.

John was now head of painting at Croydon College of Art and had been living at the studio in Battersea High Street since we parted in 1974. Now he had found a different home and wanted me to come and see it. It was a small house in Upcerne Road at the World's End in Chelsea and he was waiting, on his own, for me to arrive.

The accommodation was arranged over two floors above an empty shop with a garage at the back. The rooms were small and, like the studio, there was no bathroom. I had to agree, however, that, with all its limitations, it provided superior living space to that in Battersea High Street and we both felt happy that it would be more comfortable for him and the children when they visited. It would be referred to from then on as 'the Scottish Embassy' and in its own way would provide hospitable facilities for, among others, many wandering Scots.

However, as I drove away afterwards through Chelsea on the way to Shepherd's Bush and my interview, my spirits plummeted. Gone was the enthusiasm for whatever good would be brought about by this new job. The initial feeling I had had on seeing John's new home had quickly degenerated into sadness. It was now 1976 and although we had had over two years to get used to the idea that we were separated, all I could think of now was that his move would be another step further away, making the split ever more permanent.

I could not really engage with the education officer as she

outlined the features of prison employment and was glad when the interview came to an end. The job was mine, though, and I had the relief of knowing that I could at last support myself and the children. Yet in doing so I was veering off in a strange direction and all of it was a million miles from where my heart lay.

I would be working along with another art therapist in the psychiatric ward of the prison hospital holding the most disturbed and unpredictable offenders. I very quickly realized that our work would amount to no more than glorified occupational therapy. But during the few years I worked there, some of the men came to enjoy drawing, having never previously done anything like that in their lives. I remember a series of remarkable drawings, detailed and colourful, depicting West Indian culture. They were full of fictional birds, animals, legendary figures and pagan icons. He produced them obsessively, a steady narrative from his troubled mind. There was also a very gentle-mannered Sikh who, as he worked, cried readily when one talked to him. He held to his belief that in a previous life he had committed a felony that now trapped him forever in an eternal cycle of damnation. He really believed that he had to be punished and that the punishment would be never-ending. For him the voices would never stop and there was no escape.

Over the time I worked there I heard many of the saddest and most moving stories from genuinely sick human beings who, if they could be helped, would not find the answer in what was offered in a prison. While such desolation could be oppressive, the minefield of the mind's dark dimensions concerned and interested me to the extent that I came to accept all of it as part of the great spectrum of human nature.

The education staff was not devoid of its share of oddballs and eccentrics, among them Oxford graduates, PhD students, failed Catholic priests and nuns and hippies (the latter description probably applying to the likes of me). The camaraderie was a warm and amusing antidote to the misery that surrounded us.

In the course of time I made the acquaintance of Dr Max Glatt, who visited the hospital every week. Dr Glatt, one of the original pioneers in the treatment of alcohol dependency, was highly esteemed in the field of addiction research and had distinguished himself by setting up the first residential therapeutic centre in Britain for the purpose of helping those afflicted. His life story was remarkable. As a young German Jew he had been incarcerated, in the early days of the Second World War, in Dachau concentration camp, but along with a very small minority he managed to negotiate his way free before such an escape became impossible. He had been separated from his parents and they, and most of the other members of his family, perished in the camps. He had succeeded in reaching Britain only to be interned as an enemy alien and transported to Australia for the duration of the war. After the war he married and set up his practice and private clinic successfully in London. By the time I met him he must have been about seventy. His sharp intelligence and ready wit combined with his self-effacing personality endeared him to everyone. He was extremely interesting and interested in people in a non-judgemental way and was naturally able to draw the best out of his patients and colleagues. He managed to get me interested in the mechanics of addiction and its treatment and he asked me to go and work at his clinic in Chelsea from time to time. It was due to his inspiration that I subsequently found myself working in the field of addiction. The irony of this new direction would become apparent in time.

CHAPTER 32

University

There was always a large supply of drawing paper and pencils on the kitchen table and every day when the children came back from school they immediately set to work, as if to meet a need. Paul, especially, continued this until he was well into his teens, writing stories and making football magazines of which he was the editor, reporter, illustrator and the featured star footballer. Jonathan drew well too and Anya specialized in making intricate little objects – houses, suitcases, bags, cash registers, pieces of furniture and miniature schools – out of paper and cardboard and also endless tiny books with stories and illustrations. The best times were when we huddled together in the evening on the sofa when I read to them – *Watership Down*, *The Hobbit*, *The Lord of the Rings* and so on.

Battersea Park was our garden. It was where everything happened. The old funfair was still there, a bit shabby but still capable of providing thrills and excitement. The adventure playground and fishing on the ponds beside the Henry Moore and Barbara Hepworth sculptures were still of interest and there were special events held in the park that drew crowds from all parts of London: the Guy Fawkes bonfire and fireworks; the start of the London to Brighton Cycle Race; endless cavalcades throughout the summer months. At Chelsea Bridge, one Saturday every month, the vintage and custom cars gathered and spent the evening cruising round the perimeter of the park across Albert Bridge, along the Chelsea embankment and back across Chelsea Bridge.

The Queen's Silver Jubilee took place in 1977 and our street party filled the length of Lurline Gardens with a long trestle table laden with party food supplied by all the residents. It was a freezing cold day with icy showers but all the children were dressed up, the street was festooned with red, white and blue bunting, there were silver crowns everywhere, and the warmth of the atmosphere, the music and the dancing meant all the expectations of a great community celebration were fulfilled.

The children's schooldays had progressed fairly well. Jonathan was a good average in most subjects, Paul likewise, although he tried to avoid overburdening himself with homework. Anya had problems with reading that required considerable help. On a personal level their school reports were generally complimentary – 'Likeable, kind, well-behaved children' – but these reports consistently drew attention to the major failing that afflicted all three. They were daydreamers and the potential of each one of them was being continually compromised by this. A noble, but perhaps unfortunate, family tradition established by me in my own schooldays when I gazed out far over the sea from my classroom, well out of reach of the teacher's voice.

In the summer of 1977 a bulky envelope dropped through the letterbox: divorce papers for me to sign. I'd had no warning of this and there were no words from John, so the lawyer's letter came as a shock. We had been apart for three and a half years. I had grown accustomed to life without him and had long since surrendered hope of any reconciliation. I had over the years worked hard to pick myself up and felt that, of the two of us, I was, in one sense, faring better. All my feelings were buried deep in the past.

As I looked over the divorce papers, however, and the cold, formal instructions from John's solicitor, I felt a sudden stab of sadness. I looked at our marriage certificate and was immediately back once more in the little white church in Golspie on that sunny showery September day when we had believed that this was going to be forever. What we had had between us had been so right, had seemed indomitable and had promised so much. Still, as real and profound as that had been, it was all gone now, only a distant memory. We had not even succeeded in keeping a friendship alive between us.

Over the years of separation we had grown far apart. Guilt made John hostile and defensive. Any scraps of information he had been unable to avoid hearing concerning my life without him exacerbated his attitude towards me. He could not bear to know anything about what I was doing.

It was in the aftermath of our separation that his drinking crossed the border from enthusiastic social bonhomie to something serious and self-destructive. The person I had known and loved had now rapidly become overwhelmed by the descent to alcoholism. I knew that the vibrant, inspiring and compassionate person was still there somewhere but, for me, he was beyond reach. Sometimes I saw him briefly at his door when I delivered the children to him on Saturdays but the relationship we managed to maintain was fragile and uneasy at best, with the resentment he now attached to me for ending our marriage never far beneath the surface. We never spent any time together with the children. I was never invited to his exhibitions or to see his work. I watched its development from a distance, going to see it in the galleries on my own.

The shock of the arrival of the divorce papers brought to the surface again my deeply buried sadness. But time had moved on. This was part of the general passage through divorce and I had to get on with it. I would do as he wanted and quickly sign the papers. I believed the children were used to the situation and so I did not make an issue of the divorce papers arriving.

This was now 1978. Jonathan was about to turn thirteen and was into his third year at Sir Walter St John's grant-aided grammar school in Battersea. Paul was ten and Anya eight. Both still attended Chesterton Junior School. Up to this point my working hours, apart from unforeseen days off school and holidays, had been fairly compatible with those of the children but they were latchkey kids and had to be trusted to cope until I got home at teatime.

My work experience eventually led me to want to study psychology, something in which I had always had an interest. I discovered that London University ran a degree course that took place at Goldsmiths College in Deptford, where I had previously studied for my art teaching qualification. As the course was part-time it would extend over four years, one day and one evening per week. This I thought was manageable for me so I applied for a place on the course and was accepted. Being an employee of the Inner London Education Authority I was awarded one-day leave and my fees paid for the course. Childcare, however, was a problem.

When I began my first year, my neighbours did what they could to help and various strategies were tried out and worked for a while, but none of them was really satisfactory. Penny had by this time moved to Clapham. All of our extended family lived hundreds of miles away in Scotland and while the children continued to visit John on Saturday nights, coming back to me Sunday teatime, further help from him was strictly non-negotiable. More and more was asked of Jonathan as he grew older.

As a family we had a fairly harmonious living pattern, with the usual bickering from time to time but no serious altercations. Had it been otherwise I could not have entertained the thought of leaving Jonathan with the responsibility of the home while I was at college. It was the fact that they were easy children to trust that allowed me to take the risk, a risk that now seems irresponsible and was probably illegal.

For the first two years it was only one night a week from six thirty to nine thirty. I had based my plan on that one night per week, possibly two at the most as the course progressed. I certainly had not been prepared for the continual increase in the number of evenings required. As I started the third year it became apparent I would have to be in Goldsmiths three nights a week and was warned that for the final year it might, for a few weeks, be four. What could I do? Once I had started something I was not one for quitting but there were great difficulties with childcare.

During the third year we had Joanne, a young girl from the

one of the families in the street, who came to be with them for those hours. She was a couple of years older than Jonathan but by the time he was fifteen he was embarrassed by the fact that she had been given the responsibility of looking after them, him especially.

While I had been considering the psychology course, my mother had come to visit us. She did not think much of my plans even if, as I tried to argue, it might mean that I would eventually be able to leave prison education, which I wanted to do, and have a better job with paid holidays. She kept saying that by the time I graduated, Jonathan would be sixteen, his childhood almost over. I was aware of this, and also aware that he was now entering the difficult years of his adolescence and that Paul would quickly follow him. I was, however, so confident in my close relationship with the children that I convinced myself the going would be relatively uncomplicated, that I could juggle it all – working full-time, the hours of study, keeping regular communication with school, providing an easy-going and happy home for the children, and making good the time we were together. I had taken no account of crucial factors – the essential need, and right, of children to know that there is a parent's presence in the home and to always be able to feel the comfort, the consequent reassurance and sense of safety and security that it guarantees. For Anya in particular, feelings of abandonment began to displace many of the better things that were also part of our lives then.

Sundays, while they were with John, I used to get my essays and projects underway. On weekdays I rose at six to read textbooks and make notes for a couple of hours before we all had to get ready for school and work. At work, during the long lunch hour I found an empty room, usually a cell used for interviews, and shut myself away with my books. There was a steady backlog of essays to be worked through and handed in every week and most of the time I somehow or other made the deadlines. Social life was usually confined to Saturday nights, when I was more than willing to let my hair down.

Anya's reading problem was an ongoing concern and I was

in regular talks with her teachers. This resulted in some extra one-to-one help in her class but she was still struggling. I felt she needed more intensive help and suggested that she be assessed by an educational psychologist with this aim in view. The school was adamant that this was unnecessary. I should read to her, they insisted. But I did, every night, until college became more demanding. While there were plenty of things that I did not do with them, I had always loved reading to them and she, like her brothers, loved following the stories. She used to make little books and write the stories for them herself. She was very creative and had a lively imagination. I believed that, as far as I was aware, the level of home stimulation was good. What was needed was more help for her at school. Reluctantly they referred her to an educational psychologist but her dyslexia was not properly diagnosed until she was eighteen.

Diagnosis, of course, is only the beginning of the story. It might give her confidence to counter any claims by other children that she was 'stupid' but it did not take the problem away. In the seventies the understanding of such problems as dyslexia was in its infancy. To bring order to the jumbled letters in her visual field and calm to her short-term memory, hard work and constant struggle were required of her and she did her best, but anyone who has suffered this affliction knows it will be with you for life. In the meantime, she tried hard to respond to the only help available.

Paul was the arbiter of the family morals. He was always keen to inform us what was right and wrong. He was equally enthusiastic in defending right from wrong outside the home and did not hesitate to make his displeasure known at anything he saw as an injustice. He always had a small group of school friends around him who reflected our multicultural environment. His best friends for a considerable time were a group of West Indian boys in his class to whom he was fiercely loyal.

Jonathan was the peacemaker. Being the eldest he tried to look after the other two, sorting out their squabbles. I could rely on him when I needed help. He, like the others, was open and told me most of what was going on at school, while carefully avoiding anything that would worry me. When things came up that upset him, we talked them through, usually late at night. Adolescent years are fraught with challenge and insecurity at the best of times and those rites of passage must be the most testing and arduous any of us will ever have to face, but I felt at that time that our closeness as a family unit would see us through. I felt we were coping fairly well under the circumstances. But I was wrong.

CHAPTER 33

Skinheads

When he was twelve Jonathan came home from school and told me that during a discussion in class the teacher had asked how many boys came from a one-parent family. There was only one other boy and himself. This upset him very much. I was surprised that there were only two boys out of a class of about thirty. This was the seventies and, sadly, broken families seemed to be an ever-growing social phenomenon. Later he came home on the bus from the sports field sitting beside a boy from another school. This boy too, he told me, with relief shining in his eyes, lived only with his mother as his parents had split up. Knowing there were other boys in his predicament eased something in his mind but at the same time brought home to me his raw vulnerability.

He talked about the usual skirmishes at school and a couple of times told me his dinner money had been taken from him by black boys who carried knives. He was not the only one to whom this happened, nor was he bullied any more than most, but this kind of intimidation was widespread throughout the schools in south London. As is usual with bullying I was urged by my children not to inform the school as it would only make things worse. Like most parents I probably never knew the extent of what went on. I certainly did not know that he began to frequent the York Tavern with other boys when he could not have been more than fourteen.

Skinheads

The York Tavern was situated near Battersea Bridge, within walking distance of the school. It quickly established notoriety as a skinhead meeting place. Jonathan found a sense of belonging there, where he probably felt supported. Instead of having to take responsibility for his sister and brother and worry about me, he found that he could escape those obligations. He was apparently among the youngest of the boys who went there and the support he was given by the skinhead 'big brothers' must have given him strength that he could obtain nowhere else.

John, while living at the World's End near Chelsea's football ground, Stamford Bridge, had begun to take the children to home matches on Saturdays, and thus their lifelong support of the Chelsea team was born. Anya was persuaded to go to the matches too but they never appealed to her. Only six when they began attending, she was cajoled into going by the promise that she would see herself on TV when the game was replayed on television in the evening. She kept looking for herself in vain. About that time, racism increased at Stamford Bridge, along with its accompanying violence, but John took care to keep the children away from the area where this was concentrated and, for the boys and John, the outings were the highlight of the week.

In years to come, being a Chelsea supporter provided Jonathan with added street cred, aiding his ability to integrate with the Chelsea-supporting skinheads he found at the York, who were, unlike him or any of his other friends or acquaintances, ardent racists. At first, all this activity was concealed from me. He was soon, however, sporting Dr. Martens boots and to my dismay came home one day with a shaved head. I didn't like this but could cope if I tried to see it more or less as a teenage uniform.

Although I expected challenges from the children as they grew up, I believed my fundamental values were instilled in them. I was both unprepared and totally dismayed to hear them now voicing racist views.

It is well established that the peer group rules in adolescence, and my caring and responsible eldest son was a sitting target for indoctrination by elements he saw as providing a deterrent to the menace of street violence, the source of which he now believed to be solely black kids. He had seen some evidence for himself. Many other factors may have influenced him but I believe that the lack of family security on top of the responsibility that fell on his shoulders at home must have played a significant part in his eagerness to find a new support system. He could not find at home the strength he found with his new friends at the York Tavern.

Jonathan's school reports began to include comments on his declining attitude to his work. At parents' evenings I found the same goodwill and affection towards him but he seemed to have lost his direction. I was also becoming increasingly worried about the company he was keeping and the attitudes he was expressing and I made it clear I was in need of help and guidance from the school. I talked about the intimidating behaviour he had told me about. It would be an exceptional school that didn't feature some form of bullying but I believed it was something that should be dealt with. I felt my son's experience should be acknowledged. It just so happened that in this case the bullies were black. It didn't justify Jonathan's fledgling racist views but as with bullying of any kind it was a valid cause for concern. They agreed there was a bit of trouble from time to time and they were trying to do something about it. They would of course be happy to help me in any way they could, as they liked Jonathan and felt that he could do well in his exams if he could get back on track.

A door had opened for him, however, and he was on his way along the escape route. The loving kindness of the child I knew was there but how could it survive in such brutal and mindless company? The draw of the crowd he had become part of was irresistible and was too strong for any home values to influence. He saw being a skinhead as great sport. It was tribal warfare and it was what young people did. More importantly, it provided an escape from the pressures of home. It was where he began to leave his childhood behind.

It was not all about violence, he assured me. He also claimed that it was not about indiscriminate aggression to black people in general, but the dogma he was bringing home was not encouraging. It didn't brook any discussion. It did not matter how we talked the subject through, everything was becoming fixed in his mind. In his view I just did not understand. I had grown up in the remote wilds of Scotland, so how could I understand what growing up in inner London was like? Nothing I could offer was therefore relevant. It was like talking to the flat-earth society.

Significant events determined his attitudes. In 1981 there came the race riots of Brixton and, even nearer to home, Clapham Junction, in which cars and premises were set on fire and people were injured. It was out-and-out warfare between black and white gangs. He and his friends saw it as a duty to defend their home territory, justifying their behaviour. One night there was a party to which he was invited but which he was lucky enough not to attend, where one of his friends was murdered, again as the result of racial conflict.

These incidents might have influenced others to steer clear but by this time he had identified with and was loyal to people who acted like a family to him. He believed he should fight against the injustices being done to them.

CHAPTER 34

Juliet

After we parted John's drinking had escalated and although he did not seem particularly conspicuous in the crowd he ran with, even they were beginning to struggle to keep up with him. They were all boozers par excellence but he was now pouring his first drink early in the morning and it acted as a medicine to bring him up to form for the day. Never really appearing out of control, he quietly topped up until the evening, when he made his way to a pub or private view with friends, all of whom also ended up totally smashed. Those were the great drinking days, full of hilarious tales of legendary escapades and warm friendships. Despite this, for him painting remained the constant and obsessive air he breathed. But two years after we split up, an accumulation of factors led to a crisis, mainly the aftermath of our separation, and in early 1976 he had to spend a few weeks at the family home in Port Seton recovering from a deep depression.

Back teaching at Croydon, well after the divorce was finalized, in late 1977 he met Juliet. There being virtually no communication between John and I, all I knew was what I was told by the children and this was that she was a sculpture student at Croydon and they had begun to live together.

Juliet Gray, née Lister, came from a well-to-do aristocratic family. Her father had been the Senior Opthalmic Surgeon at Moorfields Eye Hospital. One of her illustrious forebears, her

174

great uncle, was the Lord Lister who discovered antiseptic. Her great-grandmother, 'Granny Cameron', was Julia Margaret Cameron, the Victorian pioneer of photography.

Quite soon after they got together, Juliet bought a house in Linden Gardens at Notting Hill Gate and John left the 'Scottish Embassy' in Chelsea to move in with her. To begin with they enjoyed a rather unconventional *ménage à trois* that I heard about later. The elderly woman from whom Juliet bought the house had asked if she could stay on for a while till she found somewhere else to live. This was not a problem. Apparently a curtain was erected dividing the sitting room into two compartments – one for John and Juliet and one for Mrs Mazzawi and her wardrobe of fur coats. The wardrobe was often surplus to requirements as Mrs Mazzawi frequently wandered around, answering the door, putting out the rubbish, naked as nature intended. This temporary double occupancy became more and more long term until the day a taxi was called and the furs and Mrs Mazzawi were bundled in. It was all becoming a bit too cosy and eventually exasperation had ignited the Bellany fuse. A few months later, in July 1979, the children came home with the news that Juliet had bought a large house on Clapham Common and they were moving in very soon.

It was generally better for the children if there was a female presence among the friends at John's house. It made things seem more homely. They told me about Juliet and that they liked her, in as much as they got to know her. During their first meeting with her she had what they subsequently learned was an epileptic fit, something they had never witnessed before. John had not told them that this could happen and, unable to understand, they were frightened.

Apart from that Anya especially was delighted to have Juliet around – a female friend at last in a male environment. Juliet, being an insomniac, was always about when Anya woke early in the mornings and they spent a lot of time making things together, modelling clay, drawing, sewing and talking. I felt relieved and glad they got on well together. My knowledge of Juliet was dependent on what I was told by the children and was consequently vague but Anya's random observations were always enthusiastic. At eight years old she accepted with equanimity Juliet's explanation of the burn marks on her arms. These were simply the marks where she had stubbed out her cigarettes. Their conversations, as they happily sewed or sketched together, were peppered with unpredictable topics.

'Anya, when you die, what would you like to happen to your body? Would you like to be buried in a box under the ground or would you like to be cremated?'

'What does "cremated" mean, Juliet?'

'It means that your body would be burnt in a big hot furnace. Which do you think you would prefer?'

To Anya's delight, Juliet took her on her own on trips across London on the tube and on buses. Apart from my fear of Juliet having a seizure while on her own with Anya, I as yet knew nothing about her chronic alcoholism and the quarter bottles of whisky she carried on those days out with Anya. That was their little secret.

It was impossible to broach my worries with John. Because he would rather not acknowledge them himself, his approach to problems was to brush them out of sight rather than look at ways of dealing with them. Any intervention by me was seen as criticism and not as the natural and understandable concerns of a mother. Over the next year or so, little by little, I became aware of the extent of Juliet's problems: they were deep-rooted. Along with her alcoholism and epilepsy she had for many years struggled with a severe bipolar disorder. Cutting herself was only one of the signs of her disturbed mind. She had made suicide attempts and was a regular in-patient of the psychiatric department of Epsom District Hospital. As the result of a rare period of relative stability she had enrolled in a sculpture course at Croydon School of Art where she met John.

Juliet's life was one bound by sadness and ill fortune. She had trained as a nurse, had been married and had one son, David, who, since the break-up of his parents' marriage, had lived with his father in Sussex. The nature of Juliet's illness meant that she had spent more of her adult life in hospital than out of it, and most of her days were spent struggling against the illness that tormented her. For brief spells she was able to draw strength from the safe refuge and respite she found being with her mother, but she rarely saw her son, who was similar in age to Paul. In her unexpected relationship with John she had invested her brightest hopes and throughout the darkness of her misery she clung on to the snatches of happiness it provided.

The malevolent nature of bipolar illness means that it always has the upper hand and has to be treated with respect. When she was well, things were calm for a spell and then, without warning, they veered off balance to such a degree that she suddenly had to readmit herself into the sanctuary of the hospital. Many times John accompanied her there in a taxi all the way from London to Epsom, sometimes in the aftermath of a suicide attempt when she had cut her wrists. Much of the time out of hospital she spent lying in a darkened room for days at a time. Not properly understanding what was happening, the children learned to adapt to the ever-changing situation, knowing to phone me in any emergency (though they never did).

It was through the children that I became aware of the extent of John's drinking, which no longer seemed to be purely social or recreational. Although he continued to paint they told me that he was frequently ill. Flu, he said. I told them that if they were worried when they were there with him, especially if he was on his own, to call me and I would come for them. I would also try to help him. Juliet's troubled existence just didn't bear thinking about and the outlook for their life together, from the start, did not seem promising.

By this time John had established himself as a prominent and popular personality in the London art world. Along with his post at Croydon he was a visiting lecturer at the Royal College of Art, Goldsmiths and other colleges throughout the country. He was included in most of the major contemporary group exhibitions at the Tate, the Hayward Galleries, the John Moore's Annual in Liverpool, in which one year he was a prizewinner, and those promoted by the British Arts Council and British Council that toured to Europe. He was an enthusiastic member and exhibitor of the London Group and a convivial presence at art-world jamborees.

He held regular solo exhibitions, mainly at the Drian, but wasn't making much money from his painting. In Battersea High Street a few years back, he and Norman had held Open Studio exhibitions and in the dejection of the post-mortem when nothing had sold they consoled themselves that at least by showing their work to a wider audience they had made 'invisible earnings' from which something might materialize in the future. Things were now, in 1978, much the same – an occasional sale but still mainly invisible earnings.

Despite the drinking, John's work pattern never faltered nor his passion for painting. He had eventually abandoned working on hardboard and now used canvas, which, to me, gave his work a sensuous fluidity. His painting followed a steady progression and from its solid foundations he was developing a resonant voice with its own idiosyncratic language.

From the directness of his earlier view of the world he now had found his expression in allusion, symbolism and the haunting echoes of his inner life. His work was powerful and impressive, finely and delicately worked, and sure in its conception. The boozing and carousing taking over his life brought a wildness to his vision and a freedom to the touch of his brush. I loved this work of the seventies and was excited to see its development. One aspect he had introduced was the use of masks, following in the steps of one of his European heroes, James Ensor. This added a dimension of mystery, the notion of disguise, which he seemed to me to use in an effort to conceal the torment of his inner life not only from the viewer but also from himself. Guilt was an ever-present factor in his life and his work. I was drawn to its haunting melancholy and throughout it all I could still hear his inner voice.

I had finally emerged from the loneliness of our last years together. My memories of the boy with whom I had grown up and set out on life would never fade but they were securely in the past. I had filled the weekends with my own social life. Like

John, I too was drawn to a hedonistic life and when I did not have the children with me I put all my energies into burning the candles just as he had been doing. A lot of the time there was a frantic edge to my pleasure-seeking, a slightly desperate need to believe that I was happy.

I missed the happy fearless times we had shared, united in our belief in his unique creative energy. I missed the smell of oil paint and all it had meant to me. Now there was no common ground left for us to walk together, no shared events even for the children's sake. I was no longer any part of his life. We never talked together, not even of things regarding the children's schooling or general well-being. He had an aversion to dealing with any of that, so it was all up to me. While I was banished from his life, he wanted to know nothing about mine. His animosity, however, never convinced me that he could forget the bond we had shared, how immersed in his work I had been since the age of nineteen, how deeply I understood it, and understood him, and how indestructible my belief in his talent was and would always be.

One Sunday night in October 1979, over two years after the divorce was made absolute, John rang to tell me that he and Juliet were getting married the next day at Chelsea Town Hall. I should not have been surprised but, with no warning, I was taken aback. I assumed that he was ringing to tell me this as he wanted the children to take the day off school to be there but, no, he didn't want them there. The purpose of his call was just to inform us.

My mother was with us at that time and we sat the children down to tell them news that I did not expect would surprise or upset them. It did cross my mind that he might have invited the children to join in his celebration but I didn't think too much about it. That was just typical of him. Feelings too complicated to cope with, as usual, had to be avoided.

There was not much reaction from the three of them except from Anya, who wanted to be there and couldn't understand why it wasn't possible. I did ring back to ask if he was sure that he didn't want them there, as Anya especially wanted to go, but he confirmed that they were not being invited

Just as I had made unrealistic assumptions about what the children could, or should, be asked to cope with, John had no idea that his decisions could be insensitive and hurtful to them. His attitude to children was very much fashioned by what had been the norm for us in the fifties. Children obeyed the adults and required little or no explanation. Time and time again he brushed things out of sight with no discussion because he couldn't handle them himself and he would prefer to conceal what was happening rather than explain and work his way through them with those involved.

Arriving home after school on that Monday, Jonathan went straight into his bedroom, lay down on his bed and sobbed. He lay there for the rest of the evening, never even coming through for dinner. I asked him to tell me what was wrong. He just did not feel well. Had he wanted to be at the wedding? No. He just didn't feel well. I accepted that it was all he could say. I knew then, and it became even clearer with hindsight, that it had been the end of the dreams he had always cherished that John and I would somehow come back together to live as a real family once more.

When the children visited John the following weekend, Juliet's son David told them he had been at the wedding. Paul and Anya were indignant at being excluded. For both of them the significance of the marriage was markedly different from Jonathan's. Paul's memories of John and me living together were hazy and Anya's were non-existent. They had just missed out on some event that might have been fun, where they might even have felt a bit special and Anya could have worn a pretty dress.

CHAPTER 35

Disintegration

At the time of John's marriage to Juliet, Jonathan was nearly fourteen. Paul was eleven and had moved on from Chesterton to secondary school. In spite of my misgivings he too went to Sir Walter St John's. It was the best school in the area by far and there seemed to be no viable alternative. I was worried about him following in the footsteps of his brother but to begin with he was strongly critical of what Jonathan was getting involved with.

It was to be more than thirty years before I learned that it was the music of the time that was the vehicle for Paul's change of attitude. While he still had his close black friends he began to follow Ska and Two Tone music – Specials, Madness, Bad Manners – whose message largely promoted multicultural harmony. But because the skinhead look that went with this music was considered National Front, his black friends began to make a stand against it and everyone fell out. This changed the nature of his friendships and there was a parting of the ways. Once this happened he began to change his views. Gradually he headed off in the direction Jonathan had taken and nothing I did or said had any effect.

In the light of this turn of events, in January 1982 I had Paul moved from St John's to Pimlico Comprehensive, just over Chelsea Bridge. The school was only ten years old at that time and, being based on the lines of Holland Park Comprehensive, enjoyed the reputation of being 'progressive'. Just across the river and within walking distance of Lurline Gardens, it had built its reputation on its music and arts departments. This new beginning seemed to provide some optimism.

After a year and a half at St John's, Paul went without any fuss to begin the term there. Many years on he described his first day at Pimlico. Knowing nobody whatsoever he arrived at the school, which was full of children milling around. He walked into the midst of them, feeling very self-conscious, walked the length of the long building and straight out the other end. Apparently he spent the day until it was home time just dodging around here and there in the centre of London. He was thirteen. The next day, thankfully, he found his way to the school office and joined his class, and I was none the wiser. But neither had I been aware that he and his friend had regularly bought Red Rover bus tickets and travelled from one end of London to the other at the age of eleven, hanging out with other wandering children at places about which I am now grateful to have known nothing.

Paul did make a valiant attempt at a fresh start but it misfired. Having been a skinhead for the previous twelve months the camaraderie was too powerful and too entrenched. At first he made big efforts at school but the more he became involved in skinhead activities, the less attention he paid in class. Summoned to the head teacher's office I was told they liked Paul, just as Jonathan had been liked by his teachers, but he was not conforming and very much underachieving. I, of course, knew nothing about any of this until I was informed by the school. He had come home to tell me with indignation that he had, for example, been told off by the sewing teacher for not learning to use the sewing machine correctly. His earnest insistence that he was genuinely trying hard to do what he had been asked, albeit on a sewing machine, an activity I found hard to imagine him doing as it would be a girl's thing in his eyes, gave me a moment's hope and wry admiration. However there was no mention of the detentions he was being given nor of what he was getting into out of school hours.

Until about this time I had believed our flat to be a secure and comforting refuge for the children and myself. Bringing up three children on my own involved the hard work and exhaustion that unfailingly goes with family life but the usual ups and downs were played out in relatively easy accord.

Now the bubble had burst. Now I spent hours listening to them, reasoning, arguing, explaining, giving examples of the flaws in their arguments, drawing support from references to various members of family whom they loved and admired, pointing out the effect of their racism on friends, our friends and theirs, and asking them to put themselves in the places of those they had taken against, not the violent and offensive but ordinary people like those in their own family. All I achieved was deadlock and angry rows. I exhausted myself trying to reason with them.

Out of the blue, one Sunday, I was summoned to go and collect them from Bethnal Green Police station in the east end of London. Thinking that I would never find out, they had left John's house to go to Brick Lane Market. Anya had wanted to go with them. She longed for their approval. There they had been stopped by the police after they had been seen buying racist stickers which, apart from being obnoxious, they did not realize were actually illegal. These had been sold to them from the stall run by the National Front. They had been accompanied by a man in his twenties who, on the approach of the police, had made a run for it, leaving them to face the music. All three children were taken to the police station.

There I found a petrified Anya being looked after by a female officer while the boys had been put into separate cells, with their Dr. Martens, laces removed, left outside the door. The avuncular police officer had decided to treat them like proper little criminals to frighten them and, with my agreement and in my presence, gave them a good talking to. He warned them off the company they were keeping and attempted to scare them with the prospects they could face if they chose not to heed the warning. It was the first time I had experienced support from any source, and I was so grateful to him. Although I was devastated by the whole event, his help, along with the promises I subsequently elicited from the boys, even allowed me a glimmer of optimism about the effect this episode might have. Perhaps it was possible to get them out of this whole nightmare before it took hold. After all, they were still so young.

It was a vain hope. They had quickly become entrenched in the subculture. It was a powerful drug. The more I laid down the law, the more trouble they waded into. The boys soon acquired girlfriends – half-shaved white blonde heads and full skinhead gear. In crises I stayed calm and gave the appearance of being in control; however, with each one I had to deal with, my resilience began to crumble. A beating by black kids just fuelled the fire and knife wounds were seen as trophies.

I was becoming desperate, suffering panic attacks and sleepless nights. I was convinced it must be mainly my fault. Children need two parents and, most importantly, parents who act in solidarity with each other. This ideal state is not reality for many families and even in an average family one parent often has to do the work of two, as in my case. In practice, I was responsible for the children's welfare and I had to take responsibility for what had gone wrong. I firmly believed that parents always had to answer for that.

John and Juliet were now living in a large house on Windmill Drive on Clapham Common. He was showing his work in exhibitions throughout the United Kingdom, the major one at the Ikon Gallery in Birmingham. The Tate Gallery had bought *Star of Bethlehem*, which he had painted in 1965, and Southampton City Art Gallery bought *Bethel*, 1966. Things were looking up and recognition was at last coming his way. He now had an agent, Monika Kinley, and in 1982 he held his first exhibition in New York at Rosa Esman, where work was sold to important American collectors.

His lack of interest in the boys' activities was in no way silent approval. It was born of his inherent laziness about anything that took his energy away from painting. Denial was easier and he always chose the easier way. Their behaviour was too distasteful to confront. He would rather not acknowledge what was happening; he hadn't the energy for it and hoped it would all go away. He loved his children but played his part in their lives in a relatively perfunctory fashion. He saw them for twenty-four hours a week, during which time, while they enjoyed seeing him and he them, they were scared to step out of line and incur his wrath. They were always on their best behaviour. John never had to deal with the petty rows and arguments and bickering of normal family life, far less the problems that had now arisen. They only surfaced at home with me. There was consequently no conflict. His portraits of our skinhead sons in full regalia in those early days express the innocence of young boyhood and the vulnerability of their complete unawareness of the danger they were in.

I was approaching the end of my degree course and somehow kept up the pace of study and work to be handed in. I was not a quitter, and I did see it through to the end, but my worries about the children had taken the heart out of any enthusiasm I had had and my enjoyment had begun to wane. The scientific basis and relentless testing of hypotheses, the probabilities, preoccupation with statistics, the carrying out and writing up of practical studies, the reading up of clinical research based on running rats in mazes, etc. held no attraction. The under-lying facts and theories, however, continued to fascinate me. The mechanisms of the brain, the intricacies of memory and learning, human development, the acquisition of language and the operation of the nervous system were endlessly absorbing. It was the methodology I wearied of. My subsidiary subject was social anthropology. It enthralled me and I wished it could have been the principal subject of my degree.

In June 1982 the final exams arrived. They were set over three consecutive days, two three-hour exams each day. The whole of the night before they began I spent in A & E at St Thomas's Hospital with Jonathan, who had injured his hand in the doors of a tube train, and we arrived home just as it was time to set off for Goldsmiths and the exams. I was beyond caring and indifferent to the second-class degree I obtained. It wasn't the best I could do but it wasn't the worst. I looked on it as a four-year-long disaster, upon which I had misguidedly embarked and which had landed me in the most dreadful place. My mother had been right. Working full-time, studying for a rigorous academic degree and bringing up three children on my own without help, all at the same time: no wonder things were all wrong. Worst of all was the realisation that I had in my own way neglected the children just as John had.

Looking back thirty years on, many of the boys' exploits merge into one nightmarish blur. There was never, at any time, even throughout the skinhead years, any aggression or animosity directed towards me. That was nowhere in their nature. The major issue in the home was their frustration at my inability to see things their way. They were never less than respectful of me and our home. The underlying love was always there. The company they kept and the activities they were involved in caused me increasing anguish until it finally became too much. In January 1983, I could cope no more. I told them to get some things together and go to live with John. I had often warned them that this would happen if they did not change their ways.

I was fully aware that it was not a good move; in fact, as they would much later agree, it was the worst possible action I could have taken. John was already incapable of looking after himself and Juliet. Nothing would ever get in the way of his painting – wild gestural work that I would get to see in the future – but his drinking had escalated beyond control. Juliet was a sad, haunted shadow reeling from continual bouts of illness, which electro-convulsive therapy had frequently attempted to relieve. She was generally in the Epsom hospital or at her mother's home, but on the rare occasions she was at Windmill Drive she was usually lying in her darkened room. I was aware that the boys would have carte blanche in this household, but I no longer had the energy to do any more. I was burnt out and distraught, not least because I was having to tell them to leave our home, their home.

In my despair I had searched everywhere for help. I was obsessive in my need to get them out of the world they now inhabited. I spoke to our kindly family doctor. I asked the schools for help.

I constantly burdened my friends with my worries. I talked to counsellors, solicitors, psychologists, colleagues at work. All of them listened and gave me advice to the best of their ability but none of it could touch the heart of the problem. My anxiety levels steadily increased, closing up my throat in panic attacks and taking away my breath as I tried to speak.

I read articles in newspapers and magazines, watched programmes on television and obsessively latched on to anything that could offer even marginal support. One lead I followed up on a Sunday afternoon was a meeting of parents of skinheads being held somewhere south of Lewisham. I found my way there only to come away with the usual disappointment. The group turned out to be interested in their skinhead sons' addictions to glue-sniffing to the exclusion of all else. Glue was not on my boys' agenda or drugs of any kind. They didn't even smoke. Perhaps I should have been grateful for this but it provided no comfort. I was concerned with something that was to me much more insidious.

There were no answers but I had to keep hoping that somewhere I would find a source of help. 'It's a good thrashing they need' came from one elderly acquaintance, thus confirming his own dubious views. Others, who enjoyed the luxury of objectivity, tried to lighten the subject by reassuring me that 'they'll come creeping back when they're skint and miss the comforts of home'.

John had treated Jonathan to a set of drums and Paul to an electric guitar and they used his cellar to practise in. They immediately saw the potential of such a well-meant gesture and after a few years they were working their way up as stars of the bands at the forefront of the movement. This had the effect of providing them with extra status and they were soon playing at gigs around the country.

Anya and I were now left in the flat on our own. It was as if we were in mourning and of course we were. She was now twelve and a half and desperately missed her brothers, and I was heartbroken at how our whole family had splintered into such disaster. We spent a lot of time huddled on the couch in misery.

CHAPTER 36

A New Job

After my degree course ended, in a need for change I began working in a Turning Point project for rehabilitating drug- and alcohol-dependent adults where I would be the acting person in charge during the current leader's sabbatical. To me it seemed a natural progression but I was well aware of the coincidence with John's problem. Dr Glatt had been instrumental in encouraging me in this direction and I was glad to leave Wormwood Scrubs at last. The major benefit was that this new employment would provide paid holiday and sick leave. Also, the location of my new workplace was at the end of Lurline Gardens looking on to the entrance to Battersea Park, much nearer home and Anya.

It could be said that I was going from the frying pan into the fire. What was it about working in the mainstream, in something like school teaching, which I felt unenthusiastic about? Why could I not contribute and fulfil myself in a more benign environment? Why did I seek out and find comfort operating in the relative shadows of life? I had once been told that I was a marginal person, not fitting in to a clearly defined group. The way I felt then made me believe that there might indeed be some truth in that. Perhaps I had come to identify with those whose lives were not being played out as they would have wanted.

I loved working with people, however. They and their lives interested me, and I wanted to continue in that sort of occupation. For my employment at Turning Point I was both overqualified and underqualified. My degree status stood for something but did not compensate for the fact that I had not gained the appropriate social-work qualifications. The post was really for a fully trained social worker. Perhaps my experience of prisoners who had been dependent on drugs and alcohol had won me the job. Or perhaps no one else had wanted it!

As with many aspects of my former workplace, I found much that was dreary in the new one. It was in the greyness of the administration. It was not the people. Their backgrounds, their stories and how they coped with all that had come their way always interested me. Many of them were wretched and I was fearful for them. A few were well seasoned in ducking and diving through the murky waters of life and others were heroic and truly inspirational.

The people our organization, Turning Point, was set up to help were not those who simply got a bit too merry a little too often; they were not the drunken friends whose uninhibited antics were the source of endless hilarity. The residents of the Davis Centre had been there and done that too but there was no longer anything remotely amusing, to them or to anyone close to them, about the role that alcohol played in their lives. The cross section of residents touched every part of society – teachers, doctors, journalists, business personnel and manual workers. The reality was desperation, degradation and despair. Their often suicidal fear was of none other than the Demon Drink itself. To battle every minute of every day and night against their own self-destruction they needed all the help that could be imagined, in whatever shape they could find it. Communal living-in places like the Davis Centre, with people who shared the same problems, provided initial support and rehabilita- tion. Along with this, the first rung of the ladder that provided ongoing support in the wider community was always Alcoholics Anonymous. Through AA many found a tenuous and fragile lifeline for the rest of their lives.

While working at the Davis Centre I began to feel myself sinking. Working with other people's difficulties was not to blame. If anything it provided a distraction from my own and now and then provided moments of illumination. Anya and I clung together in shared misery about our broken family. She could not understand how the boys could be involved in such activities. She had tried to go along with them in an attempt to be close to them but she was frightened and disliked everything about the life they were immersed in. She backed away in despair. Now she had to cope with their total rejection, which hurt her badly.

She had begun at Pimlico Comprehensive and for the first few weeks I walked with her through Battersea Park across Chelsea Bridge every morning before going to work. As with the boys, her teachers were supportive and helpful but her dyslexia was holding her back. She was supposed to have one-to-one help with reading and writing but in time this degenerated into her being sidelined into the remedial class (or the dunces' class, as they called it) where time passed without anything being achieved. The remedial class was full of reluctant and demoralized pupils who, like her, resented being 'dumped' there.

Anya soon began to bunk off school with some other girls and now the calls from teachers began to be about her. Repeatedly they wanted to know where she had been, but I could not tell them, as I didn't know myself. They devised different approaches to help with her problems, moving her away from other disruptive influences, interesting her in new strategies, but by this time she was on a steady self-destruct course. On top of the considerable difficulties she had to deal with in reading and writing she was a troubled girl whose family life had disintegrated. The warm closeness we shared, just the two of us, was not enough to help her. It was now 1983, she was thirteen and an adolescent with all the uncertainty that comes with it.

Eventually she stretched my inner resources beyond the limit. It was clear that things were not going to be easy with her either. All of a sudden I found myself worn out. There was nothing in my daily life that seemed to offer solace. The energy I needed for my job was waning. Home life was desolate.

CHAPTER 37

Despair

One evening, waiting at the lights on Chelsea embankment ready to cross Albert Bridge on my way home, I was idly daydreaming about my life. It had gone so badly wrong. I had warm friends and enjoyed a lively social life at weekends but the colour was draining out of it and I now felt detached from its pleasure. My inner landscape seemed to have the bleakness and loneliness of Sutherland about it, except there was none of its beauty, no place within it of refuge to go for comfort in the dark hours. What turning might I have missed that I could have taken for the better? I began to muse about what it might have been like if John and I had got back together. Only for a fleeting moment. The lights changed and the notion passed. Far too hypothetical, far too fanciful. Given my time over again I would have had to make the same decisions about my marriage. The traffic and my momentary thoughts moved on.

I assumed that John too had sometimes had regrets, as on one or two occasions throughout the years he had rung me up, usually when he had been 'out on a spree', to tell me how we had made the biggest mistake of our lives. We should never have broken up. We had destroyed something so good. We had ruined our lives. At such times he was emotional and maudlin, and it was difficult to draw the conversation to a close. I had long ceased to entertain any thought of us ever getting back together. Alcohol clouded his days and I could not find the person I had fallen in love with all those years ago. He was unreachable. I could not afford to squander my hard-won equilibrium thinking about it, but afterwards a whisper of sadness lingered on.

Those moments of regret always went underground again and our relationship reverted to the one we had become used to, one of uneasy cooperation, sometimes frosty, sometimes less so. Our only contact was minimal, regarding the children. Our lives never overlapped.

I heard bits of news about him from time to time. None of it was encouraging. Now from his first glimpse of the day to his last at night, a glass of Bacardi was his constant companion. He topped up to get on a steady keel for the day ahead. He was now teaching at Goldsmiths, the Royal College, or visiting at one of the provincial colleges. Evenings found him and his cronies at various exhibition previews back in town and after that he painted into the small hours when he got home. His painting was his *raison d'être*, as it had always been. When he painted, he was in an unreachable place. It was where his dialogue with existence took on the force of his fear and dread of death, and he followed a tenuous path in search of respite. Painting was one constant in his life. Drinking Bacardi and Coke was the other.

His time with Juliet must have provided them with brief interludes of light among the darkness. She sought the happiness and optimism she had first invested in him and, in his own way, he must have had hopes of something better and less lonely for himself too. Her chronic mental illness along with his reliance on alcohol, especially in view of her own alcohol problem, did not bear thinking about and from more or less the beginning of their relationship much of their time had been spent apart. On discharge from hospital for short breaks she often stayed in refuge with her mother. During the long spells in hospital she wrote copious letters to him, sometimes as many as three each day, and he tried to reciprocate. They had agreed that he would phone her once a week but there were never any hospital visits from him or, to Anya's consternation, from the children. Long months passed in this way. His explanation was that he could not face visiting her there and that seeing him might disturb and upset her too.

He now lived more or less on his own with a couple of cats, one of whom, Captain Baines, obviously decided to take himself off in search of improved home conditions, as he could later be seen lounging smugly in the sunny window of a neighbour's house. The other cat, Craigie, had decided not to abandon ship and to see it out to the end.

He ate when it crossed his mind. What was at hand? Boil-in-the-bag curries from his nearest shop. For someone who had relished good food, eating was now not something that he gave much thought to. As Max Glatt said of eating, 'It took up far too much valuable drinking time.' Every day they were with him he sent the children across Clapham High Road to the Pakistani grocer's, to which he had given the name 'Happy's'. They carried a simple invariable shopping list:

60 fags
B. O. B. (Bottle of Bacardi)
Coca Cola
Tin of cat food
And any treats they fancied for themselves.

In the early days, once set up with their provisions they settled down to the usual routine. When he had finished painting, they watched the *Onedin Line* (his favourite), *Thunderbirds*, *Planet of the Apes* and other things they all enjoyed, including much football. He sent them to Abbeville Road to choose videos from the chemist's shop where, incongruously, they could be rented. John invented names for everyone. The chemist himself was 'The Ditherer', which I assume related to the style of service he operated. So, 'Jonathan, all of you, go round to the Ditherer's to find something to watch tonight.'

One of their highlights was the Wine Gum competition. Who could make one last the longest? Occasionally there was a football match to attend, much to Anya's dismay. These occasions were memorable for the boys, especially the time they met Bobby Moore and George Best. There was also the phenomenal thrill of being taken through the tunnel on to the pitch at Wembley to be shown to their seats at the England v. Scotland match in 1979.

As the boys grew up, Saturday nights would sometimes find John and his friends In party mood. He would arrive downstairs while the boys were sound asleep and set about the piano in their ground-floor bedroom, his friends giving the old Irish and Scottish tunes their all. Bert (Irvin) would be on the spoons until he suddenly fell senseless onto the bed in which one of the boys was trying to sleep. As the New Year bells rang out they played football in the snow on Clapham Common beside the house, John in full flow on the accordion. Once or twice he took them with him as he and his friends made a day trip to Dieppe. John's spirit was irrepressible and memorable occasions came back to all three of them in later life that they were then able to appreciate as fun. Those were the good times for them in the periods they spent with him back then, and for John too – good moments in a drawn-out desolation.

He was by this time, however, frequently falling ill. When he was having to lie low, which happened increasingly often, he told the children he had 'the flu' or that his sickness was due to 'something I ate'.

He had, over the years, made himself known through a steady stream of exhibitions in London and throughout the country, and now he had a little money but it was still mainly the 'invisible earnings' that were quicker in coming his way. He had a beautiful place to live, a large house on leafy Clapham Common which he shared with Juliet who was seldom well enough to be there. It gave him space to paint, which mattered most, but it was not a home. He might just as well have been living in the condemned premises he had rented on Battersea High Street. Domestic issues were never of any interest to him and so he lived in chaos, his only requirements fags, Bacardi and Coke and a tin of cat food for Craigie.

The boys had been living with John since I had sent them there but the arrangement was not successful. He hadn't the patience or energy to be bothered with their antics and frequently lost his rag. Throughout all the troubled years they did remain in touch with me, and they knew they could come back and stay with me on the proviso that they turned away from skinhead activities, but Jonathan eventually left Windmill Drive to live instead among his friends of the time, at King's Cross and later on in Kent, with people of whom I knew nothing.

The children, all of them, had become very concerned about John's drinking, as he was ill so much of the time. They didn't dare talk to him about this but they did share their worries with me. I suggested that if they were scared to mention it they should write to him and this they did, pleading with him to stop. They did not want to be there when he received the letters and so had taken themselves off to stay with some of their friends. The letters were a failure. All that happened was that John was angry and Juliet wrote in reply to say he was not an alcoholic and there wasn't a problem. Once this confrontation had subsided things went on as usual and they never tried anything like that again.

The boys were past the age where I could have any influence on them. They were both lost to me and I had to cope with that. People tried to reassure me that values instilled in children take a lot to extinguish and I did hang on to that belief but I could not visualize the day when the boys I loved would come back to me. They might get into such deep trouble that they would never be able to extricate themselves.

In September 1983 John was invited to be artist in residence at the Victorian College of the Arts in Melbourne and set off to Australia for three months; Jonathan and Paul lived in Windmill Drive on their own, Juliet now being more or less permanently confined to hospital.

The Australian residency was eventful. He exhibited in Melbourne, Perth and Sydney and painted some of his most vigorous and wild semi-abstract paintings. In December he arrived back to find his parents in poor health. His father had had a stroke and his mother was battling breast cancer. His Auntie Peggy's funeral was taking place in Scotland in December after she too had succumbed to the disease. He emerged from the plane after a twenty-nine-hour flight into the full blast of the

London winter shivering in tropical clothes and the worse for wear from Bacardi. He was gaunt and weary and spent the first weeks back confined to bed, too ill to travel to Scotland. This marked the start of a steep downward spiral into ever more serious health problems.

The situation with the boys along with the growing crisis with Anya had eventually claimed what was left of my resilience. Once again I found myself lying silently curled up on the old red Turkish carpet beside the gas fire for hours at a time. I had wound myself down to a full stop. Inside I felt like John's big house – empty, echoing and devoid of hope. I had failed at everything and I had done so spectacularly. For a while now the feeling had been growing in me that I was dying inside. Everything was wasting away. I had no idea where to go next or what to do. I couldn't stop crying. I cried if anyone looked at me or talked to me. Our GP, Dr Winston, brought Dr MacLean, a psychiatrist, to assess me and I cried all the way through their visit.

Dr MacLean wanted to admit me to Springfield Hospital, which was a large psychiatric hospital in south London. She wanted me to have a complete break from my life. I was so weary, such sanctuary was a comforting thought, but who would look after Anya? Who would be at home for the boys if they did decide to come back? Also, I was frightened. Through my work I had visited people when they were patients in Springfield and what I saw had horrified me. I had not seen anything of refuge or sanctuary in that place among the deranged and drugged remnants of faded humanity wandering ceaselessly to and fro in constant agitation. If I were to be admitted there, would I ever get out again? The idea of such a place terrified me.

Instead, I was signed off from work for three months and treated with a course of powerful drugs, which had strong side effects, the most notable of which was that I could suddenly black out and fall to the ground with no warning. The other effect was that I saw in negative. As in a photographic negative, all light things were dark and dark things were white. It was agreed that I would be an outpatient of Dr MacLean and see her every week. This continued for several years.

196

At this time, my mother came to live with us. The comfort of her presence was everything to me then. We had always enjoyed each other's company but now it was my lifeline. She came to stay in a home that was no longer a home in the way it had started out. It was a place bereft of life and light. As I struggled with the medication and with the effort to regain a hold on myself, she was there to help me up when I fell down. We had always shared a ready sense of humour but it wasn't easy to make me laugh at that time. There is no place for laughter in depression.

If I write it quickly, I can make this time seem no longer or no worse than a bad weekend but, as anyone who has ever suffered serious depression knows, the nightmare descends in a blackness that permits no light or form of escape. There are no reassuring landmarks, no music that heals and soothes, familiar voices seem distant. You exist in a cage of darkness and silence, a subterranean world. Forever is the only concept you can grasp with regard to this hell.

When John and I parted, great waves of sadness had overwhelmed me for a long time afterwards but they had in time gradually drawn back. Now it was as if they had surged again with mighty force, completely swamping me. To fight back you need energy but in depression you have none; you are paralysed. Then, after weeks or months of this, a momentary flicker breaches the gloom and you believe, with overwhelming relief, that it is withdrawing at last. Hardly has that thought been formed before you crash back into the blackness. This deadly game goes on, the pattern repeating, catching you out and pulling you down again.

Later in that spring of desolation I decided I had to make a concentrated effort to pull myself to the surface. Probably the drugs were beginning to take effect. We must go out and about, to make life a bit better for my mother too. We began to visit some places in London she had rarely, if ever, been to before: Madame Tussauds, Westminster Abbey, Hampton Court, Harrods, Alexandra Palace, Kew Gardens, the Tate Gallery and to films and the theatre too. I think she was exhausted by it all! One sunny spring evening I told her I was taking her on a mystery tour. I think I saw her heart sinking – *Coronation Street* seeming to her a much better option at the end of the day – but away we went in my car. Five minutes later I stopped and parked in Westminster and we started walking.

'Where are we going to now, Helen?' she asked in a 'must-we-do-this?' voice.

To her great amazement, within minutes she found herself in the Stranger's Gallery of the House of Commons. Possibilities are endless in the city if you are able to make the effort. She was astonished and excited to be there. It was the tentative beginning of better days.

While she was with me she said how sad she felt that long years had passed since she had seen John. She always asked how he was, her fondness for him undiminished. I asked her if she wanted to go to visit him and she did. Juliet was in hospital so he seemed at ease with our visit. They were overjoyed to see each other but my mother was saddened to see him so ill-looking. He had been back from Australia for four months and was gaunt and fragile. It was a sweet, sad encounter.

Two of my friends had got married in the summer of 1984. Although I was happy for them, it nevertheless compounded my sense of loneliness. I envied them, for having had the good fortune to find that special person with whom they could share everything that mattered. I had found mine when I was in my teens and grown up with him for eleven years. Now that was gone and who is ever lucky enough to find another person as close? There can surely only be one, if that, for each person and even then they have to be able to find one another.

That summer Anya and I were invited to go on holiday to Spain with friends. We gratefully accepted. It was a refreshing escape from London, away from all the reminders of failure and despair, and it offered me a space to breathe freely for a while. Nothing was then resolved with the boys but the spell away gave me respite. When I got back, I would feel fit again to work and cope with everything once more.

CHAPTER 38

Dieppe

On 30 September 1984 Anya turned fourteen. It was a Sunday and she had gone to see John after his return from Edinburgh where he had been exhibiting. When I arrived to collect her, he invited me in. I had not seen him since my mother and I had visited a few months previously.

On his own, he was on good form this day and wanted to celebrate Anya's birthday, so he suggested we go to a wine bar on Clapham High Street for a late lunch. Anya, Paul, John and I walked down along the common to find that the restaurant was closing. To counteract his disappointment he suggested that all four of us go on a trip to Dieppe the next day instead. He urged me to take time off work as it was for Anya's birthday.

I was reluctant for several reasons. I couldn't just bunk off at the drop of a hat, particularly as I had only fairly recently returned after a few months on sick leave. More important was the fact that Dieppe was where we had gone on honeymoon and it was a very special place in memory for us both. I don't believe that John had any ulterior motive in wanting us to go back there together. He just loved the place and had returned once or twice over the years with his friends for days out. I had never been back. I knew it was bound to be emotional and I wanted to avoid a sentimental journey at all costs. I could not afford to unsettle myself in this way. It had been hard to win stability for myself and build up my life after our marriage ended, and I had just recovered from a deep depression.

Eleven years had passed since our life together had come to an end, and we both now had different lives. There was nothing wrong with a family day out. It would be the first time ever in all the years we'd been apart that we would spend any time together but I really did not want to go. There of all places.

He was fired up with enthusiasm, though, and had persuaded the children. 'Come with us, Mum. I don't want to go if you're not going. Oh, please come, Mum!'

They went on and on, John too. 'It is for the bairn's birthday!'

Eventually I gave in and agreed to go. I dreaded what I had let myself in for. Although Anya and Paul might enjoy the day off, this definitely wasn't a good idea for me.

Next morning at 6 a.m. Anya and I collected John and Paul (Jonathan was living in a King's Cross bed and breakfast by now) and we drove down to Newhaven for the early ferry to Dieppe.

John had brought his Adidas bag that accompanied him everywhere. This contained his bottle of Bacardi, Coca Cola and a glass wrapped up in a tea towel. As soon as we were on our way out of London he poured his first 'heart starter'. He was on great form. Cares and worries left far behind. He was all set for a wonderful day out.

Getting out of the car at Newhaven and taking our places on the upper deck of the ferry, in the harsh early morning light, I suddenly became aware that John was bright yellow, his face and his eyes and all his visible skin. A terrible fear passed through me as I realized that he was seriously ill. In the car he had shown me his ankles and lower legs. They were swollen and bright red. He thought it must be an allergy and I had urged him to see a doctor. As he poured himself another drink he agreed that he should but I knew that he would do no such thing. Now I was afraid for him. His jaundice meant that he had urgent problems. We were by now on our way across the Channel and wouldn't be returning until the early hours of the following day. We were going to have this day out in France and everyone was in the

mood for a good time. There were no mobile phones back then and there was nothing I could do, so I would just have to hope for the best and keep my worries to myself until we got back.

The crossing from Newhaven to Dieppe lasts around four hours so it was some time before the coast of France eventually came into view on the horizon. Soon the familiar sight of the little church high up on the cliffs that guarded the entrance to Dieppe saw us glide slowly towards our waiting berth in the harbour, and our day properly began.

Dieppe, which has captivated so many painters throughout the ages, had lost none of its charm. The harbour busy with fishermen and boats, the quays crowded with market stalls of seafood and shining fish, locals going about their daily routine, the crying of the seagulls and the sea-salt winds buffeting the towering cliffs and pulling taut the ropes of boats at anchor in the swell: it was all as I had remembered it.

It was mid-morning as we disembarked. John wanted to take a trip along the coast to visit some of the places we had been to all those years ago, so we set off, taking the road that climbed up out of Dieppe and followed the coast. In true John style everyone had been given paper and pencils with strict instructions to draw what we were seeing. He was in effervescent mood from the start of the trip to the finish, his ravaged yellow features lit with the joy of a child wound up with delight at the jaunt. He laughed and joked and cajoled us into a surge of happiness that carried us all through the day.

Only a few miles out of Dieppe, by chance we spotted a signpost that told us that Braque had lived nearby. We would go there.

Varangeville is a sprawling well-to-do village hidden in woods on the edge of the cliffs and, following the signs, we visited La Chapelle Saint Dominique, whose stained-glass windows had been designed by Braque in 1956. We followed the leafy lane that took us to the house where he had lived and found ourselves further on at the tiny cliff-top church, L'Église St Valery, where his burial place lies among those of the rest of the villagers. We were so moved to have found this place and stood in homage to the great master at the mosaic tombstone with its dove of peace. From this little cemetery we could follow the line of the white cliffs meandering along the Normandy coast, look way out to sea and watch the shipping course its way through the Channel and think of our home country invisible on the other shore beyond.

John looked around to find something to offer in tribute and out of his pocket he drew a battered postcard of one of his own best paintings, *Sea Cat*. This he placed between the edges on the large gravestone. The inspiration provided by this place had been an unexpected bonus. It had empowered him and served to camouflage the precariousness of his own plight. Sadness was, however, welling inside me, strands of memory and emotion unfurling like ribbons in the wind.

By this time it was midday and we found a pub in the village to have lunch. We decided we would try to get to Fécamp and were soon on the road again, drawing and laughing and loving the day. In Fécamp and Saint-Valery-en-Caux, as in Dieppe, John showed Paul and Anya all our haunts from 1964 and drew everything he could before we made our way back to Dieppe as the sun was setting, in time to catch the last ferry to Newhaven. There was just time for dinner on the quayside. John was sure this was a restaurant we had eaten in twenty years ago, and, of course, we must have our favourite *moules marinières* to celebrate the great occasion. But John could only pick at the food he had loved. Along with alcohol, food was now a challenge for his body to deal with. His liver was unable to process much without inducing terrible bouts of sickness.

Darkness had fallen by the time we boarded the ferry. It was too chilly to go up on the open deck as we would have liked, so we found seats inside. For the time of year there was quite a number of other passengers and everyone settled down to sleep, all except John. Next day Anya had to be back in school and Paul at the framers where he had begun to work, and tired by now, they wanted to sleep. But there was no stopping John. He had been tippling all day from his Adidas bag but as usual was not overtly drunk. He was high with delight at the day we had shared and still buzzing. Throughout the whole long day he had been at his best, his funniest and most lovable. Now he was cracking jokes and telling stories of some of his outrageous escapades and no amount of pleas for sleep would stop him. Some of the other passengers were becoming irritated and let their feelings be known.

'I'm sorry,' he apologised, 'but I just don't want this day to end.'

The ferry was moving smoothly through the harbour and heading out into the darkness of the Channel. I wanted to have a last look, on my own, at this place that meant so much to us. I had worked hard all this day to conceal the sadness that engulfed me, the sheer happiness we had shared all the more painfully bittersweet when I saw the sickness in John's eyes. I was now alone on the open deck in the sanctuary of the night, watching the passing of the illuminated church hovering in the darkness high up above me.

What a mess we had made of our lives and of the lives of our children. How had we allowed the sweet promise of our early days to become so twisted out of shape and so wasted? All that we had found in each other when we had first met and all that life had given us we had thrown away and destroyed. Now, along with the terrible aching regret, I was afraid for John's very life.

The little church grew smaller and smaller and as it faded from sight we hit the motion of the heavy seas. We were swallowed up in the dark, unable to see where we were going; we were literally and metaphorically now at the mercy of the stormy weather ahead.

CHAPTER 39

Hospital

The following morning I rang Max Glatt. From the symptoms I listed he could tell John had acute liver failure and told me I must get him to hospital immediately. I rang John to advise him to have, if he wanted, a last drink because this was the end of the road for him and Bacardi. I wanted to know who his GP was because I was going to ask him to visit, when, if John wouldn't, I would spill the beans about his medical problems. I warned him that he would undoubtedly be going to hospital.

I had tried to do this on a previous occasion. At first he had acquiesced and then, at the last moment, refused point-blank to admit there was anything wrong with him. This time he was like a lamb to the slaughter. I had the impression he was relieved that someone had at last taken control of a situation that was running away with him. He knew he needed help.

It was evening by the time the GP arrived and as I listened to John chatting her up and denying the severity of his symptoms, I was assembling a bag of newly purchased stuff for his hospital admission. After sending for the ambulance, she tried to explain to John what was wrong with him and how necessary it was for him to be treated in hospital. He was still in high spirits, enjoying the conviviality of the company and in no mood to take anything seriously. It was all part of the fun of the moment for him at this stage. The next part of the jaunt was a trip to St Thomas's Hospital.

A couple of days later, after all examinations had been completed, doctors needed to explain the situation to John's next of kin. I put myself forward as a Mrs Bellany and explained that although I had been his wife I was not the current one, but as she was ill in hospital I would have to stand in as the only adult who could be responsible for him. And so it was spelled out to me. John's liver had been damaged irretrievably. It did not have the capacity to regenerate to any degree of healthy function. He was now extremely vulnerable to infection and if he continued to consume alcohol he was facing imminent death. Even if he ceased drinking immediately he had already forfeited the chance most people have of a reasonable lifespan. The mood was sombre and the message was frankly delivered that while time was not actually being counted in minutes, it was very limited indeed.

Juliet and her mother had been informed and updated when he was admitted to hospital. My plan had been simply to get him into hospital for urgent treatment, after which I suggested he might go to Port Seton to convalesce on the assumption that there he would slowly recover. I, and the children, would then resume our lives. It soon dawned on me, through the shock and devastation of the prognosis, that my plan was severely deficient.

In St Thomas's the first priority had been to wean John's body off its dependence on alcohol. While this was being done, further tests were carried out to check the condition of his other organs. They had also taken a battering over the years. He was weak and jaundiced and in no great shape to say the least but paradoxically he was in a buoyant frame of mind. He laughed and joked with other patients and took a great interest in the life of the ward. I was soon instructed to bring in paper and drawing materials and he set about immortalizing everyone in sight. St Thomas's was conveniently in the centre of London, directly across the river from the Palace of Westminster, and, to his great delight, visitors began pouring in to see him. He held court without a care in the world and for the first time in his adult life without a glass in his hand.

It had been put to him plainly that he had only two choices

and there was no room for negotiation attached to either: life or death. Life meant no alcohol whatsoever. More alcohol meant certain and speedy death. 'No problem,' he announced. 'Life it is.'

Doctors and professionals in the addiction field hear that kind of declaration all the time. They all will it to materialize but with the benefit of experience accept that these promises are notoriously difficult to keep. Usually 'the end of the line' has to be reached before the crucial desire and determination of the person himself to give up drinking or drug-taking replaces simply acknowledging that they have a problem. John had wreaked havoc with his body but had managed to continue functioning socially without finding himself in the gutter. His friends were expert drinkers too but he could drink them all under the table. 'You knew when you went out with John it would mean two lost days of your life,' they used to say. On what he called 'a spree' or a 'spree-erama', the camaraderie was a great antidote to his largely solitary home life. But this present crisis, the grave sickness he was suffering, was this the ultimate wake-up call that would succeed where all else had failed?

The fear of death was not new to him. It had lodged itself in his bones as a little boy as, with clasped hands every night he had recited:

'If I die before I wake

Please, oh Lord, my soul do take.'

The terror haunted him all his life. In view of this, there was no choice. It was literally the fear of death that made the decision for him. He had, however, not grasped the acute seriousness of his plight. He later claimed he had, but all the evidence, along with my deeper instincts, convinced me that he didn't sense the true danger he was in. He believed if he simply never touched alcohol again then he would have a life that could stretch out as long as that of the next person.

In spite of the end of his love affair with the bottle, he was euphorically happy. The care he was receiving in St Thomas's and the affectionate concern of his friends warmed him. Gradually the jaundice began to fade and he began to feel better than he had for a very long time. He was celebrating life, life without alcohol and life that he believed had a future.

Why was his prognosis not clear to him? He was an intelligent man. He himself ought to have been able to read between the lines, as there was no subterfuge being employed by the medics. He had a fondness for walking on the sunny side of the street, avoiding the shade if he could help it. So it was not spelled out to him sufficiently, and I began to believe that was how it should stay. It was the fear of death that stopped him drinking in the first place and it was his love of life that enabled him to abide by and realize such a courageous ambition. Life in abundance was what he understood the deal to be and that promise made him feel better and stronger and more positive. He was then forty-two years old. No age to embrace the idea of dying, if there ever is one. My view was that if he was to get the most out of the time left to him he would be better off not being faced with the reality of his lifelong greatest fear.

Unless he asked. But he did not ask. He never would have done.

Again I talked with the doctors. Without alcohol he could survive. It was, however, impossible to predict the duration of that survival, only that it would be severely circumscribed. Less rather than more, sooner rather than later. His liver was extremely damaged. A precarious future of sorts then. I was warned about the perils, the dangers of infection, and in particular the possibility of sudden internal haemorrhage. It was made clear to me that in the life he had left he would be walking a tightrope.

I was devastated. The anger and hurt of our break-up had long since subsided, as had any thought of reconciliation. We had had minimal contact over the years apart, not even shared birthday celebrations for our children, our day to Dieppe the one and only family get-together in all those years. John characteristically avoided the complications of life, especially those of an emotional nature. I was never allowed to be included in occasions where Juliet or even our mutual friends were present and I was never invited into his parents' home in Port Seton if he was there, although I was welcomed when he wasn't. I never considered this trait of his as aversion towards me. I always interpreted it as being motivated by guilt and as an attempt to keep the door of his mind firmly shut on past sadness. I always heard how he was from the children, though, and, as someone who had meant a lot to me, I cared about him and always would, as I hoped that he would similarly deep down always care about me.

But now the utter tragedy of the situation crashed through all my buried regret and pain, dissolving the long years of estrangement. All I cared about was that if we could help John to get the most out of life, however long he had left, then that is what I wanted with all my heart to do.

I had no claim to him any more, however. He belonged with someone else. But Juliet needed the more or less constant care of her hospital and had done for several years. John was equally and similarly in need. Neither could look after themselves or each other. So who would help him? Bearing in mind the sensitivity of the circumstances there was nevertheless only one course of action to take. We would look after him. When he was discharged from St Thomas's, Anya and I would move into their home on Windmill Drive, where Paul already was living, and stay as long as required. There was no one else who could do this and I could not see any other way. John was overjoyed and Juliet was in agreement. I was heartbroken at what his future promised and in his vulnerable state there was no way I could leave him to fend for himself.

CHAPTER 40

Clapham Common

Clapham Common is a couple of miles away from Westminster, a flat parkland criss-crossed by paths and bordered by major traffic-laden routes into and out of London. The common, over its vast area, boasts a large Anglican church built by Christopher Wren, a cafe, children's nursery and playground, and a broad avenue of beech and sycamore trees that has as its centrepiece an ornate Victorian bandstand. It is frequented by walkers, joggers, cyclists, families with dogs, people flying model airplanes and kites, as well as the lost and lonely. An archetypical city park, it is a welcome green space a mile away from where we lived in Lurline Gardens and our own green space by the River Thames, Battersea Park.

Windmill Drive is a narrow tree-lined road that traverses a stretch of the south side of Clapham Common, on each side of which lies a lake. The two lakes are stocked full of perch and gudgeon for the coarse fishers who set up rods and shelters and wait out the hours in the hope of catching something. If successful, they throw it back into the water to catch again another day. At one end of Windmill Drive a group of Victorian houses stand overlooking the common and in close proximity to the Windmill Pub, an old coaching inn that has been on the site since medieval times. Windmill Cottage is situated between the pub and a pair of high semi-detached houses, one of which, No. 2, was where John and Juliet lived.

210

The autumn leaves were blowing into whirlwinds off the common and were piled up in drifts at the doorway as the children led me inside the large house. It was an uncomfortable feeling to be in a home that belonged to other people, but was also home to my children. The boys had been living there off and on throughout their later teenage years. They showed me round.

Their room was on the ground floor beside the front door. Among the chaos of their stuff was a piano, a pull-down sofa bed and a large ornately carved mahogany and wicker Victorian daybed. This was where they slept, one on the sofa bed and one on the daybed. The latter was called 'the Granny Cameron', as Juliet had inherited it from her great-grandmother, Julia Margaret Cameron. I subsequently learned that the daybed had been specially made for her sea journeys to and from India.

At the back on the ground floor, a room of similar size had been converted into a custom-built storage area fitted with racks holding numerous completed canvases. This room was necessarily dark, as the closely stacked paintings obliterated the light from the large windows.

What would have been the original kitchen area of the house was now full of bags of abandoned debris. All this looked out on to a small back yard enclosed in high walls, on the other side of which was the garden of the Windmill pub. From the yard a wrought-iron spiral staircase snaked its way up outside the building to the top of the house.

The main staircase, bereft of carpet, still had felt underlay and the gripper rods with protruding nails on every step – an arrangement undisturbed since Juliet had bought the house. Halfway up the stairs was a small room off to the left, serving as both bathroom and laundry, as the bath contained clothes long left abandoned in the process of being washed.

On the first floor we found the studio I had been invited into with my mother. This was a beautiful spacious room with large, high windows that looked out over the common onto Eagle Pond with its weeping willow drifting over and into the water. Beyond the pond was the Southside and its noisy thoroughfare which John had to cross to reach the shop he called 'Happy's'.

The studio was filled with light and was full of the fruits of creativity: large paintings, canvases in waiting, plan chests (for storing drawings) and a chaise longue, all heavily laden with drawings and watercolours and prints, on top of which the cat lay sprawled in the sunshine. Among the clutter of empty cigarette packets, cardboard boxes, books, tubes of paint and paint rags, old shoes and what not, a scatter of small change glittered where it had landed.

Among the other rooms was the sad little room where, I was informed, Juliet used to lie for days in the dark. At the top of the house was the kitchen where one could look out over the common and the pub and its garden, through the trees to the traffic flowing, night and day, to and from Clapham High Street and central London. Nailed up along the length of the back wall of the room was *Kinlochbervie*, one of John's most iconic masterpieces of the sixties. At the front of the building was the sitting room that also had a view through the trees to Eagle Pond.

An overpowering feeling came over me of the desolation and melancholy that pervaded this huge house. It ached of desperate lives and loneliness and neglect. Although I knew that the walls had frequently rung with merriment and conviviality, witness to the sporadic high jinks of the London art world, it seemed, that day, to be a house devoid of life and alienated from the mainstream of human existence. The heart of the house, of course, was the studio, where one sensed the energy and the fire of creativity, but even there, that day, the heartbeat seemed muffled by an enveloping sense of gloom.

John had been in St Thomas's for about two weeks and was soon to be discharged, so we had gone to the house with the intention of getting it ready for his return. The idea was to freshen it up and get some basic food in the fridge. Was there a fridge?

We decided we should clean up the kitchen, the sitting room and bathrooms, change the sheets and make up beds. This turned out to be a mammoth task. There were mountains of

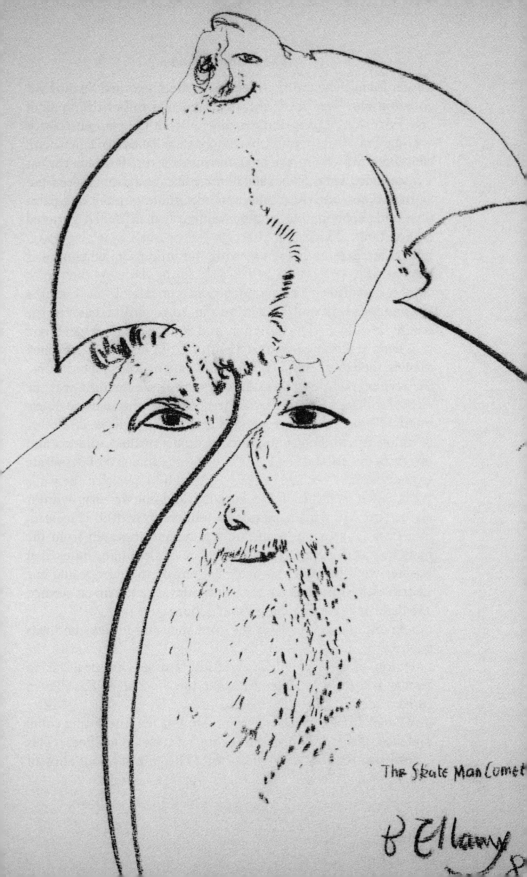

The Skate Man Comet

B Ellamy

unwashed dishes and the remains of weeks of takeaway food covering every surface in the kitchen and elsewhere. Both John and Juliet were chain-smokers and so in the sitting room there was a film of deep yellow ochre coating everything from the well-worn armchairs, the large mirror and, as I brushed against a framed drawing, obviously all the prints and drawings on the walls too. Among the books, accordions and variety of bric-a-brac lying around, a large glass-fronted box displayed a trio of stuffed birds. The room, although full of trash, was even more full of intrigue, overflowing with the unique miscellany of a creative life.

John had latterly been employed as a lecturer at Goldsmith's College and was well known on the art-school circuit, having taught at Winchester, Croydon and the Royal College of Art and been visiting lecturer at Central St Martins, Chelsea and many regional art schools, but he had also spent much time on his own in loneliness and isolation, regardless of which, or more likely facilitated by which, the stream of his productivity flourished. His inner journeys could be traced through the wealth of work on the walls or lying stacked up everywhere and in piles on the floors and tables. Every room was deluged by the output of his vision.

The work on display in the house at that time was mainly from his current and wildest phase. He had returned from Australia nine months previously and during the intervening period his body was struggling to cope with years of alcoholic abuse. This was reflected in both the work he had done in Australia and since he had returned. It was wild and almost out of control and I saw in it the raw energy and defiant edge of his struggle. It was heroic and desperate at the same time and I loved the sheer power of it.

At around this time he had completed several portraits of his friends and they were on the walls too – John Walker, Brian Glover and, in the boys' room, Micky Droy, who had been captain of Chelsea football team. Around the house there was evidence of the drawing sessions he inflicted on visiting artists – a roll call of characters from the London art scene. He had formed the habit of swapping work with these friends, and his collection, some of which was also on show, included works by Alan Davie, Sandy Moffat, Harry Thubron, William Gear, William Johnstone, Bert Irvin and many others.

It was a sad house certainly but it was a palace of wonder to me too and once we had made it a bit more habitable I revelled in its hidden gems. I cleaned the nicotine-stained glass and frames and found the most exquisite drawings dazzling with the lightness and confidence of his line. The floors revealed in shady corners a haphazard collection of ink drawings bursting with energy; in another, a cache of finely drawn etchings. All over the place unopened business letters from the bank and so on would fall out from among the heap and join the other pile of unwanted and unopened mail to be looked at 'next Thursday', as he would say. This was a world I knew. The disorganization I had not missed. It had made life even more of an obstacle race. But the living, breathing tide of creativity I had been starved of, that had so inspired me, now flooded back into my veins.

I slept in the sitting room. I was up early to get ready for work and also to see Anya off to school. John, now back home, had given up teaching because of his health and had to be given his breakfast before I left. I was instructed to continue where the hospital had left off: eggs for breakfast. Three choices: 'Biled [boiled], strangled [scrambled] or celestial.' Celestial eggs were the perfectly fried eggs made in the way he remembered my mother had taught me – cooked gently with no oil, the yolks just filmed with white but still soft and golden. No crispy bits.

He was weak but optimism and contentment radiated from his face and it wasn't long before he was back in the studio with his brushes in hand. I would ring up from work to check he was OK and we would discuss what to have for dinner. Oh, the comfort of simple pleasures.

As he grew stronger we began to attend the usual art-world events. At one of the first private views we went to, the St Ives exhibition at the Tate, I met up with people I had not seen in over a decade. I felt warmly welcomed back and basked in rekindled friendship.

Juliet remained in hospital, occasionally staying with her mother for short periods of respite but she and John felt too ill to see each other. John's many friends rallied round him visiting and sending encouraging messages. One particularly memorable one came in a letter from the painter, John Bratby:

Dear John,
Heard from Gus that you've been in St Thomas's, from work and whiskey. I drink too much and am afeard of it – Terrified.
6 days ago me 'and shook so much when I peed, my cock was here there and everywhere. I daresay you do not care to hear about that. Anyway thought I'd drop you a line. Did not like to hear of you falling by the wayside. Still we are not indestructible. Look at ol' Richard Burton: the drink killed him indirectly: broke him. It is a terrible thing drink & yet such a good companion …

Take it easy (fatuous advice)
Regards
John

That first Christmas of our reunion we spent on our own with Jonathan, Paul and Anya, and we all made an effort to make it good. Among the presents I had gathered for John was an antique wooden tray. It was an apprentice piece and carved on it was a bunch of grapes with the wording 'Load Me With Luxury'. He declared that from that day onwards this would be his motto. And I decided that I would do what I could to contribute to that end.

At weekends we went for long drives in my little battered Ford Fiesta out of London, down through Effingham woods astonishing in the burnished orange and yellow of autumn beech trees striated by long dark shadows struck by the setting sun. We found beauty in places like Friday Street, hidden away by a lake in the middle of the woods, in the view from the chalk ridge over to the South Downs and Abinger Common and on our return to London by Box Hill. Every time we followed a different route and surprised ourselves with the pleasure of being back in the countryside again. Ordinary things provided us with inner calm and comfort.

What made it possible for me to adapt to this about-turn in my life? There was no other option. John was going to die. That was enough of a reason. I was doing what I could in a desperate situation. I was doing it for him but I also was doing it for me. How could I live with myself after his death if I had not taken this opportunity to help him? Over and above all of that was the fact that alcohol had been completely and permanently eliminated from his life and now I could see him again in the way I had first known him. Now it was possible to communicate. We had so much to talk about, the sharing of thoughts and opinions and memories. We quickly slotted back into an easy affection but with a growing awkwardness in the situation. We were enjoying so much the time we spent together. The self-protective wariness that had been there, on my part, before our trip to Dieppe was fading and a new genuine happiness was being allowed to grow between us once again.

One dark winter morning I was filling the kettle at the kitchen sink and getting ready to go to work. I could see the glittering stream of traffic wending its endless way along the rainy south side of the common. The trees were bending and swaying in the stormy day. I felt sheltered and warm but there was something else too. As I pottered about it became clear to me that a great feeling of serenity and sense of well-being had gradually seeped into my consciousness. I realized that I had begun luxuriating in a comfort I had experienced once before but had long forgotten. It was a good feeling of something sliding into place. It was the divine feeling of belonging.

What I was experiencing was very real and true but the other reality loomed even larger. This blessed time could only be an interval of limited duration. It was too late for it all to be again as it once had been. The clock was ticking and the days given to us could only be the best of bittersweet.

Janus, the god of new beginnings, who looked forwards and backwards simultaneously, and whom I saw turning again and again, was throughout those days the reigning presence in that house on Clapham Common. His gaze would swivel mercilessly from the dark to the light and back to the dark in the crazy rhythm of human turmoil. His voice would at once rejoice in our rediscovered gladness, only to spin round in scorn at the unguardedness of our happiness and in so doing would turn to ice the sweet waters of my contentment.

'Don't fool yourselves. There is no future.'

My ears rang with that refrain. John, meanwhile, had no such preoccupations. In his line of vision the years stretched out forever with newly regained happiness. He began to make plans.

CHAPTER 41

Precarious Life

Anya lived with us at Windmill Drive but was now following her own precarious path. We had been close during the bad times the boys' behaviour had brought into our lives but now she was rebelling against the obvious happiness John and I were finding together. She decided that I had abandoned her, that I was putting her father first when he had done nothing when we needed help and support with her brothers. The boys were antagonistic towards her because of her boyfriends, and this made her feel isolated and lonely. She believed no one cared about her and so she set out to do her own thing in the most self-destructive manner. I was obviously not going to get away lightly with what she saw as my betrayal.

After one major incident a meeting was called at the school with the headmaster and her form teacher. They were at a loss to know what to do next. Anya was fifteen and was on the verge of being expelled. Her form teacher had been spending time counselling her but now she believed that Anya needed more in-depth help. It was finally decided that she should attend an off-school site for unruly/disturbed children where she would have the attention of a tutor specially qualified to help her.

Anya's boyfriends were mainly West Indian boys, some of whom I liked, some I did not. While I was searching everywhere for help for my own boys, whose behaviour regularly brought me distress, she found her way into increasingly dubious company. The boyfriends she favoured were also powerful tools she could use against me. If I didn't approve of any of them I was accused of racism and therefore of siding with her brothers. I used every ounce of energy sticking to my right to discriminate on the grounds of what I considered was good for her and what was not, regardless of race. In talking with Jonathan and Paul I had to defend Anya's choice of company in the same way. I was being tested in every possible respect. However difficult and draining it was, I remained consistent in my convictions. There was no other way I could be. They were my children and it was my love for them and fear for their future that infused me with strength to carry on.

The home tutor Anya was assigned was Dr Edite Mason, who was French. What Anya saw at the Home Tutor Centre near Clapham Junction did not appeal to her – troubled young people like herself, disaffected and exuding hopelessness. It was decided that she would go instead to Edite's home on the south side of Clapham Common to be tutored there. She immediately took to Edite, who was one of the great good things to come into our lives.

Edite's doctorate was in English Language. Right from the start, Anya responded to Edite. She began to come home excited by what she was learning and reading and could not wait to discuss it all with me.

The growing happiness between John and me was the core of our days around which tumultuous currents of family conflict swirled. Then there was Juliet. John never talked about her or the difficulties of their life together. What he now saw was a promise of black clouds lifting, giving way to blue skies and sunny days in which there would be him and me and our three children together once more. 'Paradise regained,' he said.

He had glimpsed it on that day trip to Dieppe, the day he had never wanted to end. Now, as far as he was concerned, it need never do so.

In the midst of our regained happiness what I saw was each of our three children already travelling at speed on dangerous roads away from all that we were, one of them hostile to the new happiness John and I had regained. I saw the spectre of Juliet in wretched despair. I saw John's death looming and fading with the turning head of Janus and I saw myself, having forfeited my defences, after it was all over, sinking, with nothing to hold on to, into the dark place I dreaded returning to. I felt I was being torn in all directions. But it was easy to immerse myself in the joy of the good things that had come our way, to love being loved and to love again, to make each other laugh as we used to and to share again all that we had shared from our young days, everything that we had both always deeply cherished. We embraced it all but in the dark hours I fought against harsh reality.

Tentatively, in time, John and I picked up our lives together, starting where we had left off eleven years previously. By then I had convinced myself it was the only thing to do. I reasoned that Juliet's mental problems were far beyond the reach of John's help. They had not seen each other for months and the times they had been able to share had been few and steadily diminishing. The solace for her that these had once provided was no longer possible.

As for John and me, the time we would have might be brief but something so good could not be wasted. It meant he would get the very best out of the time left to him. For me there was a healing of old wounds, bringing me inner peace. We lived for the day, shutting our eyes to tomorrow. I did not dare imagine what would happen to me afterwards.

John, however, surprised me one day when he said he had decided to ask Juliet for a divorce. That was a step I had not anticipated. He was quite sure, though, and maintained it had been in his mind for some time. Long before our day to Dieppe, his life with her had been a nightmare he could no longer handle.

He felt guilty that he could do nothing to help her. He felt guilty at abandoning her. He felt guilty that we were finding happiness together again. He first approached Margaret Lister, Juliet's mother, who in her characteristically open-minded and benevolent manner had no trouble understanding John's need to break away from her irretrievably sick daughter, but expressed deep sadness that a divorce was necessary. She wanted, above all things, to keep John within her family. She loved him dearly and the feeling was mutual. She had been a student of Henry Tonks at the Slade as a young woman and John had encouraged her to take up drawing and watercolours again. It was a warm and affectionate relationship that meant a great deal to both of them. Reluctantly Margaret agreed to help Juliet come to terms with what would be a deeply distressing blow, for which she possessed no resources. It was an uneasy time for all of us.

CHAPTER 42

Good Days / Bad Days

Having a car was a novelty for John but soon he began to cast his sights on something a little grander. He decided my old Fiesta had to be upgraded and thus began his passion for cars, the more luxurious the better. At Easter 1985, in a gleaming white Rover, the model favoured for police cars at the time, we set off with Anya to visit Port Seton. John's father had had several strokes and his health was in serious decline. His mother was recovering from cancer treatment. John's prognosis I kept to myself. As he was not aware of the extent of his fragility I did not think there was much point in worrying his parents in their vulnerability with the news.

It was a wonderful reunion for me and I felt back in my warm place in their family. They were relieved to see John looking better and overjoyed that he had stopped drinking. The boys joined us at Port Seton and we set off for Golspie, where we were to have a reunion with the rest of my family. John was so glad to be back in Golspie again, where he was welcomed with open arms by all his many friends in the village. We retraced our steps to our favourite places – Kinlochbervie and its remote harbour that had thrilled him so much on first sight in 1963, Lochinver and Suilven, Ullapool and Stac Pollaidh, Drumbeg, Tongue and Ben Loyal, all the little harbours from Helmsdale up the east coast over the Ord of Caithness to Lybster, Dunbeath, Latheron

Wheel to Wick. The pencil never stopped and the watercolours were flowing.

On the way back south we stopped at Port Seton again. There we enjoyed a few days with John's parents. It was the last time we saw his father at home. A few weeks later, in June, he suffered another stroke. We managed to arrive back from London just as he was dying.

John's father was a most lovable man and very popular in the community. His ready wit and instinctive kindness drew people to him. His death, on 19 June 1985, the day after John's forty-third birthday, took away from Nancy the reassurance and solidity provided by their pattern of life. Death is an ending no one can prepare for and the family was devastated. We were glad, at least, that his dad had seen John's life more settled and that their worries about their son must have been alleviated to some extent before he died.

John's health was unstable. In between the monthly clinic appointments at St Thomas's there were frequent medical crises, some more worrying than others. He still smoked, as no one (in authority) had told him not to. But alcohol was not an issue. To the great astonishment of his friends and doctors he gave up drinking instantly, totally and for good when he was admitted to St Thomas's that first time in October 1984, and it was never mentioned again. It ceased to exist in his life, as if it had never been. On his return to Windmill Drive after being discharged from hospital, I asked him what he wanted to do about having alcohol in the house. He was unequivocal. Guests had to be treated hospitably. There always had to be alcohol on offer. It was quite simple. He did not want to drink alcohol. He did not want people to ask him about it. He did not want to talk about it. He just wanted life to be normal. I never asked again and never after that did it cross my mind that it would be a danger to him. For someone who had worked with addicts I knew that the likelihood of relapse was very real but my instincts told me that here was something unique: someone whose life had depended on alcohol from morning to night for years on end had decided to stop altogether and banish it from his consciousness. I had never heard of such a thing. How many of us try unsuccessfully to give up things we enjoy even to the smallest degree? I had known of no one who had been able to forgo drinking with such apparent decisiveness. How did he do it?

Willpower had to be part of it, but it seemed to me that the overwhelming motivation was his love of life, along with the accompanying dread of dying which had always consumed him. He had come close to the edge but had been reprieved to live another day and this new day was full of promise and optimism that had been sadly lacking in the previous years. This was the day he didn't want to end. That was all.

However, his liver had been badly damaged and his day-to-day existence was coloured by the symptoms that remained. He began to suffer a dreadful itching all over his body and his skin was covered in what the doctors for simplicity called spiders – red marks like burst blood vessels spreading out in a sort of asterisk shape. His diet was carefully monitored, as it was important to achieve a fine balance of protein and carbohydrate intake. It was crucial not to overload his beleaguered liver with too much protein but it was also vital to keep up his body weight, as he was very thin and fragile. His prescription of essential drugs began to increase rapidly. Every hospital appointment included extensive blood tests, X-rays and a review of medicine. From the very start a process of juggling all the variables was put in place and while the prognosis was poor, every effort was made to bring John comfort and optimum health. He was extremely appreciative and enjoyed his clinic appointments. They quickly became social events with old friends, when the last thing he wanted to discuss were his ailments. When asked how he was feeling, he always said he was absolutely fine and glowered at me when I expressed my worries about some of his more alarming symptoms.

One day I rang him from work as usual and got no reply. Several unanswered calls later took me home to find him lying on the floor of the bedroom, writhing in agony. He hadn't been able to reach the phone. All he could tell me was that it was the worst pain he had ever had. Was this what they had warned me about? Was this the sudden internal haemorrhage? However, the doctor diagnosed a kidney stone and in hospital he managed to rid himself of the culprit. According to him it was in the shape of a seahorse! Crisis over for now.

There were frequent scares regarding his health, the worst necessitating urgent dashes to A & E and subsequent short hospital stays. There were also lighter moments that made my hair stand on end until I realised what was happening.

One night, while I was preparing dinner in the kitchen, all of a sudden I heard coming from the sitting room next door John loudly bellowing, 'Wah wah wah wah wah wah WAWAWAWAWAWAWAWAWAWWAWA ...' It went on and on, louder and louder. I was rooted to the spot. He was having a seizure! I was alone in the house with him but scared to go through, dreading the scene that would greet me.

There he was with his hands up blocking his ears and his eyes firmly shut, shielding them from the television on which were displayed the football results that were being announced at the same time. When he realized I was there, the 'wah wahing' suddenly halted and he said 'What?'

My knees gave way and I collapsed into a chair.

Surely everyone knows that if you are going to watch a football game, the last thing you want to know is the result beforehand! I would get used to this pre-match ritual in time.

From the moment I moved in, John wanted me to give up work but knowing his possessive tendencies and with my own uncertain future in mind, I had so far resisted. However, now I relented, handed in my notice and stopped work in October 1985. I wanted no regrets about time not spent together and I tried not to think ahead to what I would do when he was gone. We survived as we had in the past, relying on the occasional sales that were beginning to be achieved.

The glory of meaning everything to someone who had meant everything to me, with whom I'd had three children, who shared so much history with me and had now again become the focus of my days, was indescribable. In my wildest dreams I would never have believed that John and I could ever get back together again. After eleven years apart!

If there are such things as miracles, this had to be a mighty one. Out of the blue as it came, for me it was a glorious balm to soothe our broken lives. It has been said that women need to be needed. Doesn't everyone need that? I was needed again and he felt needed too. I mattered to someone who mattered to me. I belonged in a place that was familiar and comfortable. I had a job to do of rebuilding, making good and bringing back light and life to something that had lain dormant. I would gamble with my own hard-won stability in the long term but I embraced life again with John wholeheartedly. A burst of happiness for us both, for however long or short a time, was a gift. Gradually, and tentatively at first, but then effortlessly, our bond had been reignited and was now burning bright.

The backdrop to this good fortune, however, was perilous. I was consumed with anxiety and fear for Jonathan and Paul. Although I never doubted their love for us, their involvement with the skinhead music scene embedded them in a movement that was composed of largely aimless, disaffected drifters, herded and incited by a core of troublemakers.

My approach to crises whether at home or at work was generally fairly calm. My great fear was of the depression that might follow after my resources had been depleted, as had happened in the past. I had however always considered myself to be a strong person and not particularly anxious. Now, with the unpredictability of John's health always in the forefront of my mind I began to dread the telephone ringing not just for that but for every other reason as well.

Would it be a crisis with John or news of the latest escapade the boys had been associated with? I had lost my voice talking with the boys and asking them to question what they were doing. Everything had been said. They kept in touch but there were no more confrontations. There was no point.

If that was not enough to deal with, Anya's behaviour had taken me over the top. She had been bunking off from school, vanishing for whole days, wandering around London. She had found other latchkey kids at Pimlico School with whom to squander her days. The school used the nearby Queen Mother Sports Centre at Victoria and swimming was what she liked. Asked where she had been, she lied defiantly, 'Up the Queen Mother!' We laugh about that now, but back then there was little to laugh about in what she did. Although she was benefiting from the enjoyment and stimulation of her relationship with her tutor Edite, her behaviour still worried me because of the company she was keeping and the activities they were all involved in.

So we blundered on. I loved my children. They had been my rock and were the core of my life. They were good people but all of them had wandered away. I was used to dealing with the children's problems myself, so they weren't new to me and I tried to protect John from the worst. He had no resources to spare. My own were fragile enough and I was glad to continue seeing Dr MacLean at Bolingbroke Hospital, who listened to it all with equanimity.

Chapter 43

Moving Onwards

John's career had at last taken off and there were exhibitions all over the place to which he was invited to contribute. For the last few years Monika Kinley had been his agent. At that time she dealt also with Paula Rego and Ken Kiff. To her credit, Monika had taken on a massive task dealing with John as, lovable as he was, he could be difficult, especially when he was drinking. She had brought about several important exhibitions of his work, in particular one opening at the Icon Gallery, Birmingham, that travelled around England to Sheffield, Newcastle and Edinburgh, Glasgow etc. She arranged his first exhibition in the United States at the Rosa Esman Gallery in New York and discussions were underway for a major retrospective to be held at the Scottish National Gallery of Modern Art in Edinburgh.

After he had absorbed the shock of his hospitalization, John quickly and with revived spirit resumed his plans. He was in buoyant form and the sky was his limit. He didn't encumber himself with too much worry about anything that was not his painting.

The National Portrait Gallery had approached John with a commission to paint a portrait for their collection and had given him the choice of several dignitaries as subjects. He quickly advised them that he could only paint someone who would inspire him, for instance, he suggested, George Best, the astonishingly talented footballer. That did not go down too well with the trustees at the time. Best's colourful lifestyle was apparently considered not in keeping with an official portrait in the august setting of the NPG. John's second proposal of Ian Botham, the England cricket captain, fared better and an arrangement was fixed for us to travel to Cheshire for the portrait to be painted at the country estate of Botham's manager at the time, Tim Hudson.

With Anya we arrived at Birtles Hall on 5 October 1985 to be greeted at the high locked gates by bounding, barking Alsatian dogs sporting loud striped ties in Rasta colours around their necks. Once the dogs were quietened, their owner Tim Hudson came into view, resplendent in high cowboy boots and ten-gallon hat.

We had just made the acquaintance of someone who would light up our lives for some years to come. Tim and his American wife, Maxi (whom he called 'Mouse'), made us welcome and showed us to our suite, on the door of which he had taken the trouble to erect a brass plaque bearing our name. This, 'The Bellany Suite', was adjacent to a large room also appropriately brass-plated with Anya's name.

Later, downstairs over dinner, we met Ian and the pregnant Kathy Botham.

John had been suffering in agony with toothache and at one point it seemed we would have to postpone our trip to Birtles but, as I would see on many further occasions, it was a question of mind over matter: the show always went on. John suffered continually as his body struggled to function. Constant cramp, skin infections, swelling of his limbs and feet, stomach pain, toothache, chest infections, oesophageal ulcers, kidney stones, stomach ulcers, insomnia, unbearable itching – every part of his body was in crisis. He complained little. It was boring to talk about it and anything from a visit or phone call from a friend, an outing to a private view or dinner with friends, would see him rise above it, all in the interests of a good time for everyone. Painting, especially a fruitful day's work, would also banish symptoms to a bearable level. There was one notable exception, though. Man flu always reduced him to a whining, miserable, sorry-for-himself victim.

The portrait went ahead the next day, interspersed by Botham taking off at regular intervals for a run barefoot round the lake and the extensive grounds of Birtles. It was completed in John's usual way. After the initial presence of the subject and the main concentration on the face, he would continue on his own into the small hours of the night until he was satisfied it was complete. He would always then collapse, drained. The portrait would never be touched again.

John and Juliet's divorce had been filed and the process was underway. We had to think about where we would live; as the property belonged to Juliet, we could not continue at Windmill Drive. Although John's work was beginning to sell, any money went from hand to mouth as it had in the past. There was no assured income from any source and as usual we had to hope that something would turn up. There was certainly no house-buying kind of money.

We spoke with Alan Gordon, John's saintly and eternally optimistic accountant, and as usual he sent us onwards with hope that something could be arranged in the way of a mortgage, something neither of us had had any experience of. All I vaguely knew, at the age of forty-two, was that mortgages depended on steady income and a lifetime of good health. I had the health but not the income, but according to John we were not to worry, he was getting better every day and money from the sales of paintings would definitely come in. He was having a large retrospective at the National Galleries of Scotland, for goodness' sake. John had a great ability to persuade bank managers and financial advisors of the positive prospects of his affairs. Everything could be achieved. Alan had dealt with John's finances for many destitute years and never failed to encourage and inspire him even at the lowest ebb. He now put in motion the process of assessing John for this financial undertaking.

But I had been caught up in my own web of deceit. I had never been honest with John about his prognosis. While his excitement and optimism were soaring into the rosy future he was seeing for us, his body was failing. He was in decline. This was as good as things were going to get and it would not last. Doctors are notoriously evasive, and especially so then, and it was easy for John not to read between the lines. I could not tell him and I stand by that decision still to this day, but there were complications to fend off, as there generally are with any kind of deceit.

The first appointment for a medical assessment for the mortgage was with an independent doctor on Lavender Hill. I was prepared for disaster. The truth would emerge about John's health. Not only would we fail to get the mortgage but John would be confronted with information that would demolish his spirit. My greatest fear of his being told the grim truth was that he would then give up the will to survive. What time he did have would be diminished by the fear of death that tortured his thoughts and dreams at the best of times. I had wanted to delay the moment of truth for as long as possible so that his time could be rich with experience and achievement. I wanted his days to be good.

Nerve-wrackingly we waited in vain for the doctor's report; finally we were informed that he had felt unable to provide adequate information. We were given an appointment with a second doctor. There were delays with this report also but somehow, to my great amazement, the mortgage eventually went through.

On 5 November 1985 we moved into 59 Northside, overlooking Clapham Common. The sparkling and flashing lights of the fireworks and the carnival fairground in the distance across the south side of the common that evening were pale in comparison to our euphoria in the good fortune that had come our way. In our early days we had never considered ourselves to be the sort of people who would be property owners and had certainly never aspired to be such. Now here we were with a beautiful home with a view of green spaces in the heart of London. There was no guaranteed income and there were insurmountable health issues. We had little experience of steadiness or routine in our life together and now we were taking on a grown-up responsibility for which we would have to do our best.

We were buoyed up with preparations for the great retrospective to be held at the Scottish National Gallery of Modern Art the following summer as part of the Edinburgh Festival. The director Douglas Hall and one of the senior curators, Keith Hartley, had been staying with us in Windmill Drive to select work to be exhibited.

In the autumn there was the new Athena Painting Prize worth £25,000; John won this jointly with Paul Huxley. Mr Micawber's philosophy had served us well. Something had turned up.

BBC Scotland had commissioned a half-hour film to be made by Keith Alexander and filming was taking place in that same month. John was not new to media exposure, was always happy to participate and always expressed himself eloquently in interviews. There were talks taking place about a one-man show at the National Portrait Gallery planned for the following year to coincide with the unveiling of the Botham portrait.

Much as John valued the support and encouragement Monika Kinley had given him, Monika did not have her own exhibition space and he longed to be taken up by a major London gallery where he could show regularly and which would hopefully promote his work further afield. We had been introduced to Wolfgang and Jutta Fischer by our friend Mary Rose Beaumont, with the result that in 1985 John terminated his agreement with Monika in order to affiliate himself with Fischer Fine Art, in King Street, St James's, a gallery that specialized in German Expressionist paintings. The warm rapport we enjoyed with the Fischers would become an ongoing pleasure that sustained and encouraged John and me for many years until Wolfgang and Jutta closed the gallery when they retired and moved back to Vienna.

One of the most significant outcomes of this move to Fischer's was our meeting and subsequent friendship with Robert Summer and his wife Susan, after they had driven past the gallery one night and spotted one of John's paintings in the window. The couple were from New York. Bob was president of Sony and throughout his career dealt with all sorts of artists like Michael Jackson, George Michael, Annie Lennox and many other megastars, and his wife, Susan Kasen Summer, was a glamorous and astute businesswoman. The two of them had begun to form a notable collection of British art.

This was the start of a firm friendship during which some of the best of John's work was acquired to be hung alongside that of other major players in British art in New York and in the Summers' palatial mansion in Connecticut. Memorable times were spent with them in the United States, in Italy and the UK. The enthusiastic support they gave to John and those other artists was in the spirit of modern-day Medici, whose constant belief in the power of the creative spirit was the energizing and sustaining encouragement of which all serious artists dream.

There was so much change in the air, all of it exciting and exhilarating. Life was blossoming and was full of the promise of so much to live for. In the background, however, the divorce was something that brought anguish to all of us, not least myself. The idea that our clutching at happiness, brief though it promised to be, might come at the expense of someone sick and entirely vulnerable was hard to accept.

John was increasingly ill and we were on an unpredictable and inexhaustible merry-go-round of trips to St Thomas's Hospital, usually in the dead of night. The decree nisi would come through in mid-December and, as we had gone this far, we decided that there were no reasons for us to delay our remarriage. I made enquiries about the possibility of the ceremony taking place in our own house, as some days John was bed bound by his illness and the depth of winter cold was difficult for him to cope with. This, it transpired, would require certificates from doctors spelling out the terminal nature of his health and that was a step I wanted to avoid. We had to wait until six weeks after the decree absolute had been declared and the banns had been published for our remarriage to take place. We decided on a suitable date in January and that it would be a completely private occasion attended by just John and me, Jonathan, Paul and Anya. We would inform our families and friends after it had happened.

Chapter 44

Tragedy

I couldn't make out the message I was being given.

On the morning of Jonathan's twentieth birthday, 22nd December 1985, a phone call came from John's mother. She whispered something and I had to ask her to repeat what she had said.

Juliet had taken her own life.

Her family had not known John's new address and phone number, so they had rung his mother with the dreadful news. Juliet had been staying with her mother and had ended her life there during the night.

The severity of John's symptoms saw him turn night into day. If it wasn't physical it was mental anguish, but often both, that saw sleep only arrive with the reassuring promise of the dawn. Every night, aware that the dark hours were passing, we were thankfully sliding into oblivion at last only to be awakened again by the most enchanting sound. How desperate we were for sleep, but the blackbird's song in the darkness just before dawn every morning was a rare beauty that gladdened our exhausted hearts.

John was thus asleep when the devastating news arrived. Stunned by the tragedy of Juliet's desperate and lonely death, I waited until he awoke later in the day in the hope that sleep would give him the strength for this blow.

Christmas 1985 was a gloomy affair. There was little to celebrate. John's reserves were severely depleted and as with the previous Christmas, one had to question if there would ever be a better one or indeed another one in the future for all of us to share.

There had to be a post-mortem before Juliet's funeral could be held. That and the Christmas holiday period meant that the date for her funeral was not fixed until well into January. We had arranged for our wedding to take place on 17 January 1986 but now began to be anxious about its proximity to Juliet's cremation.

I made enquiries into the possibility of changing the date but was informed that we would have to go through the six-week waiting period again which, because of John's poor health, neither of us was keen to do.

It was a bitterly cold morning as we set off for Wandsworth Town Hall for our fifteen-minute slot at eleven thirty. The civic headquarters of our borough was a faceless concrete mass punctuated by the small regular windows and, inside, long winding corridors lit by dim electric bulbs gave it all the charm of its possible counterpart in Eastern Europe. Anya and I had something new to wear for the occasion, John had bought a new jacket and the boys had spruced themselves up too. We were all going to do our best. There is a photograph of Anya in her finery taken by Paul as we waited in the gloomy corridor. Although a truce had been called for the day, she knew that he was winding her up and her hostile teenage expression spelled out her truculent attitude to him and to all that was going on. She, who did not even have memories of John living with us when she was young, was much less than enthusiastic about the proceedings.

The occasion, bleak and unremarkable as it was, was imbued with deep and poignant meaning for John and me and the boys too. We felt Anya would thaw out in time. The registrar was sympathetic and did his best to bring a touch of warmth to the short ceremony, which added to the emotion of the occasion. Regrets and hurt and all the waste of family life were faint departing shadows on our horizons, but the scars of our mistakes were indelible in our children's lives. From that day on we hoped they might draw wisdom and strength to emerge on to a surer path, so that they could make a better job of things than we had done. Our reunion might have come too late to make amends to them but for John and me, the broken links in the circle of our bond had been recast and there was deep gladness in that.

In an attempt to introduce a sense of occasion, we had arranged to have lunch at the Café Royal on Regent Street. There is a photograph of us, among the mirrors and luxuriant palms, doing our best to look festive. It was not one of John's good days and in the morning I even thought that we should have to cancel the ceremony. He insisted that it went ahead but by the time we got to the Café Royal he was suffering badly and feeling very ill. He ate nothing and we ate little and soon we were on our way home, where he immediately went to bed in semi-delirium. The children subsequently vanished and my evening was spent keeping vigil over my newly re-wedded husband, on alert to assess if I should call the doctor or an ambulance for him once again.

When Juliet's funeral took place John did not attend. He was far from well but neither could he face the occasion. Too much guilt. Too complicated. There were no goodbyes.

CHAPTER 45

1986

That was the sorrowful start of 1986, a year that would, despite John's health continuing to decline, become an *annus mirabilis*.

In February the Botham portrait was unveiled to much adverse criticism. Television announcers asked, 'Who on earth is it?' A good enough portrait perhaps but no one knew who the subject was! There was much ridicule and the press had a field day. John had had a particularly difficult night and I did not expect him to be able to attend the unveiling. But he never failed to astonish me with his ability to pick himself up from the depth of illness if the occasion demanded it and this was a prime example. He wrapped up his ravaged frame in his thick overcoat, donned his ubiquitous black hat and he was ready to face the world.

He sailed through all the commotion with unusual equanimity. He knew it was a great painting and that was all that mattered. He had painted Botham as he saw him, as an Olympian hero whose very presence on the cricket field commanded awe in opponents. This was one of his characteristic approaches to painting portraits, especially of public personalities of whom he personally knew little. He painted them as heroes, as mythical figures. He made them into what he wanted them to be.

His attitude to the endless subsequent talk about the Botham portrait was one of boredom and any sting from the critics was lost in his pride at the collection of portraits of family and friends that comprised the accompanying exhibition that opened some time later. It was a triumph of an exhibition curated by Robin Gibson and John's pride in passing the National Portrait Gallery and seeing his name up on large billboards outside was all the recompense he looked for.

Could we have imagined seeing such a sight as we anxiously passed that way in a taxi on our arrival in London twenty years earlier? Probably not. At that point we had not thought out our future so far ahead but, as he cradled his father's precious model boat in his arms and looked out at the great cultural institutions as we rattled on past them through Trafalgar Square, the possibilities even then were endless. Right from the start, we had never been in the business of ruling anything out. So, twenty years on, thrilled and excited and proud we most certainly were but surprised at such good fortune? Not really.

Recompense would come in another more concrete form when not only did Tim Hudson commission John to paint himself and several of his own family, including his uncle Charlie, but he also bought outright the whole NPG exhibition of portraits. Henceforth they would be known as the Maxi Hudson Collection. They would go to a good home and, as a result, our own home would now enjoy some much-needed financial security.

It came as a total surprise to learn that, under the conditions of Juliet's will, John was to be given a property for his lifetime's use. Such a prospect had never crossed his mind, nor had he expected any form of consideration from her.

The summer was approaching, bringing his great retrospective exhibition near, so he set about searching for an Edinburgh property and found what his heart desired: a spacious apartment in the neoclassical New Town in the centre of Edinburgh. Its grandeur thrilled him. 'Grandeur' was very much a word in his vocabulary and he relished the style of his new abode.

John's motto 'Load Me With Luxury' was coming to fruition. Paintings were selling and he was now the proud owner of a sleek Jaguar. One of his new passions, luxury cars, was developing at an alarming pace.

We moved in to the Great Stuart Street flat in June 1986 and he immediately set up his studio in one of the large rooms. He was beside himself with excitement and the summer weather made his health issues, while every bit as severe, seem not so threatening.

John was invited to design the poster for the Edinburgh Festival that year. It was dominated by a self-portrait in the guise of a magician surrounded by some of his own personal iconography along with the emblems of theatre, music and all the arts. In my mind, 'a beezer!'

At the time of the Festival, artists and actors and musicians arrive from all over the world. Actors from the Royal Shakespeare Company along with well-known Scottish actors found their way to his studio to be drawn or painted. It was then that we made friends with Sean Connery and his wife Micheline. We attended theatre and orchestral concerts, films and receptions and many lifelong friendships were formed. Joan Bakewell interviewed John for *Newsnight* and subsequently went on after the Festival to make a short film about him, ending up with a portrait of herself in her smart orange suit.

Life was buzzing and we were carried along willingly. It was easy to forget the reality of John's predicament in spite of the bad days when he could not waken up or find the strength to get out of bed. Anyway, I argued with myself, doctors can get things wrong sometimes. While life was this good we would go with it, relishing every moment. There would be time in the future to worry. After all the misery, we were close once again. We were flying and it was a heady sensation.

The climax of that summer, of our whole lives to date, was, of course, John's great retrospective exhibition, which opened at the Scottish National Gallery of Modern Art on 16 August 1986. The private view was swirling with hundreds of people spilling out on to the lawns in the balmy summer evening. It was a triumph of critical acclaim. I was so proud of him. My belief in his work had been there from our first encounter at the age of nineteen and not even the pain of our marriage break-up had diminished it. I knew and loved what he was attempting to do. While I understood the nature of his inner dialogue and what he was trying to express, his paintings would always exude a sense of mystery which is the ongoing life force of a work of art. The key to his existence lay in the language of his work, the telling of his search and struggle to make sense of the life that was his and to place its meaning in the contemporary world. It was there that one could find his attempt to be himself and to make that worth being.

In our negotiations with Douglas Hall and Keith Hartley, in order to avoid delay as much as possible, I had confided my anxiety that John might not survive to see this triumphant day. Sometimes I could sense their near disbelief in my gloomy prediction. With friends and on occasions, especially those in preparation for this grand event, John rose above all his problems, concealing them to an impressive extent until we were alone again. Only our children knew about the dashes to hospital, the bouts of sickness, the gnawing pains in his body, the debilitating weakness. To other people it would have been understandable to assume that, in spite of his gaunt demeanour, he was untroubled by anything too serious and to write off my concern as exaggeration.

Anyway, he had made it! No one was more relieved and happy than I. It was my own private triumph that I had had some part in helping him to be there to bask in the glory. The joy of the whole event was something that enriched his days and provided him with vigour and sustenance for that formidable struggle of physical survival. He was justly proud and overflowing with the energy the acclaim gave him.

He never for a moment doubted that he was worthy of such an accolade. For all the afflictions from which he suffered, modesty (regarding his work) was not one of them. Self-doubt, on the other hand, that essential companion to the making of great work, was something that he knew only too well but that was to be worked at in the privacy of his studio and in the recesses of his mind. To have been given such an honour and such a vote of confidence at the early age of forty-four was, however, even accounting for his self-assurance, truly remarkable. Only establishment figures of esteemed maturity were so privileged in those days. It fortified him ever after and proved to be the most effective medicine he could have received.

The exhibition drew crowds from all sections of the community just as the exhibitions on the railings outside the Royal Scottish Academy had done all those years before. Wandering round the show one day I encountered a couple of Edinburgh wifies with their shopping bags. As they left a room showing the wild paintings that John had done in Australia, I overheard them astutely sum up what they had just seen. 'Aye, ye can tell he was weell drunk when he did thaim!'

It was during this time that I first met our hero from art school days, Alan Davie, and Bili his wife, who had come to see to see the exhibition. It was a considerable shock to find that he was not the jazz-playing macho presence I had conjured up throughout all those years. He was diffident and quietly spoken, and Bili was very much his guardian and in charge. John had met them previously and now I too entered into this enduring friendship. John and Alan shared the same obsession – their work – and in that way the essential bond of kindred creative spirits thrived in mutual respect.

John's work was everywhere during that Festival. His prints were on show at the Printmaker's Workshop. There were watercolours in the Assembly Rooms. He was interviewed by Paul Allen for *Kaleidoscope*, the flagship Radio Four cultural programme, and subsequently was invited to review upcoming exhibitions and to participate in *Kaleidoscope* for years to come. There were the Fireworks Concert and parties on the rooftops of Princes Street. He made portraits of everyone who came his way. We were part of everything. The energy of the city was exhilarating. John worked as hard as he partied and paid the price – a price he thought nothing of paying. Subsequent days would see him laid low with sheer exhaustion.

There was an agreement that the exhibition would travel, in whole or in part, to other venues, and we were especially pleased that the Serpentine Gallery in Kensington Gardens, London, was going to be the next host venue. The show opened there in the autumn of 1986. At the same time the Gulbenkian

Hall at the Royal College of Art had just been renovated and a grand opening was planned. The sculptor, Bryan Kneale, was to display his work in the upper gallery and John was invited to fill the lower one. Would the juxtaposition of John's two exhibitions be a problem? He was always up for more. Enough was never enough. He would have happily filled the whole of the V&A at the same time.

In the autumn Tim Hudson persuaded us to fly with him and Maxi to Los Angeles. We would stay with them at their beach house in Malibu and join up with the other London friends who had travelled across for the Art Fair and the opening of the new Los Angeles County Museum of Modern Art (LACMA). As Christmas was approaching, the shopping malls were decorated accordingly and Christmas music piped blandly throughout. Outside, the sun was setting spectacularly over the Pacific Ocean while the breakers crashed on to the sand and spaced-out dudes performed their mystic rituals on the beach.

There were several occasions in Los Angeles where we dodged along on the edge of trouble. Severe cramp in John's legs and constant nausea dogged every day and had me on alert. I suppose that no one in their right mind would have flown halfway round the world in such a poor state of health but the promise of great times always had a louder voice. We had the zaniest of times with Tim and Maxi, and the view of California through their eyes was something quite other for us. We just turned up the volume, drowned out what we did not want to hear and danced! It was a relief nevertheless that we arrived back home without incident.

John had for several years been a member of the London Group – a sort of splinter group independent from the Royal Academy – and the many good artists among the membership were his close friends. Like most serious artists he had always been fairly mouthy about the quality of what he saw in both the London and the Scottish Academies. Since his demonstrations with Sandy Moffat in the sixties against what he considered the bland drawing-room decoration exhibited in those pompous establishments his view had not changed. If change had in fact crept in to those institutions, he maintained that it was only in the form of transatlantic fashion decades too late.

Then, in January 1987, came a phone call to inform him that he had been unanimously voted by the membership of the Royal Academy to become a member. He was utterly taken aback, bemused but delighted! All antagonistic youthful principles vanished in the glow of approval awarded him by fellow artists. After all, these were strivers like himself in the great game of creativity. He would never compromise his own personal standards just as they would defend their own. The important thing was the concentration on his own work, that being a lonely and solitary pursuit. To be the best he could be. Membership of the Royal Academy would not change that. To be surrounded by the camaraderie and friendship of people for whom he had warm personal affection was a welcome bonus that he embraced. A diary from that time describes his first attendance at an Academy meeting: 'Thought for the day! "I dreamt I dwelt in marble halls"!'

CHAPTER 46

Pleasure and Pain

The Serpentine and RCA shows came to an end and in 1987 Charles Booth-Clibborn approached John with a project to complete a set of lithographs based on Hemingway's *The Old Man and The Sea*. Charles had previously organized the *Scottish Bestiary*, a powerful set of individual works by contemporary artists, and now John was fired up with this project of his own concerning a book he much loved.

We were back to his midnight visits to St Thomas's and the by now familiar battery of tests and short hospital stays with barium meals, gruesome endoscopies (Pentax down the throat, in his words), scans and the feared results. He was suffering badly from swollen legs, his body accumulating fluid it could not get rid of, with the resulting difficulty in breathing, sudden pains, bouts of sickness and a deathly pallor in his wasted features.

He loved more than anything our drives out into the country through the Effingham woods. We drove along, each lost in our own thoughts, silently taking in the beauty of what we were seeing. At those times I always had a sense of melancholy as, in years to come, I knew that I would remember those journeys as essentially odysseys of farewell. Occasionally I was shocked by a sudden glimpse of his emaciated face sitting beside me, the very presence of death.

Those outings were largely conducted in a comfortable

silence. We talked over all his exciting plans for our future and everything else that we needed to discuss, then the rest of the jaunt was spent in contented appreciation of what we saw and in reflection of inner things. It was the bliss of being together and of shared silence – the ultimate mark of deep intimacy. Now and then, out of the blue, his hand reached over to stroke mine.

In April 1987 we went on a quick trip to New York to see Rosa Esman and other friends of John's that I hadn't met before. We set ourselves up in the Waldorf Astoria, a venue that inspired a set of several paintings. The highlight of our week was a visit we made to the spacious apartment of Richard Zeisler, who lived on 5th Avenue near to the Metropolitan Museum. He had bought two paintings of John's from Rosa Esman's gallery and wanted to show us where they were hanging. We were breath-taken at seeing the company in which John was showing. 'All my heroes!' he exclaimed. There were several works by Delvaux, Chagall and Braque confronting us as we entered the apartment, Matisse cut-outs in the kitchen, Picasso drawings in the cloak-room, superior works of many of the leading European masters – and then, amid all of these, was the painting of Jonathan on Bobo's fishing boat holding a gutted fish. Round the corner, in the open-plan lounge, John's dad held court. It was the thrill of a lifetime for any artist.

In May that year we drove out one Sunday to have lunch with Robin Gibson in his garden at Hempstead. On the way we passed through some of the attractive old villages on the corner of north Essex, Hertfordshire and Cambridge, among them Newport and the market town of Saffron Walden. It was a part of the world that we had never seen before. We were not to know then what the area would hold for us.

Meantime, there were so many things going on, life was a rush of pleasure and private pain. We were up and down to Edinburgh, there were exhibitions in Australia and Ireland, Keith Alexander's film was shown on BBC television and, just before John's forty-fifth birthday, the *RCA Artist's Cookbook* was launched, to which staff and former students and associates were invited to contribute the recipes of favourite meals that they liked to cook. John chose all his favourite food, *moules marinière*, tiramisu, etc., but failed to include the only thing I ever remember him cooking – the Rolling Pin Omelette!

That year London Transport had decided to perk up its image and had launched a set of specially commissioned posters for various underground stations. John was approached to do something for Chinatown, so one winter day we took ourselves up to Soho and for about an hour we wandered around Chinatown, soon needing to warm ourselves up in a steamy restaurant over dim sum. It was another ill day that left me questioning John's ability to produce something inspired for the project.

Then in June 1987, the resulting poster was unveiled. John had composed a scene at a restaurant table of two white women being served lobster. Grouped around them were three Chinese people, one of whom seemed to be a waiter. Seemingly the acceptance of this image by the Chinese community was dependent on a significant diplomatic initiative by Henry Fitzhugh, director of London Transport Art Collection, who was masterminding the poster project. In the letter that Henry submitted to the Chinese he took it upon himself to state that the intention of the artist was to denote the innate superiority of the Chinese people over Western society and went on to point out that the evidence was obviously implied in the arrangement of the figures – the Chinese occupying the upper and larger part of the painting while the Western women were in the lower part of the composition. Accepted with no further questions!

In July 1987 we travelled to Hamburg. We were going to see Dr Werner Hofmann, the director of the Hamburg Kunsthalle, to talk about the possibility of the Scottish National Gallery of Modern Art retrospective being shown there. Our talks were successful and after exploring the museums of Hamburg, we returned home euphoric. Every time we went abroad I was anxious and watchful over John but never did I think we shouldn't go. We packed our lives with unforgettable experiences.

That summer of 1987 we were back in Edinburgh for the Festival. We had settled in to our flat in Great Stuart Street and had made the acquaintance of our neighbours, the most memorable of whom were the two elderly Alexander sisters. They came from a notable Edinburgh medical family and Isobel had been the GP for Edinburgh University. Her younger sister, Alison, was the widow of a Sri Lankan doctor who had at one time been the president of the World Health Organisation. Their rather conventional outward appearance belied the libertarian openness of their attitudes. Their range of interests encompassed all of the arts and culture, the history and heritage of Scotland and the world in general. They were founts of knowledge, total joy to spend time with and the most nonconformist and refreshing company.

The first time John had a health crisis in Scotland we realized that we had not registered with a GP in Edinburgh, so it was to Isobel that we turned in panic. She called their own GP, who she felt sure would be highly competent in dealing with John's state of health. His name was Dr Henry Gebbie, she told us, and he rejoiced in the role of the Queen's Apothecary for Scotland no less. This was just up John's street. Dr Gebbie was exactly the doctor for him. He certainly was. The very likeable and compassionate qualities of his good-natured personality, to say nothing of his dedicated professionalism, drew us into a warm friendship that also afforded us a comforting reassurance in stressful times to come.

Dr Gebbie had to be called several times and the hospital visits were now rapidly increasing in frequency. Still, portraits had been painted of some of the visiting artists – Hannah Gordon, Barbara Brecht-Schall (daughter of Bertolt Brecht) and her husband, the actor Ekkehardt Schall, Frank Dunlop, then director of the Edinburgh Festival, and others.

John had been asked to be the artist in residence at the Kilkenny Festival and so off we went across to Dublin in a twelve-seater plane full of young priests all discussing the Abortion Act. As the little plane dipped and wobbled out over Ailsa Craig and skimmed the Irish Sea, the land and water combined to thrill the senses and mercifully dull the soundtrack of their discussion.

The Festival was centred on Kilkenny Castle, where John's

exhibition was on show. The Irish know how to enjoy themselves and we knew how to join in. We were given a beautiful
old stone cottage to live in by George Vaughan, an artist, and
his wife Norah, an opera singer who entertained us with her
exquisite voice.

Aside from all those delightful distractions, all John's energy
went into the paintings. He worked in a fever of inspiration. Our
days followed a continuously unpredictable pattern. Struggling
health issues, increasingly frequent stays in hospital and clinic
attendances, sudden descents into desperation, simultaneous
abundance of the highs of opportunity and exhibition invitations, extraordinary excitement but ongoing anxiety and alarm
regarding the boys' activities in their band: all that kept apace
with John's declining prospects.

Anya, under the guidance of Edite, had enrolled at Kingsway
College in London and was to start a course of study aiming for
O and A level passes. She had responded well to Edite's help
and had developed a deep interest in literature. For the first
time in her life her dyslexia was not defeating her progress in
finding meaning and inspiration in books and learning. Dyslexia
would be a lifelong affliction but she was beginning to see a way
through and to be able to use the specialized help she was being
given. Her real ability was beginning to shine through to her satisfaction and my great joy. We were able now to share so much
of the excitement of learning and the thrill of her achievement.
For me, to see Anya's world expand in this way was the best
thing possible. It would go with her and enrich her throughout
her life.

The Self-Portrait show which included John and many of his
contemporaries with the accompanying book by Edward Lucie-
Smith opened in Bath in September 1987. John was unwell again
but we still went to Bath for the occasion. This was where we
met up with Reg and Patricia Singh, who owned the Beaux Arts
Gallery there. There was brief discussion about a possible show
of John's work to be held there the following year.

In November that year Roz Oxley, who had shown John's

work at her gallery in Sydney when he was in Australia, was going to show him again. We had been planning to go and the idea was to take my mother with us so she would be able to visit her sister in Queensland. The tickets were about to be booked but it now seemed too big a risk for John. Things were becoming steadily more serious and he was back in St Thomas's more and more. Our plans were cancelled.

The activities of the boys meant that many worthless hours were spent in a torment of dread. With youthful arrogance they believed I was simply ignorant of life in the big city and of the issues they were confronting. I tried to avoid knowing what they were doing but word always filtered back to me ensuring that I was forever in the grip of apprehension and fear.

We were having the time of our lives but the background to all of that, for me, was one of intense anxiety and fear. It never came in the way of our enjoyment, as I managed to push it into the background, but it was always lurking in wait for the hours of darkness when those feelings of panic rose up along with my fears for John's frailty. On one hand we lived a golden life loaded with pleasure, and 'loaded with luxury' as John's motto commanded. More importantly, we had regained the close unity and happiness we had shared in our first life together. Laughter and inspiration had come back into our lives. Success and recognition for John's work were growing apace, but we seemed to be subject to a relentless pattern of swinging from one extreme to the other, from crazy happiness to frantic despair.

The RCA was about to celebrate its centenary and an exhibition was planned, in which former students were asked to exhibit. The *Sunday Times* magazine was going to do a feature on the RCA celebration and in due course Lord Snowdon came to take John's photograph. There we were, in our sitting room in Northside overlooking the common, John's ravaged frame resting in an armchair with me standing behind him echoing the composition of a painting hanging on the wall behind us. I am standing as a guardian to the fragile person in the chair beside me and in the background of the painting a clock ticks relentlessly.

26. John at George Braques's grave, 1984.

27. Anya, exhibited at the National Portrait Gallery (oil on canvas 152.2 × 152.7 cm), 1986.

28. John, Jonathan, Anya and Paul, Christmas, 1985.

29. Our second wedding, 1986.

30. Portrait of Helen, exhibited at the National Portrait Gallery (oil on canvas), 1986.

31. Helen and John (photo: Lord Snowdon), 1986.

32. Bellanys and
Connerys, 1986.

33. Edinburgh
Festival poster,
1986.

34. Mon Hélène à Moi (17.2 × 15.2 cm oil on canvas), 1987.

35. Bowie and Bellany families, 1988.

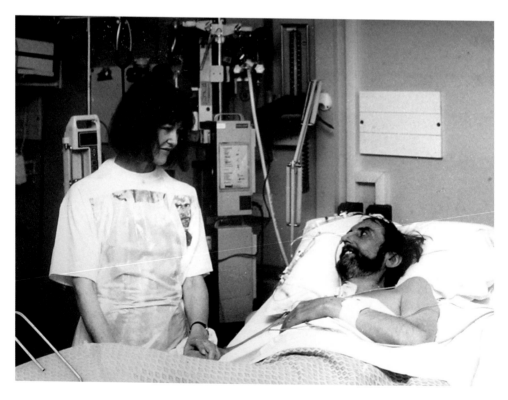

36. Helen with John in intensive care after his liver transplant, 1988.

37. Transplant self-portrait (watercolour), 1988.

38. John with Anya at Addenbrookes Hospital, recovering after his liver transplant, 1988.

39. Portrait of Helen with John, first published in Scotland on Sunday (photo: Adam Elder), 1994.

40. Helen at Buckingham Palace, 1994 (photo: John Bellany).

41. John and Helen in Tuscany (photo: Paul Duke), 2002.

42. John at work in Italy.

43. Natalina and Lolli (40 cm × 30 cm, oil on canvas), 2002.

44. John Bellany at 60.

45. John in Tuscany, 2004.

46. John and Helen at his exhibition opening at the Talbot Rice Gallery, Edinburgh.

47. John watching football with his boys.

48. John, Helen and Angie.

49. John in Glasgow, 3rd June 2005.

50. John Bellany at 70, last self-portrait (121 × 91 cm, oil on canvas), 2012.

CHAPTER 47

Desperate Days

At the end of November 1987 John suddenly, in the middle of the night, became extremely ill and lapsed into delirium. One of the most unbearable symptoms from which he suffered was continual itching, a classic condition of liver failure, and in order to calm his raging skin he resorted to having baths, sometimes three each night. This time, as I was sleeping, he ran a bath for himself and let it overflow for quite a long time before I woke up to what was happening. He was delirious and becoming very agitated. We were alone in the house and it was difficult for me to control him and get him back to bed. Trying to hold him and calm him down while attempting to call the ambulance was almost impossible. He was taken into St Thomas's A & E where we were put into a cubicle to wait interminably for an available doctor to see him. He was calling out and crying piteously. He could not be reached and was attempting to climb off the bed. I managed to call Paul, who came as soon as possible and helped me with him.

By this time it was morning and the clinics had begun in the hospital, for one of which John had an appointment. We waited on and on as it is usual to do in A & E, frantic as we were, not sure what was happening or how serious John's condition was. I was tempted to run round the corridor to the liver clinic where John's regular consultants, all of whom we knew so well, would be working. I was so frightened that he was going to die but, not wanting to cause a fuss, I restrained myself. If a similar situation ever arose I would react differently. I believe that you have to fight for vulnerable people in any situation in which they cannot fend for themselves and especially your loved ones.

He was eventually taken up to a ward. I was advised that he would come out of this delirium, so I stayed with him. There was no sign of this happening and by the middle of the next night I was exhausted and was advised to go home. I asked them to call me back as soon as he came round, as I believed he would feel very disoriented and scared. He came round as daylight began but of course I was not called. On opening his eyes he couldn't work out where he was. The ward being on one of the highest floors of a tower block, all he could see was the blue sky and fluffy white clouds of early morning, so he eventually came to the conclusion that he must be in heaven! He asked for a piece of paper and a pen and tried to draw. Panic set in. He could not make any sense of his drawing. *He could not draw.* He had to be dead! He asked for Helen and they said she would come. She did not come. He asked over and over again. Where was she? Where was he?

A nurse turned up at the start of her day shift. Her name badge said 'Helen', which confused him to begin with. But then she convinced him that his Helen had been called and would be with him soon. She sat and kept a close watch on him and gradually he began to calm down and to believe he was not dead after all. When I did arrive, he was very upset that I had not been with him – 'Where on earth were you?' So relieved to see me, he begged me never to leave him alone again. He had been seriously afraid and the experience haunted him for a long time after. He was kept in hospital for a couple of days and as usual I was requested to bring in the watercolour paper and paints. Before he was discharged he completed a portrait of the nurse, Helen Batterbury, who had given him vital reassurance at a time of his greatest fear, the fear of death. It was a beezer, an exquisite watercolour and one that he always wanted to keep nearby. It became a talisman, a guard against the possibility of such a terror coming back to him.

John was discharged from hospital but within a couple of days was readmitted, extremely ill again. His body was in serious decline. Once again the Pentax went down the throat but this time he had to undergo painful cauterization of ulcers in his oesophagus. Never one to make a fuss about his ill health he was beginning to lack the strength to pick himself up again and after this particularly painful treatment he just lay back in bed drained of colour and life. He remained in hospital in this weakened state for a couple of weeks and every day without fail our friend David Brown arrived to keep him company, sitting by his bedside. I frequently arrived to find them both fast asleep and completely undisturbed while visiting time proceeded around them as usual.

Dr David Brown was one of life's bonuses, highly intellectual and wonderfully eccentric with a consuming passion for art. He had trained as a vet and had worked in Africa for many years but then in later life turned his back on all that and enrolled at the Courtauld to study fine art. He spent several years working at the Scottish National Gallery of Modern Art in Edinburgh and now was an assistant curator at the Tate. I remember introducing him to some of John's doctors when they were on their rounds, explaining that David was a curator at the Tate, whereupon he nodded in agreement then in a loud voice declared himself to be a veterinary surgeon!

Many of the old friends visited. Sandy came, bringing other Scottish artists with him, and Bert Irvin, another of his closest friends, was among many of the London ones who visited too. It was obvious that John was going downhill rapidly.

In the middle of December he underwent more painful treatment to his oesophagus and was lying semi-sedated looking very bad. It was relatively silent in the ward. None of the patients was able to do other than lie quietly. In John's words he was again in the 'no hopers' ward where many were at death's door. Faintly, in the distance, the unlikely sound of an accordion was approaching, and slowly and cautiously round the corner and into the ward came a friend playing ever so softly. It was like the raising of the dead. All those who were able to raised their heads for a moment or opened their eyes, drawn by the life-giving tones of the accordion. All the old much-loved Scottish melodies following on from John's signature song of 'The Road and The Miles to Dundee'. In his agony, he was suddenly restored to life by the kindness of a friend and my heart was lifted.

On 21 December he was discharged just in time for Christmas but the good feeling this should have engendered was tempered by the information given to us by his doctors on their last ward round. I was there as they gathered round his bed and announced that he would be going home. John began to look pleased but the consultant continued, 'and, I'm afraid, John, that there is really nothing more that we can do to help you. We have run out of options.'

Panic-stricken, he asked, 'What exactly does that mean?'

'Well, we have done everything we can to help you but your health is now in an extremely precarious condition. Your life expectancy has been vastly reduced.'

I remember those words so clearly, as they turned my blood cold. I had so dreaded this moment. I had expected it for a long time and now here it was. He was being told that the future he was so joyously sure of and for which he harboured so many hopes and ambitions just did not exist. What now?

I didn't dare look at John's face but I heard him ask them if they meant that he was going to die. They did not answer that but made it clear that all they would be able to offer him from now on would be basic monitoring in the clinics.

I could not imagine what he would be thinking after this bombshell. What on earth could I say to him? How could I possibly comfort him or help him to accept what now was inevitable? God help me! How could I cope with this myself? I did not want John to die. He *could not* die.

My mind was jangling as I heard him protesting and telling the group of doctors, 'But I want to live as long as Picasso!'

I amazed myself by hearing my voice asking about the possibility of a transplant. This idea had never consciously crossed my mind. I knew nothing about transplants except that they were relatively new and, as far as I knew, still experimental. I had never talked to anyone, far less John, about such a thing. It must have been sheer desperation and panic that made me bring the subject up.

There was no enthusiastic response from the doctors. They just said they would see him in clinic in the new year, so I assumed a transplant was not really an option.

I began to wonder, with reason, what John would make of the idea of a transplant anyway. He, who was plagued all his life with nightmares about death, probably saw death and a transplant as one and the same thing.

In the lift a little while later I met one of his doctors, who asked me if I had previously discussed a transplant with one of their team. Assuring him I had not, he explained that they had briefly discussed such a possibility. As over the four years since he had first become their patient no one had ever proposed such a thing for John, I assumed that if the idea had been raised, after consideration it had been dismissed. In retrospect, I am left to wonder if he would ever have seriously been considered for a transplant if I had not spoken up. He was certainly in poor shape, extremely weak and emaciated. His breathing was laboured, he was having great difficulty in swallowing and could digest very little food, while he was devoid of energy. Alcoholics were notoriously unreliable candidates for intensive and expensive treatment but it had been four years since he had had his last alcoholic drink and all his tests bore this out. Since then he had complied to the letter with everything advised by the medical profession with no other motive than an overwhelming will to live. He had continued to smoke because the perceived difficulty of remaining abstinent might be compromised by trying to wean himself off cigarettes at the same time. Nevertheless, his smoking had declined markedly and, if they had advised him to quit, he would have done so immediately, without question, just as he had instantly dismissed alcohol from his life. Such a will and determination with regards to addiction is extremely rare and it would be reasonable for the medics to question his integrity but I knew how committed he had been to banish self-destruction from his life and I knew how he could never have forgiven himself if he had ever put at risk the efforts of the medical profession to help him recover from such serious illness. The strongest asset he had was his spirit and the love he had of life.

Christmas 1987 was grim, with the five of us trying to find comfort in being together and doing all we could to act as if it was a normal celebration. This one had to be the last one. As usual, he had drawings and paintings to give each of us and at the table, all of us wearing festive paper hats, using all of the little energy that remained to him, he made us laugh with anecdotes of his past adventures with his friends, his ravaged features a grotesque semblance of one of the death's heads of one of his heroes, James Ensor.

Hogmanay arrived. We would not be going out celebrating at night to Janet and Patrick Caulfield's party as we used to do. During the day a friend, Peter Griffin, came round to see John. He had brought the singer, Ralph McTell, whose 'Streets Of London' always evoked our earlier days. Their company livened up the atmosphere and we spent the afternoon laughing over old times.

As the old year passed and 1988 began, John and I were alone but after midnight the phone calls came from Scotland and from our friends everywhere. He wrote in the diary: '1.30 a.m. New Year phone call from Sandy and Ricky Demarco from Edinburgh – good laugh!'

The knowledge that the doctors had now no other help to offer engulfed us with a feeling of abandonment. Every minute of every day people are told that their lives are in the final stages. We were in that company now. There is no alternative to just facing things as best you can. You are not thinking about your own grief at times like those. You are not really thinking about anything in detail. It is about living in the minute. It is not bearable to think further ahead than that and I remember little more of those days.

CHAPTER 48

A New Chance of Life

There were exhibitions coming up. In January John would begin showing with Ruth Siegel in New York, the centrepiece of which would be the great diptych he had painted in 1987, *The Presentation of Time*, a banquet scene transcribed from Rubens' *The Feast of Herod*, in which John, with Juliet sitting next to him, is surrounded by friends including Alan Davie, Sean Connery and other actors and painters. They are all looking on as I appear at the table offering John a ticking clock, the gift of Time.

In May he would show for the first time with Reg and Patricia Singh at the Beaux Arts Gallery in Bath. Some time later they opened their gallery in Cork Street in London where they continued to show his works for almost thirty years. There were also several group shows including the *British Romantic Painting* opening in Madrid and the Royal College of Art print portfolio exhibition. His Dublin show at the Hendricks Gallery was just coming to an end. There were television films scheduled and much to look forward to.

On 4 January he was back in St Thomas's. He stayed in overnight once more and tests were done, after which it was decided he would be referred to King's College Hospital, where he would be seen by Professor Roger Williams (who would at a future time treat George Best).

Apparently this was the first step in being assessed for a

possible transplant. There had been a reconsideration. We could not believe our good luck. At least John would be given a chance and we had temporarily been reprieved. We were, however, told not to expect too much as there would be many tests John would have to undergo to determine if such a massive procedure would be possible. His body might not be strong enough for such an invasive operation.

Our frantic dashes to A & E increased. Fluid was drawn off his stomach in order to help his breathing. His diet, which I had to keep adjusting almost weekly, was becoming ever more specialized – less protein, no red meat, more empty calories, sweets galore but no chocolate, no salt, Coca Cola but no milk, more this, no that. I was learning every day the intricacies and applications of food values to the most infinitesimal degree. As I described John's latest diet of sweets and sugary drinks, a friend, Eileen Martin, summed it up: 'Oh, that's just the Scottish diet!'

The appointment with Professor Williams was set for 14 January. On meeting him for the first time he jovially told us that he had not expected John to turn up for his appointment as he had just that weekend read his (John's) obituary in *The Times*! I subsequently searched and found what he had read – an obituary for a Mr John Bella(m)y (of Westside), Clapham Common. Our address was Northside, Clapham Common. The coincidence was a step too close for comfort, especially as Roger Williams went on to cheerily inform us that, 'We lose so many of our patients on the waiting list. They fail to make it and die before an organ becomes available.' Too much information! Far too close to our precarious circumstances.

The main transplant programme in the UK was run jointly by King's College Hospital in London and Addenbrooke's Hospital in Cambridge. The preliminaries were largely dealt with in the London hospital and the operations in Cambridge. Generally the aftercare was also provided by King's. Three days of tests were completed in King's before John was discharged.

All this while we were continuously involved with time-consuming preparations for various exhibitions scheduled for the spring. We also attended the opening of the RCA centenary exhibition and celebrated along with our friends. The SNGMA 1986 Retrospective was to travel to the Museum in Dortmund and there were endless issues to be dealt with for that. His exhibition in New York at Ruth Siegel opened on 10 March, from which we were informed that the Metropolitan Museum had bought three paintings.

Exhilarating news. We were over the moon but John, back home again from King's, was once more at the mercy of fate. We had no alternative but to go on with living life on a day-to-day or, rather, an hour-to-hour basis, scared to look or think further. The vulnerability of fending for ourselves without the reassuring oversight of medical help was onerous. Decision-making was a knife-edged operation, as each choice, however small, might be crucial to his survival. He could not breathe easily. He could hardly swallow anything and things were never small enough for them not to stick in his raw throat. He would make great efforts to take the medicine prescribed for him only for it to cause paroxysms of coughing and choking when it would not go down. I felt that I had his life in my hands and I was increasingly conscious of my inadequacy in carrying such a terrifying responsibility.

The urgency of our dashes to A & E accelerated in pace with tests being carried out at King's. We were waiting for the all-important visit to Addenbrooke's and for final tests to ensure John's body would be strong enough for the transplant if he was ever lucky enough to receive one. We were stepping cautiously through each day, and every night was full of fear and apprehension.

Entries in John's diary tell of numerous details of exhibition preparation, hospital appointments and, among them: 'Buy the new Pogues album!'

Optimism still lived. And the blessed blackbird still sang in the darkness.

Some time previously we had been given the exciting news that a couple of paintings had been bought from the Serpentine exhibition by David Bowie. Apparently he had been a long-time admirer of John's work and wanted to meet him.

We were in those days engulfed in the blackest and bleakest of times. The fact that John was dying was always with us, but we were continuing to do our best to block it out of our minds while looking for the best each day could offer. At the end of February 1988 David came to have lunch with us. He brought with him his friend Coco, and Duncan, his son.

John had always possessed a strong sense of occasion. He astounded me during those traumatic years by making sudden supreme efforts to rise above his pain and weakness, gathering all his dwindling energies to try to be the fun-loving person he had always been and so get the best out of times, if even for brief interludes.

That day David came to see us was one of those occasions in which I saw life surging back once more into his frail and wasted body, a light of hopefulness shining in his weary eyes and a spirit that soared up and away from the dark despair that was enveloping him more every day.

Who wouldn't have been thrilled to meet someone like David? He was a phenomenally talented person, known and admired the whole world over. That he loved John's paintings fascinated us. It was a colossal vote of confidence from someone we recognized as a visionary musician and actor, a vibrant and intriguing personality. Like most people this was all we knew of him – the famous icon that belonged to the whole world. But that was not who turned up at our door that day. Within the first few minutes we slipped easily and warmly into a camaraderie that only occurs between kindred spirits. David had discovered John's work when they had both been students, David at Kingston and John at the Royal College of Art, and he already owned several of his paintings. This was the starting point of a relationship that encompassed many mutual interests and passions across the whole spectrum of the arts and an ongoing dialogue that ranged from the deeply philosophical and spiritual to the mundane madness of daily life. Punctuating the conversation also that day was a buoyant repartee full of personal anecdotes that had us all rocking with laughter. *Joie de vivre* had been a feature in our lives together and here it was again transcending John's weakness and frailty, filling the day with energy and shared inspiration.

All the children were present and it was a memorable occasion, a wonderful boost for John's flagging spirits, and mine. It's the best possible form of empowerment when one recognizes in a fellow traveller a validation of all one is striving for. It certainly affected John in that way. It strengthened him and gave him courage.

Later, as we waved them off from the top of our steps, the daffodils and crocuses were in bloom in the garden below, the trees the merest haze of green and the afternoon sun was sweeping away into the distance over Clapham Common. There was a glorious life-is-good feeling in the air. The relentless stress and anxiety of John's desperate health issues had been lifted, allowing our spirits to soar for a few hours.

The next morning John was back in St Thomas's in severe pain. He stayed for over a week. Easter weekend came and there were worse places to be than in the wards of St Thomas's high up looking out on the spectacular view of the Palace of Westminster, up the shining Thames towards the towers of our old home environment, Battersea Power station. It gave John some degree of comfort to see the cupola of the Tate Gallery on the north bank of the river – a feeling of being in the company of friends, still connected to the life he knew. In the other direction, down river, past Big Ben and Westminster Bridge, he found comfort in the gothic features of the Thames-side apartment block in which his friend Sidney Nolan lived. Both those vistas provided inspiration for watercolours and drawings that were eventually translated into oil paintings in which he gave a small nod to Oscar Kokoshka's landscape of Edinburgh. I marvelled at the colour and energy in those works created by a seriously sick man. It was with pride that we presented one of the paintings in this series to St Thomas's Hospital in due course as a gesture of gratitude for all that had been done for him.

Back home again the only pleasure for him was to be driven out in the car and this we did nearly every day. His diary records 'a wonderful trip to the coast. Returned via Arundel – glorious day'.

The following day we had an appointment with his consultant, Dr Wing. He told us that it was now urgent for the transplant team to take over John's care and an appointment was made for next day at King's. In the night, however, I again had to rush him in to St Thomas's A & E. He was in agony. I parked on double yellow lines and ran in to get a wheelchair for him. It was nearly daylight by the time I left John to be looked after in an acute ward and remembered my car.

This time he had gallstones, to add to everything else. I was desperate by now. I suggested to John's mother and his sister, Margaret, that it might be a good idea to come to London to see him as he was far from well, and they quickly came for a few days. Their visit perked him up but after they left he was unwell again and back in St Thomas's.

In desperation I took it upon myself to ring King's College to speak to one of the doctors we had been seeing there. All protocol swept aside, I told him that John was back in hospital again and begged him to get him the appointment at Addenbrooke's. I remember telling him that if he did not get there in the next few days it would be too late. I was as sure of that as anyone could be.

This was a Friday, not the best day to get decisions made as the weekend was approaching. The young Australian doctor promised me, however, that he would personally ring Addenbrooke's himself and call me back when he had any news. I stayed by the phone. Eventually he rang and said that a bed would be waiting for John in Addenbrooke's on the Monday. That was in two days' time, on 25 April. He was to present himself to the transplant unit.

I brought him home from St Thomas's that day. We were grateful for the appointment but there was no euphoria. We were way beyond that. We still had the weekend to get through safely. Please let him survive till Monday, until he got to Addenbrooke's, where there would be help. It was his only chance. The last chance.

A New Chance of Life

That Saturday John wanted to go for a drive to distract himself. He wanted to go to Hastings to see the sea and the boats. We would also call in to visit our friends Gus and Angie Cummins. It was a long drive but the countryside was beautiful, the day full of sunshine and birdsong and spring life.

We each had our own thoughts as I drove along. Our companion of many months came everywhere with us. There was no escaping the dark presence of Death but the pale figure within his clutches beside me was relishing the outing and the idea of seeing the sea again. There were no references to how bad he was feeling. No complaints. There never were.

There were no guarantees about what would happen at Addenbrooke's the following week. We were only too aware of that but the opportunity itself was the thing we were holding on to. The door was still ajar, if only ever so little. On that meagre raft of light we set off for Hastings. I wanted this to be a day to remember, as it might be all that we would have.

To see the sea and the fishing boats always made his heart beat a little faster, he would say, and later on it was good to be with our friends in their home high up overlooking the bay. To get to their house we had to park further up and descend a fairly steep grassy incline. Slowly we managed to do that but on the way back to the car it was too much for John. An icy wind had sprung up by this time and he was exhausted and shivering with cold. Gus took off his own jacket and wrapped it round him. With his arms around John he managed to help him get back to the car, stopping every few steps for him to find breath. Halfway up we made for a seat on the hillside where he had to rest for some time in the freezing cold before we could help him on to his feet once more to tackle the final short climb. It was a pitiful thing to witness the agony of his struggle and the labour of love of one friend for another, an image I wouldn't forget.

When we started on our journey home and he had finally got his breath back, he whispered that he had thought that he wasn't going to make it back to the car. It was a near thing, he said. He was still gasping from the effort when one of his teeth fell out. His whole body was disintegrating. Every organ was failing, the power in every limb dwindling, everything shutting down. His teeth had been coming loose from his gums and now he had lost another one. This was the last straw!

After a few choice expletives, his current favourite, Sibelius, be damned, he put the tape of the Pogues into the player and turned it up full blast.

'FUCK IT!' he shouted.

And with the last ounce of strength remaining in his body he started hoarsely wheezing out in time with the music. The Pogues roared and the drumbeats picked up the spirit, shaking and reverberating it back to life. So off we went back to London.

'DROWN THE WHOLE BLOODY THING OUT!'

And the refrain blasting away: 'If I should fall from grace with God.'

CHAPTER 49

Transplant

There was little preparation for our trip to Cambridge on the Monday. We had never been there before and had no idea where the hospital was. As I helped John to the car, the thought occurred to me, would he ever come home again?

We found our way out through the east end of London and on to the M11. I didn't dare look John's way. I did not want to acknowledge the apparition of Death that had displaced this person I was fighting for and whom I was willing to keep on holding on to life at all costs.

What were his thoughts?

All the way we travelled in silence. There was nothing to say. There was only the being as one on this journey. Words were standing by, composing themselves in readiness, but neither of us made a call on them. They would have fallen far short of any adequacy for the circumstances.

Just as we left the M11 on the first exit to Cambridge, I drew into a lay-by. I had prepared a flask of soup in the hope that he would be able to swallow some of it before we found the hospital. I parked and left him in the car. If he was alone, it was sometimes easier for him to swallow things. His effort failed, as it mostly did, and the soup did not stay down.

It was with great relief we arrived at Addenbrooke's. The normal friendly banter of the nurses and doctors who admitted him soothed my jangled nerves. They would sort him out, no worries! I could almost believe them. I so wanted to believe them. I *had* to believe them.

The transplant unit was at that time on the ninth floor of a modern hospital block, the large windows of the wards looking out over the fields of Magog Down and the open countryside south of the city. It was a bright environment and, for us, there was optimism in the air. Or was it purely the huge relief that we had at last arrived at the only place that might offer something other than the imminent death that was stalking him?

We understood that he would now undergo a series of tests lasting the best part of a week. I found a hotel and began looking for somewhere within the vicinity of Cambridge to rent. After several days I found a cottage at the end of a leafy lane in the village of Little Eversden. I was told it would be available for me to move in on the following Sunday.

Every afternoon when I visited John that week I found him on good form. He gave me all the details of his tests, which monitored his lung and heart function and his stamina. He had given up smoking, which he stopped in the same manner as he gave up drinking: totally and immediately. There could be no transplant if he continued to smoke. He found all the tests strenuous but gave the very best performance he could, especially the one in which he had to 'cycle upside down all the way to Brighton!'

On Thursday we were informed that he had miraculously scraped through the fitness test and consequently would be considered for the transplant. We knew that now there was a wait of indeterminate length that, as his stamina and state of health were rapidly dwindling, might defeat him before his turn came. I was glad that at least I had fixed up accommodation nearby where, in the meantime, we could live.

John was still being sick at every attempt to eat and was in general extremely ill. I was so relieved he was at last being looked after in hospital where he would get the help and vigilance that I could not provide.

On the Friday of that week I had been with John when the evening meal came round and as usual I left him on his own in the hope he would manage to swallow his food. Coming into the ward afterwards I found the curtains drawn round his bed and my heart sank as I assumed he had failed once again. But one of the other patients whispered to me, 'It's good news!' Good news? How on earth could it be good news?

Then the thought occurred to me that he had persuaded the doctors to let him out of hospital as he knew I had found somewhere for us to live. Not an unreasonable suggestion, I suppose, as they could not keep him in, waiting indefinitely, but I dreaded his discharge back to me. If this happened, I would have to take over, once again, the awful responsibility of keeping him alive. My crestfallen face elicited repeated reassurances of 'Good news' from the patients while I waited until I thought the staff had finished working with John.

I could hear him enthusiastically talking about a need to finish a drawing he had been doing of one of the young doctors 'beforehand'. From how he was speaking, my fears were confirmed. His powers of persuasion never failed him. He must have told them that he was feeling fine, as he always did when he wanted out of hospital, and they were going to let him out.

I went in to his bedside in a state of panic, only to be told that they had been trying to get hold of me – still no mobile phones then – as they wanted to tell me that a liver had become available. It was compatible and suitable for John's blood group and they were asking him if he wanted to accept the offer of a transplant!

The news took my breath away. It was too sudden and too enormous for me to process.

John was overwhelmed. I just remember our looking at each other and my murmuring, 'Please.'

It was around seven thirty on Friday evening. The operation was to begin at six the next morning. Preparations would begin immediately. The anaesthetist would come to talk to us shortly and we would meet as many of the operating team as possible to talk through the procedure.

What did John want me to do? I wanted to contact our children so they could come to be here and perhaps see John before he went to theatre. I also needed to go to London to get things in preparation for a long stay in the rented cottage so that I could be with him continually after the operation. All of this, of course, was secondary to what John wanted now at this crucial moment.

It was explained to us that the operation would be a lengthy and highly complicated procedure, with most of the major organs being disconnected and for a period of time maintained mechanically while John's liver was removed and the new one introduced. There would be critical moments and tricky manoeuvres throughout the eight hours it would take to complete the surgery. The talk was frank and we were well aware of the statistics associated with such a major undertaking. Two out of three patients survived the operation and the survival figures after one year were not any more encouraging. The one out of three . . .

But we could not give much thought to that. We were too excited. This was it, the big chance! All of a sudden we were being allowed to glimpse the sun. We could only think of the 'yes!' of things, of blood that would sing in depleted veins again, of jaded eyes that would see anew in true vibrant colour, of strength that would flood back into wasted limbs that would embrace the beating heart of life once more, of all the infinite possibilities, good and positive, in this wonderful, astonishing chance of a future that was being held out to us.

We were rendered inarticulate with the enormity of what was happening. I was advised that as John would be given sedation in a short time to help him sleep I should go to London, find the children, do all the stuff I needed and be back as soon as I could. The doctors told me that I could accompany John down to the operating theatre at six in the morning. I assured them that I would be back in time to be with him.

John was preoccupied with finishing the watercolour of the young doctor from Dundee, Kim Jacobsen, who had been looking after him. He told her that he would give it to her as a gift and, as it might be the last thing he did, it could be worth a lot of money. She readily agreed to sit for him again!

By this time it was around 9 p.m. on Friday night. I could not contact any of the children. They were all out. I rang Port Seton with the news. I rang my family too, and Sandy and Al and all our other close friends. I wanted all of them to be thinking about John during such a momentous crisis. Privately I asked for him the strength and support of our friends' loving thoughts. Please let him not be the one in three.

I set up a hunt for the children, roping in my friends to help. I found Anya and told her that I would be back home in an hour and a half or so and she was to be ready. I set off from Cambridge, my mind racing out of control. The first disc that came to hand in the car was Handel's *Messiah* and on it went, blasting out to the heavens above, all the way to London.

My Kyrie Eleison: Watch over him. Protect him. Help him.

If there is anyone listening, please hear me.

No one deserved this opportunity more than John. He had been the architect of his own physical destruction, of that there was no doubt, but the courage and determination with which he had faced up to changing his life, accepting the guidance of the doctors in whom he placed all his trust and the gratitude he held for all that had been done to help him by their efforts, was the driving force in his will to survive this far. Over and above that was his love of life, the life we had found once more together and that offered so much promise.

In London I quickly packed my things, leaving messages for the boys, and before 3 a.m. was back on the road to Cambridge with Anya beside me attempting to sleep in spite of the crazy volume of Handel's great choral music. It had to be that way. My heart was beating to deafen me and my blood seemed volcanic, surging with emotion.

In our approach to Cambridge over the Magog Down we could just pick out in the pre-dawn dark the distinctive towers of the hospital, which always make me think of arms upstretched to the sky. Our arrival was in the dark of 4 a.m. Somewhere high up among the concrete buildings, the echo of the blackbird's song. The intensity of its beauty, our familiar comfort in darkest times. We entered the silent ward and quietly made our way to John's bedside.

I gently stroked his sleeping face, down over his smooth temple into the hollows of his wasted face. He opened bewildered eyes to smile with gladness at finding us there beside him.

Again, as before, the words did not exist for such moments and we just sat holding hands as daylight began to push its way into the sky and the fields of springtime came into view through the large windows of the ward.

It was soon time to go with him to the theatre. We followed his bed out through the unit and into the lift, with John trying to make us laugh and all of us trying to pretend it was a fun outing.

In the anteroom of the theatre, just before the anaesthetic was administered, Anya and I hugged him. He assured us that he would give it his all and we said that he'd better do just that.

Then the doors swung shut.

This was Saturday, 30 April 1988.

I had made arrangements for us to move into the cottage that day and now Anya and I went there. As we left the hospital, a vehicle was careering up to the entrance. Inside were Jonathan and Paul. After they got my message it took them some time to find each other and by the time they got to Cambridge and the hospital it was too late to see John. They were upset they had not been able to wish him well but they followed us to Little Eversden to wait for news.

Driving round a corner in the hospital grounds, I suddenly saw a large dead rat lying on the road. I had never seen one before, dead or alive. But rats! John's serious lifetime's phobia that could not be spoken of and to which any reference had to be spelled out rather than the actual word uttered. Even a tiny mouse was a rat to him ever since one had been thrown at him when he and his friends were playing in the fishing boats as children. His recurring nightmares were of rats and he used to wake up dreaming that one was going for his throat. My mother always said that to dream of rats meant a death was in the offing. Rats and death were one and the same thing to John, as the two combined formed the greatest terror of his life. This was all superstition of the fishing world, but at a time like this I had to make it right with myself all the same.

Rat = death. But a dead rat? Might the fact of it being dead not cancel out the threat of death? A double negative might therefore suggest life? And, into the bargain, I had also heard the blackbird sing in the darkness before this morning's dawn. These had to be significant omens.

Now I prayed that the surgeon had come to work that morning a happy and contented man. Please let him not have had a row with his wife as he left home that day. Please don't let him have had a late night out and be suffering from a hangover. Please let his football or rugby team be winning. May there have been no traffic jams or car breakdowns on his way to work that morning ... All this also applied to the anaesthetist and the junior doctors and the nurses and every member of the operating team on whom the responsibility for John's survival now depended. May all the conditions and circumstances be in place to give him the very best chance.

Please do your best for him, all of you. His life is in your hands.

Please give him the strength to withstand the physical trauma of this.

Please just let him survive the operation.

Please don't let him be the one in three.

In the cottage everyone tried to get some sleep but I was far too wound up for that. I paced about restlessly, watching the clock. We had been advised that the operation would not be completed until after 1 p.m. and there would be no news until then. We returned to the hospital and found the relatives' room just outside the Intensive Care Unit in which to wait.

We shared this room with a West Indian family whose teenage daughter was undergoing surgery at the same time. The family was fractured, the parents separated, and the atmosphere was uneasy and tense for all of us.

One-thirty ... two-thirty.. The West Indian family went to be with their daughter who had returned from theatre to Intensive Care. Three o'clock ... three-thirty ... No news. Why was it not over yet? Why was he not back?

Repeated requests for news finally brought forth an explanation. There had been a complication. There had been internal haemorrhaging and it was proving difficult to deal with. We were assured that everything was being done and we were not to panic. Don't panic? I could hardly breathe. Silence descended and we hardly dared look at each other.

Four-thirty. At long last the doors swung open. A bed was being rushed along the corridor accompanied by the theatre team in masks and gowns. As the bed rattled past us I momentarily caught sight of him unconscious underneath swathes of masks, tubes and monitors and drains, machines whirring. Through my tears I had an impression, so fleeting, of a face, so crucially suspended in the balance between life and death, that spoke to me of *life*.

An illusion? Wishful thinking? A purely transitory state?

What I saw was a body artificially enhanced by the massive dose of steroids required at this crucial post-operative stage but as his entourage rapidly disappeared into the Intensive Care Unit my first impression, based on nothing tangible, was of life.

After he was settled in the ICU I was allowed in to see him. It was similar to gazing at my newborn babies. Full of wonder. Overcome by the heroic things that had been done for him and his own heroism of facing up to and going through such an overwhelming ordeal. He would now need all his courage and strength to withstand the pain and challenge of recovery. The family were admitted to see him for a short time before we reluctantly left him to the watchful attention of zigzagging tracings and whirring monitors and bleeping machines to sleep on at the mercy of the fates.

It was a cold, blustery but sunshiny evening as we made our way into Cambridge in search of something to eat. We hadn't thought about eating or sleeping for a whole night and day since the news came through about the transplant, and now sheer exhaustion and relief kicked in. All I really wanted to do was sleep. After our meal the children went to Little Eversden while I had a bed in the hospital allocated to me.

I returned to sit with John for a while in the ICU and then, satisfied with the reports of his stability, I made my way to where I would be sleeping. I was given assurance that I would be called immediately if there was any change in his condition. The room was nearby and contained two beds. I discovered that I would be sharing the room with the West Indian mother whose daughter had undergone surgery that day as well. Her daughter was eighteen years old and suffered from congenital liver disease. She was very poorly and a tracheotomy had been opened in her throat to help her breathing. She was also in the ICU and I had sensed that she was causing considerable concern. Her mother and I chatted anxiously for a while before we turned off the light. I remember the coincidence that they also came from London and they lived at Clapham Common, North Street, while we lived at Clapham Common, Northside.

Sleep was instant oblivion.

In the morning I wakened wondering where I was. My friend's bed was empty. Suddenly everything came flooding back to me. I saw from my watch that it was eight o'clock in the morning. Panic-stricken, I jumped up and ran as fast as I could to the ICU. How could I have been sleeping so long at such a time of crisis? I was petrified to find out what was happening now. Would he still be alive?

Gowned and masked, I moved near his bed. There he was among his vital machinery. We saw each other in a blur, his eyes in a glaze above his oxygen mask, mine misted up and flowing over just at seeing him alive. When I asked what had been happening and how he had been in the night and how he was now, my questions were answered by a smiling nurse.

He had begun to come round and had been trying to say something to them. He was not able to make himself understood through the oxygen mask and tubes but he had made some kind of sign that they thought indicated writing. Eventually they worked out that he was asking for pencil and paper. When they brought it to him, they saw that he was trying to draw! I immediately understood what he was doing. He was testing himself out to see if he was alive or dead. I remembered the time in St

Thomas's when he had been unable to draw, and suffered the horror of believing he must be dead.

But this morning, in the haze of his confusion, he had made an attempt at drawing one of the nurses and had convinced himself that he was still in our world. There, on a piece of paper for all to see, was an eye here, a slash of a nose careering down off the paper there, and an attempt at a mouth somewhere in an interesting position of its own. Scrambled over the page was a barely decipherable declaration:

'I . . . WILL . . . get . . . well!'

CHAPTER 50

Reborn

Four days later John was moved from the ICU into a single room near to the nurses' desk in the main ward and six days after the operation he was given his first solid food. A biopsy had revealed only 10 per cent rejection of the new liver. This result, I was informed, was encouraging and the next day he set about his first drawing – a portrait of Professor Sir Roy Calne, the renowned transplant pioneer who, although he had not performed John's operation, had witnessed it.

The transplant surgeon Keith Rolles had been the hero of the day and we met him regularly on the ward rounds. When I told him of the perfect conditions I had wished for him as he commenced the operation and for a stress-free transaction to take place, he admitted that he and some of the other doctors on the team had been trying to complete the operation in time to watch an important rugby match in the afternoon! They had in fact missed the whole thing, as they had had to work on for four extra hours in the urgent attempt to contain the problem of John's internal haemorrhaging.

Almost immediately I was instructed to find an art shop in Cambridge and bring in sheaves of heavy-duty watercolour paper, paints and brushes without delay. So there I was in the crowded lift full of anxious visitors, struggling with massive portfolios and bags of painting gear. Every day I arrived at the hospital to find more new watercolours completed and ready to be Blue-Tacked to the walls of his room.

A few days after leaving the ICU John had a relapse in the shape of a severe infection that caused him great pain and turned him bright yellow. Analgesics didn't seem to do much to alleviate the symptoms, so he began to draw. Throughout the night, using a little hospital shaving mirror and a red Conté pencil, he poured the energy of his agony into capturing what he saw in the mirror. The result was probably the best drawing he had ever done in his life. Of all the vast body of exceptional drawings he produced throughout his career this one was in a class of its own. He would say that while drawing it his awareness of pain ceased and it seemed to be something that drew itself. This self-portrait is now in the collection of the Scottish National Gallery of Modern Art in Edinburgh and still has the power to make me gasp as it did when I first saw it.

Among his first visitors at this time, our close friends Bert and Betty Irvin were impressed by the buoyant spirit emanating from such a fragile and deeply jaundiced wreck as John was in those first post-operative days. Bert declared that his friend resembled a curried chicken!

Within a short space of time the ice-blue walls of his room were covered to the ceiling with watercolours. In the days of Matron I doubt he would have got away with it but it had not crossed his mind to ask permission and everyone and everything that came within his line of vision was drawn and painted.

He craved colour and was thrilled by the vibrancy of a striped rugby shirt Tim Hudson had sent him. He asked me to bring in more things of bright colour to drape around his room on which to feast his eyes. He was amazed by the clarity of his vision and felt that pre-transplant he had been living in a monochrome world. He wrote to Sandy about the importance and necessity of colour. 'Colour is everything,' he declared. Every day seemed to bring an awakening of the senses. He described it as like coming out of a half-life of shadow into the full beam of the sun once more, like a dying flower being watered and instantly being filled with a new vigour for life. Every day he was being reborn.

In due course the infection receded and his colour returned to normal. He was still gaunt and ghostlike but there was a sparkle in his eyes that told of the euphoria he was experiencing. Every day everything brought joy to him. He was enthusiastic and hungry for it all. Visitors were arriving to see him and his friends were writing and sending messages. One day someone rang up and asked to speak to him. On being asked who the caller was, the voice said, 'Sean Connery'. The nurse came hurrying into John's room to say that there was someone on the phone who said he was Sean Connery. When we nodded and said we would take the call, she was in shock to think she had been speaking to such an idol. The whole place was buzzing.

To the alarm of unsuspecting visitors, John enthusiastically showed off the gruesome scar in the shape of a Mercedes Benz badge that covered his torso. All and sundry were treated to the spectacle, however squeamish.

One day when I arrived he was gasping to tell me of the wonderful thing that had come to pass. He told me I would never believe it, as neither could he. What great event could this be? He was in raptures to tell me that at lunchtime he had been allowed to have biscuits and *cheese*! He said he felt like Ben Gunn. It was the first piece of cheese he had eaten in many years as, due to its protein content, it had been one of the banned foods that would have been too rich for his diseased liver to process. Sheer ecstasy! He had never tasted anything finer. He realized he could now eat anything he wanted.

One day I was helping him to change into a different shirt as he was still attached to drains and tubes. I was massaging his back when I suddenly became aware that his skin was clear. This time I told him that he would not believe what *I* was going to tell *him*. Your spiders have gone! We both gasped in disbelief. The rash of spider-like burst blood vessels that had covered his body in the years of his declining health, a recognized symptom of severe liver failure, had vanished.

Now he looked in a mirror and was astonished.

'I've been purged!' he shouted. 'I've been purged of my sins! Whoopee!'

He was soon up and dressed and sitting in a chair to watch the Cup Final, a bag of bones enveloped in a shirt of many colours.

Shortly after the transplant, Patsy Calne, Professor Calne's wife, came in to visit John and me, and she invited me to go for tea a few days later. She showed me the files of the research and history of transplantation in which she also had played her small part in the early days, supporting the pioneering research Roy had carried out in the field of organ transplantation. It was a truly heroic story of courage, integrity and persistent hard work. Originally pioneered in the United States of America, where Roy had begun his studies in transplantation, he returned to carry out, in 1968, the first liver transplant performed in Europe. Now, twenty years on, it was still relatively early days in which new developments were continually unfolding, with outcomes still unpredictable but exciting.

'Make the most of every day you have together as if it's your last,' Patsy advised me. 'Look on every day as a bonus.'

Survival for a transplant patient depends on a massive prescription of powerful drugs that are required for the rest of life. The primary health hazard is rejection of the organ and in order to combat that, the immune system has to be more or less dismantled. This in turn leads to the second greatest danger – increased vulnerability to infection. All the drugs have side effects which clash with each other to greater or lesser degrees but the most traumatic are steroids, which are needed in large doses, especially post-transplant. In the early days of recovery their effects were not too visible, however, and we knew not to look too far into the future.

We were not concerned with the future in any case. Those days we were living through were heady and full of promise. We had lived with death since we had been reunited in 1984. Now energy and optimism were flooding back.

The winter was over; the world was springing back to life. The cherry trees at the entrance to Addenbrooke's were storms of white blossom. The daffodils were giving way to tulips and bluebells, the trees were all green mist and, from the windows high up in the transplant ward we could see fields of rapeseed stretch out into the chrome yellow distance. The days were becoming longer and the golden light was perfumed with new growth. It was the perfect time of year to reclaim life. The sense of regeneration and rebirth was overpowering and we joyously allowed ourselves to be carried along in its momentum.

Five weeks after I had delivered John's cadaverous dying body to Addenbrooke's, I collected him from hospital, still with a line of access (in case of emergency) in his chest, and supported by sticks. I brought him back to the cottage in Buck's Lane, Little Eversden, where we had decided we would stay in the meantime. He had been offered follow-up care at King's College Hospital in London but we were glad to be able to opt for this to be carried out at Addenbrooke's instead.

We could scarcely comprehend the complete and dramatic turnaround of our circumstances. For John it must have been truly miraculous. For me, it seemed I had lived forever in ceaseless anticipation of John's imminent death and now here we were, facing away from death to embrace life. Crazily, all doubt had vanished and in its place surged an instinctive optimism that this overwhelming gift of good fortune would now be our forever.

At Long View, the cottage in Little Eversden just outside Cambridge, in the idyllic country lane with its Georgian farmhouse and quaint cottages among the cornfields, we were surrounded by birdsong and wildlife. We watched a flock of goldfinches playing in the long grass, searching out thistle seeds. There were no more shadows, only sunny days, bright fresh colour and abundant life.

The transitional existence of a recuperating invalid was not to be for John. Life was eager to get hold of him once more and the feeling was mutual. While he was still weak and fragile, and before he really knew what was happening, he was caught up in the whirlwind of his new life. Chapter Two had really begun and we hit the ground running.

After John got out of hospital on the Friday afternoon, Roy Calne was on the doorstep the next morning eager for the painting lessons John had promised him. If his consultant surgeon approved of such a brazen resumption of life, then the way forward was clear. We lost no time in accepting our friends' Joan Bakewell and her husband Jack's invitation to dinner in the garden of their nearby country cottage and a couple of weeks later we found ourselves in the best seats at David Bowie's concert in London, where we met up again with Pamela and Billy Connolly, who enquired whether onions had been served with the new liver too. We were invited to dinner at Trinity Hall, one of the Cambridge colleges where Roy was a senior fellow. This quickly led to that college appointing John a Fellow Commoner, an honorary fellowship subsequently also awarded to Terry Waite after his release from capture in the Middle East.

At the end of June, four weeks after John had left hospital, we briefly returned to London for the evening to attend the opening of the Late Picasso show at the Tate, where we happily met up again with all our friends. While my fear of infection was real, neither of us could contemplate anything going wrong now with what John called the 'new Rolls Royce engine' inside him. Our happiness was sublime. A truly modern miracle.

CHAPTER 51

Chapter Two

In mid-November, seven months after the transplant, the exhibition was to open in the Hamburg Kunsthalle, hosted by the director Werner Hofmann. We were there for the occasion, after which we travelled to Berlin. Anya was with us and we made a memorable visit to the Berlin Wall. The weather was below freezing and the stark snowy scene was at its most powerful as we watched rabbits play in the icy stretches of no man's land between the barbed-wired barrier walls. Only one year later it fell to the sounds of angry jubilation on both sides.

John and I remained in Berlin for a further few days and travelled on the U-Bahn through to Friedrichstrasse in East Berlin, where we met up again with Ekkehardt Schall and Barbara Brecht at a performance by the Berliner Ensemble of *The Threepenny Opera* at their theatre where they performed a steady programme of Brecht's repertoire. After the performance we had dinner with them and the cast, and by the time we thought about returning to West Berlin we found that we had overrun the curfew. Our U-Bahn station for returning west would now be closed. There was panic as we had no permission to stay in the east. Our hosts bundled us into a nearby Trabant and made for Friedrichstrasse in the hope of getting us on some kind of train back. No luck! Our plight had all the drama of a John le Carré film as we screeched our way round corners and made for Checkpoint Charlie, our last hope. The family and friends of

Brecht and indeed the cream of the art world in East Germany were the elite, as was the way in Communist countries, and so, with the intervention of Ekkehardt Schall, we were favoured in being allowed, after a wait of half an hour or so in the freezing cold, to be put on to a worker's train back through to the west, arriving at our hotel there well after 2 a.m.

In August 1988 we were back in Edinburgh for the Festival and greedily lapped up the delights on offer. One of the highlights was our introduction to the Ninagawa Theatre of Japan, in which the leading actor of their performance of *The Tempest* was Haruhiku Joh. Several portraits later our friendship was well established. John Adams' opera *Nixon in China* was being premiered and Muriel Spark was being feted at Demarco's gallery. Everywhere you looked, inspiration abounded and into the bargain the preparation for John's 1986 retrospective travelling to Dortmund was well underway.

In December of 1988 there was a memorable moment when we were introduced to Dr Jean Borel, the Swiss scientist who had made the discovery of cyclosporine, the immunosuppressant that had been such a breakthrough in organ transplantation and which was keeping John alive. His monumental work in the field of immunosuppression meant not only that John's new liver would have a fair chance of not being rejected but that thousands of other people's lives would similarly be transformed and saved. This modest unassuming man, being an amateur painter like Roy Calne, only wanted to talk to John about painting. Years further on, our friendship endures and the uses of cyclosporine have been extended to other forms of medicine and its effects now are truly manifold.

We celebrated the passing of the year 1988 at our friends Janet and Patrick Caulfield's Hogmanay party. The theme was scarlet. Scarlet for life. Scarlet for passion. Scarlet for beating hearts. What a year it had been!

Among all the whirlwind of activity there were constants. Hospital check-ups were regular, advice was given and all of it adhered to. Of course we respected the importance of this, and no venture was considered that might put at risk the phenomenal gift of a second life John had been given. Nor did he want to jeopardize the efforts of pioneers like Roy Calne and Jean Borel and all the expertise of the medical and nursing personnel who had given him so much. John always sought the advice of the transplant team, albeit generally in the spirit of 'We are going to Los Angeles. That OK?' but we were never advised against any pursuit of pleasure. To the contrary.

'Go! Live for the day!'

John had been invited to visit the British School at Rome for a few days. He was accompanied by the printmaker Alistair Grant, and while he was away I spent an afternoon with Juliet's mother Margaret, visiting the Edinburgh Dovecote Tapestry Company's exhibition near Trafalgar Square, where there was on view a commissioned tapestry of one of John's large paintings, 'The Pianist', that had been created by the celebrated master weaver, Harry Wright.

Margaret was a truly remarkable woman whom I was instantly drawn to and grew to love. I marvelled at her warmth and generosity of spirit to me. She was the most loving and open-minded person. She adored John and never wanted to lose touch with him. Not only was she fond of him but he encouraged her to keep drawing and painting, and this gave her a purpose, one that brought her great pleasure and fulfilment. Her open acceptance of all that had happened was astonishing to me. The sadness of Juliet's death was softened by her gratitude that, after a lifetime of extreme mental distress, her daughter was finally at peace.

Openings of exhibitions, including those of Sidney Nolan and other friends, dinners and lunches and all sorts of other events crowded our days and nights with enjoyment. Then at the beginning of February John was invited by Roy to observe a transplant operation. I was doubtful if he could cope with seeing such a procedure but this was the new life, under new management, and not only did he attend but he also produced a series of moving drawings and etchings of the transplant of a nine-year-old boy, Robert Blades, whom we would subsequently visit as he recovered in Addenbrooke's.

Every day brought pleasures great and small. Letters arrived awarding life membership of the Chelsea Arts Club or a commission of a portrait of an inspirational person or an invitation for John to contribute to a radio or television discussion on the arts. In March we went to Paris with Roy and Patsy to see the Gauguin exhibition at the Grand Palais and while there we were entertained at the home of one of the leading European transplant surgeons in the company of others, some of whom had been trained by Roy and for whom John was a proud example of clinical success.

One of the major excitements at that time was the making of *The Heart of the Matter* – an hour-long BBC2 feature about John and his dramatic transplant. It was introduced by Joan Bakewell as part of her series on social issues and was an emotional and inspirational film shown on Easter Sunday that year, almost exactly a year after the transplant. The story was told with the focus on John's positive and life-affirming approach, with the emphasis on how his creativity carried him through the experience, defining its emotional and profoundly spiritual triumph.

There is a strict code of conduct followed in the procedure of a transplant operation, as there is in regard to any surgical treatment. Every aspect of the patient's health is first examined and tested and taken into consideration. Physical and psychological responses are monitored and probabilities are assessed in an attempt to make a general prediction of the patient's ability to survive the operation. Every detail is talked through with the patient and the family concerned. There is one crucial omission to this. There is never, at any time, any reference made to the donor, without whom this life-saving opportunity cannot take place. For sound ethical and personal reasons recipients are not allowed to know anything at all about the donor and vice versa. The occasion of the operation is not the time to reflect on this. All efforts are then concentrated on the survival of the recipient and getting through the whole trauma of the event. But in the quiet times, particularly at moments of surging happiness at the great turnaround of events in our lives, we thought of the donor and the bereaved family. At many such moments, and on anniversaries or birthdays that would never have happened, we thought silently about the gift that was given to John and therefore to us all, the gift that was borne out of another family's grief. It was never forgotten. It was always remembered in private thanksgiving.

On 23 April 1989 John's 1986 Scottish National Gallery of Modern Art retrospective opened in Dortmund and on the first anniversary of the transplant we were flying back home from the United States, where we had spent a week visiting the Goya Exhibition at the Metropolitan Museum, hearing the wonderful Jessye Norman sing at the Carnegie Hall and Pavarotti and Kathleen Battle at the Met, having tea at the Plaza, dinner at Les Pleiades and caviar at the Russian Tea Rooms.

Back home, in Eversden, we moved across into the old schoolhouse in Bucks Lane opposite Long View. In one corner of the building was the separate dwelling of Sarah Webb, her small stature more than compensated for by her large personality.

Sarah had lived in the Eversdens all her seventy plus years. She loved to regale us with her family history, about her mother who had died when she was young, her father whose name was King Webb, her brother who had been the black sheep, and her cousin Edgar who cycled to see her every week.

Sarah had been very attentive in asking about John's progress while he was in hospital, this preceded by a battering on the door, usually before I was up in the morning. The first time I was baffled about where the noise was coming from, as looking out the glass window of the front door I could see no one. Opening the door there she was, a tiny bent-over figure peering at me through her thick glasses. 'Ew's yor 'usband?' she would ask and then launch into a stream of the latest gossip. I got to know more than was strictly necessary about the sex lives of all in the vicinity, including that of their dogs and cats and pigs. No juicy detail omitted.

Once John was out of hospital she trailed across the lane every Sunday with a plate laden with 'chicken thois, tatoes and veg'. 'Here's some dinner for 'im', she would say, listing everything on the plate. 'E needs proper looking after, e does', her assessment of my looking-after-abilities barely disguised in her expression. There was never any dinner for me, mercifully, and never any mention of one.

Now we were living in the schoolhouse she sometimes joined us for a cup of tea in the overgrown garden. On one occasion a friend who was visiting her from the village joined us and after a while chatting about this and that, the friend got up to go.

'Bye bye, me duck, see you next Thursday.'

'Bye, Sarah, take care, dear.'

Before the friend had made a couple of steps in the direction of the gate, Sarah's voice rang loud and clear: 'She's had *three children*. One from her *father*, one from her *brother* and the other one from the *old boy what lived next door to her*.'

Sarah took the bus into Cambridge market once a week but other than that had been nowhere else. She did not even seem to be familiar with Royston, a small town about four miles away. One exception to this was when she had been taken with the choir to sing at Westminster Abbey in London while she was still a schoolgirl.

Her life had revolved around looking after her father and brother until subsequently she worked in service for a pair of farming brothers who owned the house we all lived in. When the shooting was on, she would hide her favourite pheasants in her tiny room until the guns were quiet again. 'You stay in 'ere with me, mite, till them guns are gone,' she would say to 'Benny' or 'the Parson' or 'Oswald'.

Now and again John drew her. She sat in her little dark room with her window looking out on to the vivid green of the summer woods from where she watched the birds and wildlife. The low-ceilinged room was furnished with a cluttered table, her easy chair near the comfort of the Aga. A considerable proportion of the remaining space was occupied by an enormous prickly cactus that flowered gloriously once a year, nourished by its diet of tea, porridge and whatever else it was administered. Through from this room was a small, even darker bedroom. There was a sink somewhere with a cold-water tap and a toilet and that was it.

Her lifeline was Fred, who lived along the lane with his family. He and the milkman were the mainstays of her well-being, bringing most things she needed. She was a steady fixture at the local cricket pitch at the far end of Bucks Lane, where she always won the prize for best supporter.

It was a long time before she would admit to the open tumour on her chest and when she was finally diagnosed with breast cancer her GP asked her why she hadn't shown it to him far sooner. She replied that she wasn't going to show him her private parts if he wasn't going to show her his!

At the end of June, just after returning from the Basle Art Fair, we made our first-ever visit to Italy. This was our first conventional holiday. Taking Anya with us we rented a villa for two weeks at Segromigno in Monte in the foothills of the Apennines just to the east of Lucca. Was our appreciation of Italy enhanced by the fact we were well into our forties before we encountered sites of historic beauty and wonder that students and tourists generally sample at much younger ages?

The country seemed to be overflowing with colour, sunshine and light, luscious with plant life, fruit and exotic vegetables and, of course, all the food and wine for which it is celebrated. There was something supremely benign and carefree about the atmosphere, blowing away the shadows of gloomy London years. Florence showed us the masterpieces we had feasted on only in books and we marvelled at the magnificence of its historic churches and palaces. We also explored the countryside around Siena, San Gimignano, Pisa, and one day we followed the River Serchio up the valley that ran right up between the Apuane and Apennine Alps. We reached Castelnuovo di Garfagnana, which during the hours of siesta appeared like a deserted ghost town.

After a snack, we turned round and retraced our way back down the Serchio valley to Lucca. Five minutes out of Castelnuovo we must have swung round a corner passing a bridge off to the left that took a road winding up to several medieval villages along the mountain side.

Although it would have been hard to miss, we probably did not register the large stone house on the hillside up above the bridge, but I like to think that it saw us.

CHAPTER 52

Loss and Life

Although our joy about John's second chance at life continued, once our new normality was established we also had to deal with the sorrows that inevitably come as the price of loving others. At times our lives seemed, in the space of a day, to plunge from the heights of the absurdly frivolous to the depths of black despair.

There was the invitation to the Buckingham Palace Garden Party to which Jonathan delivered us in his rusty Cortina, drawing up to a screeching stop at the gates for us to enter. Next day a call came from Jeanne Gordon. Her husband Mel, one of John's closest friends, had gone missing. Apparently he had been suffering from depression and after leaving home in agitation, had not returned. At first we were not unduly alarmed, assuming it was just due to a quarrel that would resolve itself.

The weather had been relentlessly hot that July and would remain so for weeks to come. Clapham Common was burnt dry as I walked over to Jeanne's house on the other side. She was fearful that there was something wrong and had already reported him missing, but after the most obvious leads had been followed there was nothing else to do but wait.

Almost three weeks later on 31 July 1989 Mel's body was found in Isabella Gardens in Richmond Park. He had killed himself on 13 July, the day he had vanished. Mel, the reliably constant life and soul of any gathering, had been an attentive companion to John, part of the boozy circle of friends who kept pace with him through thick and thin; Mel who had been kind to John's long-suffering children on their Saturday visits; Mel, friend to all, could no longer play the game and had opted out. There was no note left and none of us would ever know why.

In August we found respite and inspiration at the Edinburgh Festival once more, which as usual was milling with the great and the good. Edna O'Brien, of the lyrical word and the beautiful voice, made a visit to our flat and had her portrait painted. One of the Festival highlights of that year was a performance of *Salome*, which dazzled John into a series of extraordinary paintings and drawings. In November we were off to New York again, staying with our friends and collectors Bob and Susan Summer, where, early on 9 November, we were wakened by a phone call from Scotland.

It was John's sister Margaret. Their mother had died suddenly and unexpectedly. She had just spent a spell in hospital for investigations into a suspected cancer shadow on her lung. She died one day after her seventieth birthday. By midday we were on a plane back to the UK, stunned by the news.

This was 9 November 1989, a momentous day in the history of Europe. This was the day that the Berlin Wall came down, bringing a great surge of hope of democratic freedom. The joy and excitement of this extraordinary event was in stark contrast to the devastating grief for John and Margaret, and the rest of our family, at losing their mother.

We drove to Scotland for the funeral and ten days later 20 Golf Drive was cleared and handed back to the council to be re-let. The paintings in the garage had fortunately already been removed for John's 1986 retrospective. Such were the harsh practicalities that saw the warm and loving family home, at a stroke, cease to exist and that whole part of John's life was consigned to memory.

On 1 December, back in London, we moved on in our lives by moving back into 2 Windmill Drive. The house had come back on the market after being completely updated and developed, and now the cellar that the boys had used for playing their electric guitar and drums had been extended and opened up to form a basement room with a galleried dining area above. On seeing the house again, John decided that this basement room would be a perfect studio for him. Everything was fresh, light and attractive – not a brown cigarette-stained wall anywhere to be seen – and the stairs were now carpeted all the way up to the top. We agreed that the comfort and convenience of this much-loved house could not be resisted. We would buy it. It was going back, which they say should not be done, but we had already gone back, to each other, and that, we agreed, was the best decision we had ever made.

We knew the house and it held a significant period of John's personal history but among all the airy light innovation no trace, not even a splodge of paint on a floorboard, could be found anywhere. Almost echoing the demise of the family home in Golf Drive in Port Seton, all elements of previous occupancy had been wiped out. However, here, in this house surrounded by the stately trees and lakes and green stretches of Clapham Common, we would start again, creating the next episode of our history.

In 1990 there were exhibitions in Berlin, Glasgow, Bath and New York. Paintings were steadily being acquired by notable collectors in America and Europe, the Tate Gallery added to their Bellany collection and the Trondheim Museum in Norway bought the early diptych, *Homage to John Knox*, a sale that particularly pleased us as we believed that such a key early painting of John's had found the perfect home.

John was painting well during this time, always on a large scale, for example *Sabbath Vigil*. He was also much involved in contributing to Radio 4's Arts programme, *Kaleidoscope*, and similar programmes on television. We were whizzing around to Glyndebourne, the Aldeburgh Festival, Berlin, the Chicago Art Fair and Washington to stay with friends and to see the *Matisse in Morocco* exhibition at the city's National Gallery. We went to Amsterdam and for a holiday in Portugal with Jonathan and Anya and to New York for John's exhibition opening at Ruth Siegel. While in New York we attended our friend Susan

Summer's lavish birthday party in the half-built grandeur of their country mansion in Connecticut and served as witnesses at our friends Paul Huxley and Susie Allen's surprise wedding at City Hall.

We were speeding along blissfully but came down to earth with a bang on hearing of the sudden death of our friend Peter Fuller, the art critic and writer, in a road crash. He had been in the process of writing a book about John's work and a photograph had just been taken by Lord Snowdon for an article about this in the *Sunday Telegraph*. The photograph was spectacular. Snowdon had demanded an enormous halibut (king of fishes) to be flown down from Shetland that day and John was posed holding it, wearing his trademark black Borsalino hat, for all the world looking like the conquering hero proudly returning with the spoils of war brandished on his shoulder.

Peter Fuller was with us, enjoying the commotion as the photograph was being taken, and left just before we packed up for the day. He vanished out of the front door on to Clapham Common to get his cab, calling over his shoulder as he took his leave to remind us that we would meet up in two days' time. We never saw him again.

That autumn, death remained in the air as towards the end of October our cat Korky, who had lived her life almost totally confined to our small flat in Albert Palace Mansions, joined John's cat, Craigie, as they both were put to sleep. One morning I had come down and found Craigie lying breathing her last on the kitchen floor. Korky, never the friendliest cat, had for some time shocked people by her matted coat and her horror-movie appearance as she tottered around like a wraith. When the vet came, it was decided it would be kinder to let her go with Craigie, as her life now had no quality.

Later that same day I had to drive John up to Cambridge to a dinner at Trinity Hall. We felt the loss of our old cats keenly. I delivered John to college and decided I would go to visit Sarah, who had been taken into hospital in the city earlier that week. When I got to her bedside, I saw that she too was on her final journey. A few weeks earlier, in the aftermath of a cancer operation, she had been taken away from her cottage in order to receive the care she required. She was admitted to a nursing home in Toft, a village only a couple of miles from Little Eversden, but there, worlds away from the freedom of her wild flowers and pheasants, chicken thighs and gossip, she switched her light off and turned her face to the wall.

I stayed with her all evening and just before I had to leave to collect John she passed away. There was no family there for her and I don't expect that my presence would have been much comfort to her if she had known. She was alone as she had always been, and alone she took her leave of the world. I think, however, that she would have approved of her two black feline escorts, Korky on one side of her and Craigie on the other, as she made her way to the pearly gates.

CHAPTER 53

The Clock House

A new era in our lives began on 1 December 1990 when we moved in to the Clock House, the central part of a converted Georgian stable that had belonged to the Shortgrove Hall estate near Saffron Walden in north Essex. Its defining feature was the tall clock tower that dominated the building and from which a panorama of the surrounding countryside for miles around could be seen. The extensive gardens offered a haven only about twenty minutes from Cambridge and an hour from London.

When John had come out of Addenbrooke's to recover from his transplant operation, he had instantly fallen in love with the countryside around him. He quickly decided that we must buy a house in the area and he had set about searching. Cuttings from the local property pages had been sent to us by friends, one of which was of the Clock House. The photo did not do justice to the building, making it look like an army barracks, but its size interested John, so it had to be viewed. It was situated between Saffron Walden and the small village of Newport. Through an imposing wrought-iron gateway we followed a winding tree-lined drive crossing an old stone bridge over the River Cam and up to the top of the hill where we saw the weathervane of the clock tower gleaming in the sun.

This one visit was all it took and on 1 December we moved in. The plan was to divide our time between the Clock House and Windmill Drive. John instantly turned the large drawing room into his studio, its immaculate luxurious carpet just right for his turpentine, oil paints and ink, etc., bare, rat-infested floorboards most definitely being a thing of the far-distant past. We spent a lot of time gazing out of the windows to the extensive lawns surrounded by woodland. The pheasants were strutting along the old walls where the red berries of the cotoneaster glowed. The most astonishing feature of the garden was the yew bushes that had obviously been planted over a hundred years previously. Now they were almost surrealist in their size and shape, resembling giant Christmas puddings, especially with a dusting of snow on top.

The Shortgrove Estate had a long history going back to medieval times, first mentioned in the Domesday Book. It had changed hands many times and the stable, having lain empty for some years, had eventually been divided up into three households sharing the stable yard with two other converted barns. We had the middle section of the stable and this included the clock tower with its functioning clock running on its original mechanism.

The spring of 1991 began with a solo exhibition of John's work in the Fitzwilliam Museum in Cambridge. For this he painted two major Titian transcriptions and to our great delight his painting *Sarah Webb, daughter of King Webb* was bought for the Fitzwilliam collection. Sarah, enshrined forever in the annals of Cambridge life and art. She would have had a thing or two to say about that ... 'in with all them high and mighty'.

Exhibitions continued as usual and commissions for portraits included a couple for the National Portrait Gallery, one of Sir Roy Calne and the other of Lord Renfrew, master of Jesus College. The fellows of Trinity Hall asked John to paint Sir John Lyons, the master. I believe it was one of John's more interesting portraits but not being in the traditional academic style, it took the fellows a bit of getting used to in the great hall. Indeed it has only recently found its place there after a good few years in an outer corridor. Perhaps, apart from the lively colour, it might have been the indeterminate shape that seemed to be hanging up behind the subject that could not be accommodated, the shape that I knew to be one of the dresses of the master's glamorous French wife, Danielle, implying her sexy presence.

A great pleasure for both of us was when the Scottish National Portrait Gallery commissioned John to paint the composer Sir Peter Maxwell Davies, and he came to Windmill Drive for the sitting. One inspiring person inspires another and John was proud of the portrait which now hangs in Edinburgh. Max's strong sense of his own identity along with his self-effacing manner and lively interest in all aspects of humanity, stayed with us and left a warm impression on our lives, as did the meeting shortly afterwards with Picasso's friend and biographer John Richardson.

John was then off to Amsterdam with the young and energetic Tim Marlow on *Kaleidoscope* business, enjoying thoroughly the company and the chance to see that year's huge Rembrandt exhibition, a review of which he would contribute to the programme. Later we travelled to the north of Scotland, to have a small exhibition in Wick and to stay with our friend Dick Zeisler from New York at Keiss Castle, the home of his childhood sweetheart, Dixie Millar from Columbus, Ohio. Returning to Edinburgh we joined the whirl of social occasions with friends old and new.

Life was full, full of inspiring people and exciting events.

While John followed faithfully all the medical advice given to him, we had no time to give to illness or even to think about it. It was a thing of the past. We could not believe the happiness we had regained, the closeness and the love we shared again after all we had been through. This life regained, however, had a way of allowing us almost dizzy moments of happiness immediately followed suddenly and unpredictably by disaster.

While out at the Cricketers in Clavering on 30 September 1991 celebrating Anya's twenty-first birthday, unknown to us an event was taking place far away in East Germany that would cause us immense distress and heartache.

The next morning the telephone rang. It was a red-top newspaper and with no preliminaries I was asked for a comment about our son Jonathan. In what respect? Well, a voice languidly informed me, just that he had been taken into custody in an East German town called Cottbus. The band of which he was a member had had a gig there the previous night. There had been trouble and an East German youth had been stabbed and was now in a critical condition. Five young men had been arrested, including Jonathan.

The music stopped.

John armed himself with paintbrush and disappeared into the studio, leaving me to get on with it. It had always been like that and probably for the better, as his reserves of patience were limited.

While still in shock I quickly made contact with the British Consul in Berlin and got his version of events. He put me in touch with an organization called Prisoners Abroad. From both those sources I received constructive advice and information to enable me to find out what had happened. In due course they also put me in touch with the East German solicitor who had been assigned to Jonathan's case. Paul was not a member of this particular band and so was not involved in the incident.

For years now both boys had been mixed up in something I could not understand and all the tireless efforts I had made to help them question their views had only ended up in fruitless exhaustion and depression. All three of my children had spent their adolescent years and more wringing out every drop of my energy. It had continued and grown force even while John was severely ill in hospital and now, notwithstanding their obvious happiness at the new chance he had been given to live and to have a reunited family once again, they were still continuing along roads that took them further away from all we could offer.

I had for years lived in hope that there would be a final crisis that would prove to be a turning point. It was a constant challenge to retain my belief in the good I knew was inside them. If my reactions had been different, either more detached or more authoritarian, then perhaps the whole thing would have petered out more rapidly. But for that to happen I would have to have been a different person.

What do you do in such circumstances? What can you do?

What was the point in trying any more to save them from themselves? They were adults and whatever cards they had been dealt in life, they had to be responsible for the decisions they made. This was something I could accept in theory but giving up trying and hoping is never an option. Every time a crisis occurred I tried to steer a way through it, get my breath back and carry on, each time a little more depleted than the last.

After talking with the British Consul and finding out the facts of the case, I quickly deduced that Jonathan was not guilty of the stabbing. I had never considered him capable of such a thing in the first place but, in the heat of the moment, among a peer group who would use violence as their first and only tactic, or in an effort to protect himself, anything could happen. I had to make sure also that the boy who had been stabbed was going to survive. It had been a clash between East German neo- and anti-fascists, and the ringleaders had been quick and vicious in their attack before escaping, leaving the British band members to be arrested.

That this was the case was fairly obvious from the start but fearing the current rise of neo-fascism in Germany, the authorities were anxious to be seen to prosecute and to demonstrate their hard-line approach. We did not send bail money or offer help, as we expected the case to be heard within the following weeks. Anyway, what was the use of doing anything in support at this time? If Jonathan continued to choose such company and such activities then what more was there to be said? Being locked up in an unfamiliar country unable to communicate and with no idea of a possible release date would not be an easy experience but there was a vain hope that it might prove salutary.

The lengthy preparations for the court case got underway, but dates set for a hearing were cancelled at the last moment. After a few weeks, as it was unclear when the case would be heard, we sent the bail money. Then bail was refused. The case was to be heard, a new date was given and we were advised to attend, as the outcome was uncertain. One of the options was that the case would be held over indefinitely, as there was a significant lack of incriminating evidence, but this was outweighed by the desire and need to prosecute.

We did not talk about this to many of the family or friends. We were appalled and unable to comprehend, or help anyone else to comprehend, what the boys were involved in.

In the middle of November John and I flew to Berlin, where we met the British Consul. We had been advised that the case was to be heard at last and we were given a rough idea of the procedure of the East German courts. He stressed that in spite of the fact of our son's obvious innocence of the specific charge there was no guarantee that the case would be dismissed. The Consul had made an appointment for us to meet Jonathan's solicitor, who was based in Cottbus.

It was an early start, before daybreak the following day, 20 November, as Cottbus was far away on the Polish border and the train journey would take about three hours from Berlin. The hearing was to take place at 10 a.m.

There was a bitingly sharp frost as we changed trains around the halfway point. Other people are a fascination and often a welcome distraction as they unknowingly wander into our lives. Waiting with us were a little girl in a fluorescent shell suit holding her mother's hand, an older man with his dog, young boys with trainers and tracksuits and cigarettes, and an elderly couple with heavy bags on their backs: a typical railway station scene but in an alien landscape. These ordinary lives went on in parallel with ours, but none of those people knew what our mission was that day. Perhaps they had much more serious concerns.

My spirit as I travelled through the endless pinewoods of East Germany on this day was as flat as the landscape we were passing through and I was numbed by fear. I wanted so much to be back in our own familiar surroundings with all being good with those I loved. How on earth had our lives brought us to this place?

After we arrived in the dreary industrial town of Cottbus, a taxi delivered us to the courthouse, where we waited and waited. Eventually, after much telephone activity, we were informed that the case had been postponed at the last minute – again – as only two out of the five accused had turned up in court. The others had jumped bail and stayed away. We managed to bring forward our appointment with the solicitor, a pleasant young woman who gave the impression of labouring under an unworkable system that, especially in the aftermath of unification, lacked structure, cohesion, and most of all, money. After a long discussion she arranged for us to visit Jonathan, who had no idea we were there.

My first act had been to establish the facts: that Jonathan was not guilty, that he was safe and also that the East German boy was out of intensive care and expected to make a full recovery. I had not, however, had the inclination to contact Jonathan. What was there to say? I had said everything. Over and over again.

After a few weeks I had received a long letter from him. We had always been close. He had borne so much, far too much, when he was only a small boy and we had always had a close and honest bond. In this letter he declared, at last, that this, for him, was the point of growing up and changing for the better. He would make me proud one day. It was a promise.

There are so many troubles that individuals have to face in this world which render our day in Cottbus a mere picnic; however, I never want to experience anything worse than having to visit my own son in prison.

The prison in Cottbus was as all prisons are – and who would know better than me – grey, grubby, comfortless, devoid of hope and humanity except in the most meagre and deprived form. The light was beginning to fade when Jonathan was brought in to a small waiting room. He was overcome with the surprise of our presence and all of us were blinded by the grim awfulness of the occasion. For a long time we sat, all three of us, tearful, unable to speak.

That evening as we returned to Berlin, leaving him there in prison, despite our physical and emotional exhaustion, we felt more optimistic about him than we had for years. Seeing him there was unbearable and leaving him there was worse but we had seen someone who had, in a desperate situation, given himself time to think about who he really was and what he wanted from life, and who finally realized that there was another better way to go. I did feel that the turning point had been reached but only time would tell.

On 7 December we were back in Berlin. The whole process was running out of steam and the case had been postponed until the spring, when Jonathan would be required to return. It had been suggested that if we paid an amount of money to the court then the whole thing would be wound up. I was not prepared to do that, as I feared possible future implications of guilt where there was none. It was agreed that if there was another court appearance he would attend. In the meantime he was told to get his things. He would come with us. He had been in Cottbus for more than two months and we all wanted him home.

It was dark by now, the blackness of the journey punctuated by flashes of festive decorations in the passing houses. It was a long weary way back to Berlin, which, when we got there, sparkled with Christmas light and bonhomie, reflecting, even in our exhaustion, the warmth and relief of being close, all three of us, and in a better place, together again.

A nightmare was receding with the passing of this day. Surely now our sons would finally emerge from the darkness in which they had submerged themselves and instead invest their energies in more positive aspirations. Above all things I hoped they would find again the place they had come from and get back in touch with the people they truly were.

CHAPTER 54

Travelling

In the following months correspondence from the solicitor in Cottbus dwindled but the issue continued to hang over us for some time. She had always made it clear that there was never a shred of evidence against Jonathan but that it was common in the GDR for cases to be kept in limbo indefinitely and nothing much had changed in this respect since reunification. Eventually it just faded away. It was never formally concluded but she informed us that in her opinion no further action would be pursued. It meant that the nightmare years would now also fade away at last for everyone in the family, as both our boys dramatically turned onto new paths forsaking all that they had been caught up in. They didn't look back and neither did we. The future was better for all of us.

In March 1992 John and I set off on a trip round the cities of the former Iron Curtain countries which lasted for over a month. This was a project aided in a small way by the British Council. We had been given the use of an artist's studio apartment in Vienna as our base camp and from there we set off in our hired car armed with only the most basic map. It was an adventure for gap-year students and we relished the view of worlds we knew of mostly from newsreels and novels.

We saw the elegance of Budapest alongside the destitution of its flea market of rags and rubbish; the enchantment of Prague with its crowded Charles Bridge; and the heart-stopping beauty of Dresden, its history shamefully raw and the wounds of World War Two still not properly healed. In Dresden much had been done and we were proudly shown what had been achieved and restored. The Frauenkirche was almost ready to be rededicated and the museums were rich in treasures but the tragedy underlying Dresden still seemed to linger as a terrible reminder of the nightmare of war.

Just outside Prague we drove one day to Terezin, the former concentration camp that had been used during the war as a flagship exhibit in an effort to conceal the pervading evil of such places. The small town comprised several long straight streets that still seemed to be inhabited but it was melancholy in its silence and stillness. The camp was on the edge of the village and had been preserved well enough to evoke the sinister madness of its purpose and the eeriness of its environment.

After leaving Dresden we had intended to visit Halle, the birthplace of Handel. I was excited to see where John and Sandy and Al had been in 1967 when they were guests of the GDR at the Halle Festival. We had intended to find somewhere to stay for the night so we could explore the town and visit the places they had visited but the view we were given of the outer suburbs was a scene of the utmost desolation bathed in a sour air of defeat. We were tired and fled to Leipzig. This I regret as I never saw anything to tell me of their experience in that communist time.

Although since the transplant John had taken on the life of a normally healthy man, he was robust only in spirit. The life we were leading demanded stamina for those in the best of health and he tired easily, but his will always found a way to keep up the pace as much as he could. There were good days and bad days but he made little of any discomfort or weakness. There was too much exciting, stimulating living to get on with. Most people do not possess his courage and appetite and few who did not already know would have guessed how vulnerable was his daily life. The show had to go on and it would last as long as he could make it, and I was in total agreement with that.

Vienna was an oasis of art. The Kunsthistorisches Museum, which we visited time and time again, blew us away with its comprehensive collection of European masterpieces, especially their Pieter Breughels, all of them major favourites of ours. There were also the drawings and prints in the Albertina. It was a visual feast. Living in Vienna we enjoyed the romance of the bevelled glass, polished brass and mahogany of the cafés imbued with their history of turn-of-the-century Viennese bohemia. In our minds we saw Egon Schiele, Gustav Klimt, writers, musicians and architects, come and go.

All the while the pencil, watercolours, oil and canvas were in action and the evidence can now be found around the world as well as in our own collection.

On our return to London I was to learn of the death of my beloved Auntie Mary and I went back to Golspie to see her laid to rest in the churchyard at the top of the brae in the fields beneath Ben Bhraggie with her brother-in-law, my father, and her mother and father lying nearby, to be joined in future years by her sister, my mother.

A few weeks later we were off to Italy. It was Susan Summer's fiftieth birthday and she and Bob had flown across from New York and invited a large number of friends to be guests for a week in an hotel in Forte dei Marmi, the upmarket resort on the Mediterranean with the marble peaks of the Apuane towering in the background. It was exotic fun and games and we had no inkling then that this place of beauty with its umbrella pines and oleanders would become familiar ground in years to come.

Over time, John had perfected the practice of turning night into day. This had taken root in the largely solitary life he lived when only alcohol was his steady companion. The resulting ill health had exacerbated the anxieties of the dark hours and now post-transplant he continued, if possible, to sleep the morning through.

One November morning I picked up the post from the front door; seeing a white envelope sent from the Prime Minister's office I couldn't think what it could contain. We were used to being invited for drinks at official functions so I thought it must be something like that. Or most likely something in line with the letters from Her Majesty's Service that used to bear nothing of any good, tax demands and the like, so I thought John should be wakened up to open it.

After stretching and groaning and complaining, he managed to focus on the letter and tore it open apprehensively.

'Bloody hell! I've been given an OBE,' he shouted. 'Whoopee!'

Totally dumbfounded, we could only laugh in disbelief.

Both his mother and father were gone. This was another thing that, after all the worrying years they'd had with John, would have amazed and delighted them and I wished they could have known this news.

'I'm telling my mother,' I said.

'Not supposed to tell anyone it says.'

'I'm telling her this.'

I dialled her number and he read the letter, still in shock, for a second time.

I was busy telling her the news when he yelled in the background, 'It's not an OBE! It's a f****** CBE!' Great guffaw of astonished laughter.

John had no trouble in accepting. The possibility of such a thing had never crossed our minds, as the honours system was not something that entered our consciousness. Such qualifications were irrelevant, especially in the world of creativity, but the joy of being given such a vote of confidence was supreme, as it would be for anyone in whatever field. For him it was a spur, especially on days of struggle. He loved the fuss of pomp and circumstance and was warmed by the wholehearted support from fellow artists.

Those years brought accolades and honours, gifts and goodwill in abundance. Not a month went by without something turning up to delight and invigorate us. In our first life together we had had nothing and then, in times of desperation, John would always invoke Mr Micawber in his belief that something would turn up. It generally did, usually in the shape of a borrowed fiver, and we were thus able to breathe for the moment again. Now Mr Micawber was triumphant and delights great and small regularly surprised us.

The greatest joys were personal ones, as in the gradual reunification of our whole family. Witnessing our children finally finding their way through the desolation of their youth to make good lives brought by far the most profound happiness. In my eyes the miracle that they did turn their lives around, in spite of everything, by their own efforts, to make full use of their potential as good people with warm and generous hearts, is the source of my greatest pride.

It took courage for both boys to forsake lives that had given them some kind of identity and structure, when they had felt they had nothing to hold on to. I still do not fully know how they achieved this. I do not want to know. I am proud of the fact that both boys had the strength to do so and to turn around and begin again – as John and I had.

In June 1995 John and I were present in the cobalt-blue reflecting glory of Liverpool's Catholic Cathedral to watch Anya in her graduation gown collect her first-class degree in History of Art and Classical Literature. Another unbelievable and emotional moment for all of us. Through her own hard work and her natural ability she had defeated the self-doubt and negativity that goes with dyslexia and with constant encouragement and dedication she had climbed to the top.

What right had we to be playing the role of proud and happy parents when we had messed up so badly? We were proud of all of our children, seeing them gradually find happiness and fulfilment by their own efforts. We were, at the same time, feeling the bonds of the family circle strengthen in warmth and love. Of all the great things that had come our way since John and I had become reunited, that was the best in the world, our greatest and most enduring reward – to be able to luxuriate in warm family unity for the rest of our lives.

CHAPTER 55

Mexico

Over the years we received a steady stream of mail of all sorts ranging from the seriously wacky and brazen fakery to the innocent and sad. Genuine letters often came with encouraging information and strange surprises that caused excitement and sometimes almost disbelief.

One such missive arrived in the spring of 1996, forwarded from John's London gallery, Beaux Arts. It was a letter from a Mr Christophe Armero from Mexico City. Seemingly he had begun to collect John's work on visits to London. He believed that the vibrant culture and heritage of Mexico would interest and inspire John and so he was inviting us to be his guests for a few weeks in that country. He would provide the hospitality and John would paint. That was the deal.

How wonderful!

What did we know about this Mr Armero of this spectacular offer? Nothing at all. Reg and Patricia Singh at Beaux Arts had met him once or twice when he had bought John's work but didn't know much about him and they had never mentioned him to us.

The lack of information did nothing to deter us or dampen our excitement, so on 31 October 1996 we found ourselves flying in to Mexico City. We had no idea who we were going to meet or what he looked like. Our assumption was that he was Mexican and so most likely dark-skinned and perhaps not

307

particularly tall. We had been told he was married and had three children but that's all we had to go on.

Our plane had landed a little early, so we waited in the arrivals hall for our host to appear. Like all airports it was buzzing with people purposefully making their way through the throng. Outside, cars and taxis were arriving and departing, all clamour and flashing lights. There was so much to see.

All of a sudden – 'You must be John and Helen Bellany! Chris Armero!'

Chris Armero? Tall and auburn haired and decidedly not Mexican!

Chris was young, in his thirties and spoke perfect English. He was Anglo Spanish and had been educated in England. He worked in Mexico for a multi-national company. He had a car and driver waiting for us and soon we were off through the city, making our way up the Paseo della Reforma to his home to meet his wife, Sue, and their three young boys.

It was crazy. We had landed at night, on Halloween, and this only accentuated our first impressions of the place. Skeletons and masked figures with candles appeared out of the shadows and disappeared as we crossed the city. Chris assured us that this was only the start. We were so excited to be in such an exotic place and meeting new people. We were exhausted by the long flight and energized in equal measure.

After dinner with the family we were driven to a house that we were going to have to ourselves for the duration of our visit. It was a few streets away in the same residential area. Like the home of the Armeros this was a detached house behind high security walls. It was explained to us that Mexico City had a high crime rate and such precautions were essential. We were advised not to walk anywhere but to use the car and driver Chris had put at our disposal.

We had immediately taken to our new friends and our first impressions had been warm and enthusiastic as we fell asleep that night. Next day the first thing I saw as I opened the curtains was a tiny hummingbird dancing from one flower to the next on the bougainvillea that covered the walls outside our window –

an omen of beauty and delight, a harbinger of the weeks to come.

On our arrival Chris had informed us that we would not have much time to recover from the flight as we were all going into the country the following day to take part in the traditional celebrations of the Day of the Dead. Later that afternoon we set off, leaving the city behind, our eyes feasting on everything – the villages with clusters of people in brightly coloured clothing, the run-down dwellings and dusty roads, and the arid landscape where cactus and vivid flowers bloomed in haphazard defiance. In the relentless sun rural poverty was evident everywhere, with groups of men bumping along in the back of open trucks, children playing and dogs running about. Vivid colour wherever we looked.

After a journey of about two hours, we arrived at our hotel and as night began to fall we set off again into the Michoacan countryside. All we knew of the Day of the Dead we had gleaned from the memorable novel *Under the Volcano* by Malcolm Lowry, which we had both read many years previously. It provided all the enticement we needed. The celebration, of course, has become a great tourist attraction but nevertheless it still managed to retain its mystery and deep spiritual significance at the time we were part of it and I believe this remains so today. But today, Chris assures me, there would be too much personal danger involved in revisiting the places we saw that night.

Mexico is a country predominantly and devoutly Catholic but with enduring foundations in pre-Christian religion. In Mexico there is all the magnificence and theatre of Catholic ritual, the splendour of its art plus the power and the mystery of the colossal pagan intelligence of pre-history.

Chris had been right. Of course John would respond to Mexico. Our senses were assaulted by the vibrancy around us of the buildings, the people's clothing, the flowers and vegetation, the street markets, the intricate craftwork on display, just a sense of being enveloped in the brightest colours of the spectrum and by such a medley of traditional music, dance, song and magic it was as if we were reconnecting with primitive forces that lie dormant within us all. As in all Catholic countries there is always a feast or a celebration to be had and the celebration is always full-blooded. Presbyterian celebration, on the other hand, always seemed to me to be characterized by humility and strict self-discipline and there was always something to abstain from or banish from thought. The Presbyterian way of death was compassionate and kind but always restrained, and the dead were decidedly restricted to their places among the shadows in the churchyard. Here though there was something life-giving in the way the Mexican Catholics venerated their dead. Their dead lived on. The Day of the Dead was a celebration of Life.

It was a still, calm evening and the sunset was dying away when we boarded a small boat to be taken across Lake Pátzcuaro to the Island of Janitzio. The ripples of the boat's wake, catching the rosy gleam of the sun's setting rays, startled a couple of large white egrets and as they rose from the still waters the beat of their wings above us was the only sound as we drew near the island. All we could see as we approached in the rapidly falling darkness was a rock formation reminiscent of Mont Saint-Michel in miniature, a somewhat dark pyramidal mass rising out of the water in candlelit shimmer and presided over by a dominating illuminated statue of José Maria Morelos, vastly out of proportion to the rocky island on which it rested. Morelos was born in poverty and became a revolutionary priest who subsequently assumed control of the Mexican Independence movement. He was a national hero.

As we disembarked on the island, its mysterious beauty revealed itself in the islanders' homes, which were decorated with garlands of yellow marigolds (the flower of mourning), lit only by candles, with a profusion of illuminated skeletons, masks and other fetishistic objects which enhanced the personal shrines that had been erected in honour of their departed loved ones. Each shrine was a personal testament to the particular person that had left the world, with a much-used pair of slippers or shoes, a favourite pipe and the preferred brand of tobacco, a necklace, a beautiful dress, sweets and favourite foods and beer and rum. There were skeletons sparkly and scary, sometimes formed in sugar and chocolate and other sweet stuff, sometimes clothed or wearing hats and sitting at the door or dangling from the ceiling. Talismans and good-luck charms in the departed one's life were also displayed. Surrounded by crucifixes were photos of all the dead family members who were expected to return to their homes again for that one night of feasting and reunion.

Although there was an element of performance contrived for visitors, there was undoubtedly a feeling of poignancy in the air, especially in regard to the recently bereaved. This, as the night progressed, gradually gave way to celebration. The celebration of life and the acknowledgement of death were seen as parts of the same journey.

It was impossible not to feel a sense of trespass as we climbed up the island but the islanders talked openly about their dead and told us about them; all of this Chris translated for us. They shared with us the sad story of their most recent loss, and enigmatic aspects of the ritual were explained for us. All the doors to the houses were left wide open to welcome the dead person and their way was well lit and strewn with marigolds in order to guide them home. Dogs were muzzled in case they did not at first recognize the loved one returning and so attacked them by mistake. The favourite chair was awaiting them with all the home comforts they had enjoyed in life.

As we left Janitzio in the boat and watched the island receding into the night, a swish of oars would draw our attention to a silent canoe gliding close by in the darkness, and thus we became aware of many other Indian canoes making their way soundlessly towards the island from all directions in the black waters.

To the cemetery on the other side of the water next, where by now the preparations for the feasting were well in hand. One grave was devoid of decoration and sparkle, where two young children sat in vigil at their mother's resting place with just a candle to light them through the night. Another grave was deserted but for a single child's shoe to indicate who lay within. There were many such graves of the destitute looked after by remaining family members and they were to be found in the darkest part of the cemetery in marked contrast to the lights and liveliness of the centre from where the music now blared, the wine began flowing and the festivities had begun. Food was offered to all whom the singing and laughter was beckoning and there was beer for the taking. It was now time to turn away from the sadness and to embrace all that was good in life again while the spirits of the much-loved departed were celebrated and lived on in remembrance and glory for those special hours of darkness.

The party would only end with the dawning of the new day. The Day of the Dead was a major event in the Mexican calendar but this country was full of ritual, full of Aztec significance that permeated so much of contemporary life. There were many more celebrations to come and more spectacles in this country that proudly perpetuated its rich mystery.

Back in Mexico City on the Sunday night, John was champing at the bit to get canvas and paint, so early next morning Chris took us into the city centre to an art shop. Driving through the city, dodging about in the four-lane highways, there was a spectacle to be witnessed on every corner, especially at the traffic lights. Within seconds of the lights turning red a human pyramid four or five high would be instantly assembled, all jugging and wearing masks of cartoon characters, current politicians and world leaders. Predominantly the Mexican president was featured in a mocking satirical charade and often accompanied by the likes of Bill Clinton and Boris Yeltsin. Within the time it took for the lights to change, money was collected from the drivers and the pyramid dismantled to wait for the lights to change back once more. Brilliant performance art, and an energetic but lucrative venture.

We had been told that there would be armed guards on duty outside banks in the city but it was startling to find them at the doors of the art shop as well. Any place where money changed hands needed protection, it was explained, even the humblest of businesses.

John stocked up with all that he needed. We now returned

to our house and set to dismantling the large dining room and making it into his studio. He was fired up and ready to go.

I wanted to see everything and so each day I asked the driver to take me into the centre, where above every municipal building there fluttered gigantic Mexican flags. He dropped me there while I visited the Zócalo, the grand square around whose extensive perimeters stood the cathedral, the National Palaces and museums which housed the great murals of Diego Rivera and paintings of Orozco, Siqueiros and Tamayo. John and I went together to see the paintings but I also wandered round often on my own.

One day Chris, John and I visited the famous Blue House in Coyoacán, the previous home of Frida Kahlo and Diego Rivera, which has been preserved as it was when they lived there. We also took a trip out of town to visit Teotihuacan, the ancient site of the pre-Columbian city of pyramids that had housed a population of hundreds of thousands of people. A place of incomparable wonder. There, in the month of November, there were few visitors so we wandered virtually alone in the great Avenue of the Dead, listening to the haunting playing of Mexican pipes in the distance. The sophistication of this multi-ethnic pre-Christian civilization, leaving aside their practice of human sacrifice, astounded us. How on earth had we come to believe that we, in the present day, had invented and discovered a superior way of life?

Chris and Sue and their children came with us at weekends and showed us more of the country. We visited Oaxaca, Cuernavaca and Puebla, a Spanish colonial city in the dusty volcanic countryside and home of the well-known Talavera ceramics, where Popocatepetl, the legendary and still active volcano, can be seen for miles around, releasing on the wind a constant ribbon of sulphurous ash. Sue and I drove to Taxco, the town of the silver mines. Everywhere we went there were markets selling exquisite hand embroidery and lace, wooden and ceramic wares, jewellery and every other possible craft of the finest handwork. The food stalls presented exotic food we had never seen, including a variety of edible worms and insects.

Chris and John flew to the west coast to visit the sugar fields and watch the dramatic burning of that year's crops. I was unable to go due to illness but John described it, telling me how deeply affected he was by what he had seen.

Chris took us to meet a retired university professor who had collected a comprehensive array of original Mexican masks and from him we absorbed their cultural significance and began our own collection that we brought home to the UK and which would feature in John's future work.

Festivals abounded, and we found the colour and sound of the Mariachi bands and the performances thrilling. One town we visited happened to be celebrating the fertility of the fish. As we watched the beginning of the ritual dance, the dance of the fishermen, I had to gasp as each fisherman emerged wearing a mask that bore striking resemblance to one Port Seton artist, down to the last detail, beard and all! John was dumbstruck!

All we saw fed into John's imagination and his work. Here he identified with the juxtaposition of the pious and the pagan, the sacred and profane. The colour and vibrancy inflamed him and the deeply primitive spirituality found resonance in his inner being. He painted with a fever and he wanted, above all things, to exhibit the work that he had completed before we left for home. Nothing unusual in any of that – John always wanted what he wanted today, not tomorrow. Chris obliged by introducing us to Maria Maldonada, who kindly rearranged her schedule so John could have his exhibition in her Galería Kin, situated in the San Angel area of the city, and John was well pleased.

Sometimes I went out on my own to the Tamayo Museum and the great Museum of Anthropology in Chapultepek Park. After a while, in the daytime, I went out on my own as I saw plenty of others doing. Outside the museums in the park I remember the Indian figure diving from the top of a tall pole to fly round and round, suspended by a rope, in mesmerizing circular motion, reminiscent of a bird of prey, accompanied by the melancholy strains of the pipes. The Voladores performance of a traditional ritual was made for a tourist audience but gave out a haunting echo of the pagan past.

A few days before we left Mexico, my last solo day out was to the Basilica of Guadalupe. Our Lady of Guadalupe is the patron saint of Mexico and the feast of Guadalupe was approaching. It is the major festival of the year and takes place on 12 December. For this event pilgrims travel from all over Mexico, many on foot. Arriving in hordes at the basilica many proceed to the interior of the holy place on their knees. Travelling through Mexico in the preceding days many pilgrims could be seen, days into their arduous journey towards the citadel, on foot, on horseback, motorbike and a variety of vehicles. To go there was to witness scenes of devout faith in a mass of believers, the like of which we, in our world, might only see at a football match or a rock concert. It was almost impossible to negotiate the crowds and it was only due to my guide's knowhow that I found myself in the queue to file slowly past the icon of Our Lady of Guadalupe. I was told that this long, slow-moving pilgrimage to her shrine is a daily event.

Just before Christmas our wonderful trip came to an end. We had already extended our stay and now it was sadly time to go. It had been an unforgettable time and the value to John's work was colossal. Our friendship with the Armeros was cemented warmly in our lives and our memories enriched for all time. It was now time to get back to our family, whom we were, by this time, missing badly.

Checking in at Mexico City airport, John suddenly and dramatically fell to the ground. Chris and I stood in shock while, over the tannoy, an urgent call was made for a doctor. Then everything spun into action. A wheelchair was rapidly brought to the scene and an oxygen mask clapped on to John's face before he was rushed through the crowds to the medical centre, with us trying to keep up behind him.

Because of the altitude of Mexico City, the air is thin and the pollution level is usually well over the safety limits. The pollution is so severe that children at nursery are not allowed to play in the open air on most days. We had been warned we might be affected by the high altitude and may feel unwell and breathless at times but John and I had thus far been unaffected and had therefore not given the problem any thought. But as we were about to board our plane home his blood pressure had suddenly plummeted, causing his collapse. Why it had done so was unclear.

What now? We had been all geared up for the long flight home, the stress of which may have contributed to John's condition. Now I assumed we would not be flying that day after all. We were badly shaken up and frightened. Since his transplant eight years previously, the condition of his health, although weakened, had been relatively steady. Perhaps we had even been beginning to take it for granted. This was a wake-up call out of the blue.

After about an hour on oxygen the monitors seemed to indicate that things were returning to what was normal for John. What was the advice? After some consultation, the doctor agreed we could fly and that John should be able to cope with the flight. There was oxygen on board should he require it and the crew would be informed.

Would we take the risk? He wanted to get home. He wanted to go. If he did, so did I.

Safely back home, Christmas was coming and our home was festooned with crazy Mexican masks; our talk was all of the wonders we had seen.

CHAPTER 56

Bonvoyagers

It was always a problem thinking about Christmas presents for men, especially fathers, and here was Jonathan asking advice as usual. What could he get John? Neither of us could think of anything. Then I remembered driving in Mexico. There was so much corruption in that country that when the police pulled you over on the highway, in order to save time and get to the point, it was best to just ask how much bribe money was required for whatever trumped-up offence they had in mind and hand it over so we could go on our way. In an attempt to reduce pollution, city dwellers were restricted to driving their cars for only two days per week in the city. The problem was simply sorted (if you had the means) by having two or three different cars. As for learning to drive, it was possible to buy a driving licence. I had at one point thought of buying one for John as a joke present.

Thus the idea came into my mind. Why did Jonathan not buy him one driving lesson? Had John ever expressed a desire to learn to drive? Never! After we got together again he did become very interested and knowledgeable on the subject of cars but still never indicated that he wanted to drive. He always maintained that the human race was much safer without him at the wheel. He was happy to be driven. How would he react to such a gift?

Christmas Day and the presents are being opened. Jonathan

hands John a small package and we all watch. He opens it, takes a look and puts it down on a table beside him.

'Thanks, son. Very nice.'

I ask him what Jonathan had given him.

'I don't know!'

'Well, look again!'

He opens the packet properly and out comes a copy of the Highway Code.

A bit bemused, he thanks Jonathan once more.

'That'll be to help with your back-seat driving,' says someone.

He puts the package aside and we ask if that's all there is. He is beginning to lose interest so we urge him to look again.

An appointment card for sometime at the end of January for – 'What's this? British School of Motoring?'

Exasperated by the suspense, Jonathan blurts out that it's an appointment for his first driving lesson. What has he got to say about that?

Disbelief, horror and a bellow of laughter!

We all laugh at the joke, as none of us really expects him to take this up. John is essentially lazy. All he wants to do is paint and he works hard at that. When he is not painting, he reads and takes a nap, and when he is doing none of these he loves watching football. Even to contemplate a driving lesson would be too exhausting. Or so we thought.

At the end of January a BSM car rolls up to the house and Mr Innocenti introduces himself. Just a trial run for Mr Bellany and then we'll see what to do next. Off John goes without any fuss. We expect that that will be it. End of the afternoon's outing, end of story.

John and Mr Innocenti hit it off big time and the driving lessons became social events much looked forward to. Every Wednesday of that year John and his buddy, Mr Innocenti, sailed forth on to the public highways with the L-plate blazing the way. At the end of that year a driving test was arranged following a theory test that had been passed successfully (did we ever hear the end of it?). He sailed through the driving test first time – 'a piece of cake!'

The very next day, with the ego of Toad of Toad Hall, he donned his best tweed coat and black hat and announced that he was going to London.

Alone.

In his car.

To the Royal Academy, in the centre of Piccadilly.

He had never driven in a city before, never mind London. We gasped at the very idea but he had no time to discuss the matter further. He was off! We watched his Jaguar purr through the gates and vanish off down the drive. Heaven help us – would we ever see him alive again?

This became his new passion. There was no stopping him. Before this new venture he loved to be driven about and was always wanting to go on little jaunts. On days when I had other things to do he used to complain that if I went out and left him in the rural isolation of the Clock House, even although he was painting, he felt imprisoned 'like Rudolf Hess!'

Now he was free. He could take off to London or even Scotland on his own. He was king of the road! Having appointed himself undisputed expert of the horseless carriage, he also became unbearably superior in his criticism of my driving. 'You didn't indicate early enough! You're following that car too closely! Slow down for f**** sake!' And so on.

This freedom could be a dangerous thing. If he went out to get a pint of milk (as if!) he might just come home having bought another second-hand car. And another. And another. All bargains! At one time we had five or six cars outside our house and one or other battery was always needing to be charged, having been left unused for too long at a time. One lifetime couldn't provide the energy or opportunity to drive them all regularly.

They all enjoyed luxury limousine status but it was the number of vehicles that alarmed the gamekeeper. He kept an eagle eye out for trespassers on the estate and so, on the sudden appearance of so many strange cars, the farm gates were shut without warning. Many collisions with those gates were narrowly avoided, especially in the dark. There were no lengths the gamekeeper and the self-appointed lord of the manor wouldn't go to keep out the spivs they imagined were trespassing and casing the joint or massacring the pheasants.

None of this bothered John in the slightest. As far as he was concerned there was nothing sweeter than cruising about the countryside in a posh limo. If he hadn't been able to do that in his earlier life, then he would make up for it now. And this we certainly did. It brought an enormous amount of pleasure to his life. We drove out together, seeing and talking and sometimes just thinking. His hand would reach out to take mine or he would often stroke the back of my neck. This for him was the epitome of happiness.

The nineties brought solo exhibitions far and wide – New York, Berlin, Brussels, Mexico, Boca Raton, Florida, Dublin – and we travelled to them all. At the same time there were invitations to participate in countless group shows all over the world.

In the UK the most memorable of the major solo exhibitions was the retrospective in 1992 in Kelvingrove Museum, *A Long Night's Journey into Day*, the fiftieth birthday tribute curated by Julian Spalding, the dynamic director of Glasgow Museums. It was a comprehensive overview of John's life's work including all the major paintings throughout the decades and featuring a concentration of work from the seventies. Like the great retrospective at the Scottish National Gallery of Modern Art in 1986, it had an impressive impact on those who went to see it, not least on John and myself.

Seeing again the paintings from the seventies took me back mercilessly to that dark time when our marriage was breaking down. For me they were raw and full of sorrow. They were hauntingly beautiful and vibrant with colour, and I saw them again on the walls of our flat in Lurline Gardens with our little children playing on the old red Turkish carpet in front of them. They were, undoubtedly, what he would call 'beezers', extraordinary works of full-blooded integrity and to know, all those years further on, that such personal anguish could bring forth such creative mastery was almost (almost) reward in itself.

In 1996 a major exhibition of the Summers' collection entitled

An American Passion was held at the Royal College of Art in London before it transferred to the MacLennan galleries in Glasgow, and formed a highlight of those days we shared with Bob and Susan. John always enjoyed a strong sense of identity and unshakeable belief in his own work but, as with all serious artists, self-doubt and self-criticism were also constant companions. Without all of those factors, great art can never be created. At the same time, people who understand and support what artists are trying to do provide the all-important confidence that must be kept afloat. Bob and Susan Summer were such people.

Freda and Izak Uziyel were another couple who, over the years, consistently gave strength to John. Izak was Turkish, from Istanbul. Freda was Polish and she had a twin sister, Eva, both very beautiful and striking women. Their lives had been indelibly tainted by the loss of most of their family members in the Jewish Holocaust of World War Two, and their story was illuminated by tales of courage and sadness that followed them throughout their lives. They were secular Jews and, like most people of their faith, highly cultured. They were life-loving and the best of company.

They drew us in to their inner family circle. We attended the spectacular weddings of their three daughters, which were held in the amphitheatre of Caesarea on the coast of Israel, Fiesole in Italy and at the Banqueting House in London. The rituals and customs of the Jewish weddings were in fascinating contrast to our simple Protestantism and again were food for John's imagination – as were our trips to Israel and Turkey with them.

After our meeting with David Bowie in 1988 there were frequent memorable times spent with him. He had dinner with us in our Edinburgh flat. He came to have his portrait painted at Windmill Drive in London. We were guests at his concerts. He travelled to see all of John's exhibitions including *A Long Night's Journey into Day* in Glasgow to which he had loaned one of the pieces in his collection and he even made a personal visit to John's home town of Port Seton, where he wandered unnoticed around the streets making himself familiar with the original source of inspiration. Standing in front of the house in Gosford Road where John had been born, he noticed that the next-door house was named 'Dar es Salaam'. He had just fallen in love with a girl from Dar es Salaam he told us and soon afterwards he brought Iman to meet us in London.

David was a deeply lovable and compassionate individual with the vision of the true artist. He was someone whose curiosity and wonder about life in all its dimensions, from the absurd to the sublime, was his *raison d'être*. He wanted not just a close friendship; he wanted to get inside the mind of the artist, to explore the inner life.

To John he was someone of that unique creative fraternity he held in the highest esteem and on whom he would bestow his greatest accolade in proclaiming him to be 'a true brother of the brush'.

Frederick Kwok was a Chinese businessman, Nicolette his tall, elegant Dutch wife. She was passionate about contemporary painting and sculpture. Like Bob and Susan and Freda and Izak, they now hold within their collection some of the most outstanding pieces of John's work. She and Fred eventually formed the Red Mansion Foundation and proceeded to promote contemporary Chinese art. Over the years we valued the warm friendship we all enjoyed and the generosity of the memorable trips to China which they sponsored and these sparked off another new phase of John's work inspired by this oriental culture so starkly different to our own. Along with our other collector friends we have them to thank for the faith they had in John's work and for the confidence that gave him. The contribution all those couples, along with that of Chris and Sue Armero, made to the richness of our lives, cannot be adequately described.

CHAPTER 57

Italy

We had been living at the Clock House for ten years now and although we still had Windmill Drive in London we were spending much less time there. We made up our minds to sell the London house and John decided we would then buy a place abroad. There was so much of the world I wanted to visit if we could, that I was not too interested in acquiring another home to look after but once the idea had formed in John's mind there was only one course of action that would be taken. He began scouring the property pages one Sunday and one or two things caught his eye. Well, one thing really. He spotted a chateau, a massive crumbling affair in the Lot region of France, where no less a person than Coco Chanel had spent summer holidays. He decided that was the one for him and set about booking tickets to fly to see it *tout de suite*. I was unable to go, so I got Jonathan to agree to accompany him and watch what went on so he could report back to me. John needed a wary eye kept on him.

They were in France for about four days, during which time they viewed several properties with each of which John fell in love. As I anticipated, my pleas not to rush into anything fell on deaf ears and soon Jonathan was ringing to urge me to get on a plane and join them as soon as I could.

'Dad is about to sign on the dotted line for a massive place! He says it reminds him of Edinburgh College of Art. I think you should get out here fast!'

I knew what John would look for. He would only be interested in something massive. Huge rooms, and lots of them, lots of high empty walls with not too many windows (not conducive to hanging paintings), space for storage and a good view. At least on the latter we were in full agreement. Any other considerations were of no importance to him. Dry rot, heating, electrical or plumbing problems, the condition of the roof – any structural faults he did not see and he wanted to hear nothing at all of any disadvantages or practical downsides of the property.

Jonathan got it in the neck. 'I told you to tell her nothing!' he raged. 'You've clyped on me [told on me] and f***ed the whole thing up!'

It didn't make me feel good to put the kybosh on the feverish momentum of his property spree but that is exactly what I did once I got there. The relief I felt was to be short-lived, though, and I was only too aware of that. He was not, as they say, best pleased about my putting a spanner in the works.

I saw the half-dozen chateaux he had fallen in love with, including Chez Chanel and 'Edinburgh College of Art', each more grand and over the top than the last, and managed to stall the procedure by pleading for a little more time. Less than one week had passed since the idea had first surfaced and he and Jonathan had set foot in France but he could not understand, for the life of him, why there was any need to take things any slower. In his mind he had already taken up residence in his new French atelier and would have been virtually placing his best beezers round the walls. All we had to do was to get the coffee and croissants on the table!

All very lovely, I agreed, but if we were going to buy a place abroad, why did we not look around in Italy, where we had spent one or two memorable holidays? We had loved that country and all its charms. Why did we not go there before we made up our mind? This was the Friday and we were on our way home in the plane from France. I was really just stalling for time but this kind of talk only fired him up again. His sulk began to wear off. We would go to Italy on Monday!

Sure enough, on the Monday we were Italy-bound. Realising

he was determined in his quest I had cast my eye over Italian properties on the net. If a house was to be bought then I would prepare myself so that my own preferences would get a look in as well. He had asked the family to search the net for him and to contact estate agents in the particular area of Tuscany that might interest us. Appointments were confirmed to view about half a dozen properties within the duration of the five days we were to be there.

On our flight to Pisa, gazing down over the snowy peaks of the Swiss Alps passing underneath, he turned to me and, with a fierce glint in his eye, said that I should have no doubts that he had every intention of buying a place in Tuscany. That very week. By the time we were on our return journey on the Saturday he could assure me that, no matter what I said, he would be the owner of his very own Italian palazzo. I could argue all I liked, but that, he warned, was what was going to happen. I was resigned to this. I knew, only too well, that he would not be beaten twice in such quick succession.

The first property, of course, was 'The One'. A grand Italian mansion between Pisa and Lucca in which he quite clearly saw himself at work. Huge rooms! Plenty of wall space! All he needed! He just hadn't noticed that the window frames had been destroyed or that part of the main door, having been used as a dartboard, had also been burnt to a cinder, that floorboards were rotten and any period charm of the place had been ripped out and destroyed by the previous owners and that there were houses in close proximity hemming the property in. The drains didn't look that great either and made their presence known from a fair distance away.

Wouldn't it be a good idea to see the other houses we'd planned to see first? There might be something that he would like better. We could always come back to this one if he really liked it so much.

Of course there was something to interest John in all the other places we saw but he was getting tired now. We were three days into our search. The next day his spirits rose as we rose up and up and up through the steep wooded slopes of the Apennines, the backdrop to Lucca, that wonderful medieval walled city we had visited over ten years ago. The mud tracks took us further and further from civilization until eventually we arrived at a long-ruined stone building which boasted its own (ruined) chapel. The convent had been abandoned many years before and the church was now trying to sell the property.

The romance of the place was dizzying, literally. What was the history of this once consecrated spot that looked down as if from the height of an aircraft on to the ribbon of river in the valley below? Here, among the trees and rocky outcrops, there was nothing, only eagles and buzzards soaring on the thermals and only wild boar, deer, foxes and snakes as earthly companions. The cries of the wild world and the sound of the wind in the trees was all there was, and the endless circuit of the sun and moon.

The half-hour we took to wind our way back down through the trees to the valley floor once again was long enough to dismiss any thought of such a challenge and so we made our way further up the valley to view the last property. It was the one that had interested me most when we saw it on the net, but it had been represented by a very blurry image.

We followed the River Serchio further up the valley that lay between the Apuane Alps and the Apennines, and just before we reached the town of Castelnuovo di Garfagnana we turned off right at the sign to Fosciandora, passed over the bridge and the railway crossing and stopped at the cafe, the designated meeting place. There we were to meet someone who would show us round the old manor house we had come to see. Michael Biagi, the estate agent, was Scottish Italian, a convenience that pleased us, as there would be no confusion with language. He pointed upwards to a long stone house on the slopes above.

That was where we were going.

What was it called?

Sepulicchia.

Life is full of surprises. John would want somewhere that he could just walk into, get the paints out and get started. That, and a bed, plus perhaps a table and a couple of chairs were his only concern. Building works and disturbance and intrusion were not for him. That I knew.

We were shown into the main building through a large, heavy wooden door and what we found was a dark shell of an interior with rough cement floors with cables and pipes emerging at strategic points throughout. The original stone stairways were open and without railings, there was no glass on the windows and no doors to the rooms. Here and there a solitary electric light bulb dangled from a loose cable in the ceiling.

This was the best stage in which to buy a property, I was informed. The basic plumbing and electricity had been installed ready to be connected but everything else would be determined and chosen according to the buyers' taste and economic capability. I could see the logic in that but I couldn't see John falling for it. We wandered through the sitting room, the large kitchen with its massive hooded open fireplace, through to the laundry room, up one floor to find an enormous open room with two anterooms adjacent and on the other side of the house a large bedroom and bathroom. Up again to the top floor and into a large bedroom and bathroom with floor-to-ceiling balcony windows looking away out and over the valley to the grandeur of the Alpi Apuane, beyond which lay the Mediterranean Sea. This was it! I saw myself here watching the sun rise over the mountains and the moon fading from the day.

Several other bedrooms and bathrooms later and we were opening the front door on to an old stone balcony outside from where, yes, we could watch the sunset and see the fireflies sparkle in the dusk. Just beside the house was a ruined stone barn with an upper floor supporting the battered tiled roof. Inside at ground level, on dislodging the heavy creaky door, we found the gigantic wooden vat in which the wine of the property, once of some reputation, had been made.

Nudging up against this cantina was a dense wood of chestnut and walnut trees stretching up the hillside and down into the valley. Our wood. A cart track led through the trees to another stone ruin that belonged to the property and had once been a barn for the animals, surrounded by more vineyards. Through the wood and further on from the stone building, a steep, narrow, cobbled pathway built by the Romans formed the boundary of the property. It would have been the original mule path that connected all the walled villages on the mountainside and nowadays still functioned as a footpath from the river on the valley floor up to the furthest villages high above.

Now we were descending the mud slope below the main house. The commodious cellars were being pointed out to us and next to them a stall for the pigs that, it was suggested, would make an ideal self-contained apartment. Following the high wall that separated the garden area from the yard where the animals would have roamed we came to the *pièce de résistance*: the *limonaia*.

This was a building narrow and as long as the main house. Its principal features were six high arched windows devoid of glass, their wrought-iron casings bent and twisted in rusty decay. The uneven earthen floor was scattered with mounds of hay, old furniture and assorted debris with a large metal cage at one end where at one time dogs had been kept. The roof had fallen in and we were advised not to enter the building, as it was structurally unsafe.

Going into the garden we found a line of scraggy old fruit trees that had known better days, among which yellow daffodils had pushed their way through the long grass, winter after winter. There was also a magnolia tree and, the pride of Sepulicchia, a gigantic three-hundred-year-old camellia that leaned in against the sunny walls of the *limonaia*. In spring it would never fail to bring forth masses of red blooms with bright yellow centres.

There were two long terraces one below the other on the slope beneath the house and *limonaia*. Both were encased in high stone walls, below which the property continued descending to the hairpin bend much lower down.

There were acres of land surrounding the buildings. This had been the major property in the area. It had been owned by an influential aristocrat, Conte Valentino Carli, who had at one time run a school of architecture in the main house. After his time the property had passed into the hands of other landowners who had run the place on the feudal *contadini* system and many families had spent time living in the house and working the land for a pittance. In time to come we would meet many of those who had been born and lived in Sepulicchia. It had a history that would fascinate us.

There was no battle over this one, but I was amazed that John was prepared to put up with all the work that had to be done before it could be occupied.

Michael Biagi was not only an estate agent but also had his own work force that would carry out the necessary construction and finishing of the house. All civic and legal transactions would also be arranged for us by him and his wife, Rosanna, and everything would be explained to us in English. What could be better?

John had only one question. How soon could we move in?

Michael gave a commitment that we would be able to move in at the beginning of August – in four months' time.

The deal was done!

The next day we had a few hours before our plane left Pisa. We bought a pair of garden chairs and headed for Sepulicchia, where we set them up under the nearest walnut tree and sat gazing up at our new home. There was so much to look at and to imagine, so many possibilities for our future life. It felt right. We had come to a good place.

On 1 August the whole family with their partners, three carloads of us, left Pisa airport and, after following the road round the walls of Lucca, wound our way up the Serchio valley. As we approached the turning for Fosciandora the house came into view. Our excitement was palpable. We were about to open a new chapter of our lives. What would life in Italy bring? What would we find here?

After the bridge, the railway crossing and one more bridge over the river Ceserana, the way to Sepulicchia was up a narrow steeply winding road of hairpin bends, with the possibility of a precipitous descent into the forest at the least wavering of attention. The sign at the bottom of this road proclaimed it '*Strada Pericolosa*' (dangerous road). As we hadn't a clue then what the sign said, we proceeded blissfully unaware of this warning, as we had on all the other unknown roads of our lives. Whatever challenges now confronted us, we would take them on as we had the others.

The house was habitable that summer, if you overlooked the fact that there were no doors on the bedrooms, some areas had no lighting and we had yet to acquire most household necessities. We had managed to have enough beds installed and the basic kitchen equipment but John's mission was to unpack the consignment of canvases that Bird & Davis had sent out from England for him and to set himself up in his studio. He had chosen the long room with the two anterooms on the first floor and had had a stone staircase and new door erected at one end of the house in order to have direct outdoor access.

His next quest was to find an art shop in the vicinity. Those were available in Lucca, forty minutes away, or in Viareggio, one hour away. However his luck was in the ascendant as, in the valley, in the nearby village of Gallicano, two brothers, Glauco and Mario Aiosa, not only could provide all painting materials but would stretch and frame canvases to his heart's content. Glauco and Mario were hard-working and endlessly obliging to John's needs, and they also made it easy for him to work in Italy. The relationship between him and them was one of warm affection. John always wanted things to be done yesterday and somehow they managed to deliver the impossible and still retain their will to live.

Arriving in Tuscany in August, one is immediately caught up in the dizzy whirl of the cultural life. During the summer there are festivals and celebrations in every town and village in which the whole population is involved – babies in arms, teenagers, the whole family hierarchy right up to the oldest members. Everyone has a place at the table, with special veneration for the elderly and infirm. Enthusiasm and the joy of living, traditional food and dancing and music that lasts well into the warm balmy nights. Why would one not fall in love with all of this?

Then there was the backdrop of rugged mountains, grassy hillsides with old stone dwellings perched on rocky ledges, wave upon wave of wooded slopes stretching far into the distance. There were the medieval walled hill villages crowned by their ancient churches and *campanile* all around us, softly illuminated by night; the green valley of the river Serchio far below us; the swallows nesting in the eaves and swinging out at speed to dart and dive in the sun; the sound of the sheep and goat bells from the wooded hillside across the valley; the eagles hovering and coasting above us as we looked across to the abandoned village on the crest of the opposite hillside. This was the Garfagnana, where, the saying goes, time stands still, a designated wild place, land of the wild boar, the fox and the deer, the awe-inspiring timelessness of marble mountain and rocky terrain.

As we began life in Sepulicchia there was all I have described and more to enchant us. There were no harbours or boats in the vicinity and the Mediterranean Sea was an hour's drive away through the Apuane, but despite this we felt an almost immediate sense of belonging. We wanted to gradually become part of our new community and to contribute as residents. We did not want to barge in but we also did not want to be *stranieri* (strangers). What we did not know then was that the sense of homecoming we felt had more significance than we knew and in fact had we been aware of this phenomenon before we bought Sepulicchia it might have put us off the whole idea of settling there.

Michael Biagi was Scottish Italian, as was Claudio Donati who owned the bar/restaurant at the Ponte di Ceserana by the railway crossing. He had been born in Fosciandora then moved with his family to Scotland before returning and marrying his Clementina and opening his award-winning restaurant.

On our first trip into Barga, one of the two nearby towns, keen to try out my pigeon Italian in shops, I would stumble out my pathetic shopping requests only to be answered by kindly voices: 'Is it bread you're wantin, hen?' Thus we discovered that we had put down roots near to 'the most Scottish town in Italy'.

It was Italy and Italian life we wanted. Much as we adored Scotland, we already had it. At home and in our very hearts. We were not looking for it here as well! Any dismay, however, was short-lived, as we would find that there was nothing that was not Italian in Barga or the area of the Serchio Valley. That same voice asking if we wanted bread would immediately turn to someone else and continue a rapid conversation in fluent Italian. The place was through and through Italian but with an extra dimension that, as we learned about it, enhanced our sense of the history of the place and introduced an awareness of the heroism that was the essence of the Barga–Scottish connection.

It was a story of hardship, poverty and hunger that in the earlier part of the twentieth century had inspired the wave of emigration from the area. It had demanded courage and determination in order to establish a means of escape from the pervading destitution. Emigration took the people of the Serchio valley as far afield as Scotland, the United States of America, Peru, Argentina and Venezuela, as well as Australia. Wherever they settled, they worked hard and long to build up their own businesses and their efforts were rewarded by the respect and affection of their adopted countrymen and women. In Scotland it was ice cream parlours and later fish and chip shops and in time renowned restaurants serving the produce and dishes of their own particular regions of Italy. But however far afield the emigrants travelled to make their lives, their loyalty to the homeland never diminished with time or distance. Financial support was sent home and unbreakable links were forged down through the generations. In this way strong links were forged between the west of Scotland and the medieval town of Barga.

A major event in the local calendar was the Festa delle Emigrante, the annual celebration held when those who had left the mountains to make their lives in other countries returned for their summer holidays and to visit their families. A generous gesture in later years was to extend an invitation to the celebration to the *immigrante*, those who had come to live in the Serchio valley from all parts of the world. And so, for many years, John and I and all of our family visiting us at the time would join in, after the feast, dancing the night away to the old-time romantic Italian music blasting out over the mountains, finally making our way back down the twisty roads to Sepulicchia in the moonlight.

CHAPTER 58

Natalina and the Garfagnana

Now Natalina, 'my Italian sister', entered our lives and immediately found herself a comfortable place in the heart of the Bellany family. She brought with her Bruno, her husband, her dog, Lolli, and her family of three grown-up children, Angela, Luca and Evelin.

She was my *insegnante* (teacher) in all things Garfagnana. Both she and Bruno had lived in Fosciandora their entire lives, working the soil from which they obtained everything they needed. They lived higher up, near the village of Fosciandora, and their surrounding land included *la stalla* (cowshed), where they reared one cow every year for milk which, when it produced a calf, was slaughtered and parcelled up in carefully cut pieces to lie in the freezer until required for the dinner table. This cycle went on continuously year after year.

Around the *stalla* there were a tethered a goat and a large coop full of chickens that always ran scared of the fox which from time to time succeeded in wreaking havoc. In Tuscany there were no rabbits in the wild so they kept several cages of beautiful fat rabbits bred for the pot. Their *orto* (vegetable garden) produced potatoes, carrots, onions, leeks, zucchini, red and green peppers, acres of tomatoes, basil, oregano, mint, sunflowers and also banks of flowers, most of which were destined for the cemetery. Their trees gave them apples, pears, apricots, plums, walnuts and chestnuts, while the rest of their land was

334

taken over by vineyards and olive groves which in the autumn saw the traditional ritual of the *vendemmia* (grape harvest), and the gathering of the olives to be taken to the *fattoria* to be turned into oil.

I learned about it all and became an eager witness to this dying way of life that had echoes of the earthiness of the years of our childhood in the fifties of Scotland. No visit to a neighbour was undertaken without a gift of eggs or a newly baked cake or bottle of their own oil. Tasks were shared within the community, taking turns in the *vendemmia* of neighbours, in the gathering of the olives and the harvesting of chestnuts in the autumn and the cutting and gathering of the hay in the summer.

Not only did Natalina help in the house but both Bruno and she, while attending to the intense labour demanded by their own land, insisted on cutting our grass and scything the long hay that rapidly covered the vines and olives of our extensive property. They arrived by tractor, Bruno driving all the way down the steep windy roads from Fosciandora with Natalina sitting in the trailer with scythes and hoes that had been in use by their family for generations. In May they planted out the geraniums and pineapple plants and bougainvillea and oleander that would produce a riot of colourful blossom lasting all summer.

Every year on 18 June a party with all our Italian friends was held on the terrace of Sepulicchia to celebrate John's birthday, where the food prepared by Natalina was always sumptuous. Sometimes it was a pizza party with all the pizzas prepared by Bruno and cooked by him in the original bread oven at our back door.

The most spectacular birthday party of all was John's sixtieth in 2002, when a long trestle table was set up beside the *limonaia* for more than forty of our family and friends. As usual, Natalina and Bruno and their daughter, Angela, had excelled. This time, however, they had a couple of surprises that even I was not party to. Halfway through the meal the babble of voices suddenly stopped and on the balcony above us appeared Luciano, the accordionist from Barga, playing all the much-loved old Italian songs. He played on and on, the dancing started and later in the evening fireworks soared up into the night sky from the terrace below.

Natalina had quickly got the measure of *il pittore scozzese* and her way with him was laced with ready good humour. Neither she nor Bruno had a word of English and John had no Italian but that did nothing to get in the way of the deep respect and warm affection they shared. The house rang with their voices, long stories that necessitated much high-decibel repetition and vigorous hand movements, stories of the surrounding area, sometimes sad or tragic, as in the instance of a death in the community when tears were shed, but most times the stories were hilarious and often at her or Bruno's expense. It is from them that I learned to become fluent in Italian. Someone had to learn and it took a lot of listening to something that often sounded like rapid gunfire, albeit of a musical nature. What they were telling us was of such interest to me that my curiosity spurred me on to try to keep up with the conversation. Natalina taught me so much. I did try to teach her the odd English expression but all she managed to say, before collapsing in hysterics, was 'Appy Beh day, Joh!' for a film Paul was making for John's birthday. She did not succeed in passing on any Italian to him but she told him off when he was shouting and getting too agitated.

'*Con calma, Joh! Con calma! Joh, con calma!*' Be calm John.

She often brought him things she thought he'd like to paint. Her instinct was faultless and everything she brought delighted him. It might be some of the best sunflowers from their *orto*, or a dead weasel she had found in the wood, or a bowl of fruit she had collected from the upper terraces of Sepulicchia, or most especially the spectacular barn owl that had flown too low over our swimming pool and tragically met its end. She sat for ages holding the beautiful dead creature until John had drawn it to his satisfaction. She told him about the fox that had crept into the ruined barn by our house to die and he watched them as they made a bonfire to burn its body. '*Poverino*' (poor thing) she murmured, while he made mental notes for a painting. She caught *topi* (mice) in the cellars, but because of his phobia of rats, John wanted to know absolutely nothing about them. She knitted bedsocks and made special food for him when he wasn't well, and Bruno advised him on what medicine or therapy he should try, anything from the thermal spring water at Pieve Fosciana to the faith healer at Castelvecchio Pascoli.

Now and then Natalina announced that she was going to bring her little bag of what might be called her 'pedicure implements' with her as she could see that John needed his feet attended to. Toenails first! His foot was placed on to a cushion on her lap and then the squirming and squealing began.

'No, mamma! No! No, mamma!' he yelped until the job was done and both of them had ended up helpless with laughter.

Neither Bruno nor Natalina had ever been out of Tuscany, so we invited them to come to the UK, to the Clock House, with us. Such a journey held no appeal for Bruno but, more importantly, his mother was still alive and in her nineties and he was devoted to her care. Although they had never flown before and the thought terrified both of them, Natalina decided she would risk it and visit us for a short time.

The worry for us was, how would we entertain her? Her daily cycle of work was all she knew. It was her only way of being in the world. She was used to getting up before six every morning and heading off along the hillside track in the winter dark or as the sun rose over the mountains, to help Bruno milk the cow and collect the eggs before the other endless daily tasks got a look in. The physical laziness of our lives in Italy was one thing but in England for a whole week it would be a considerable challenge for her.

The first morning after we arrived back at the Clock House, I opened the curtains. It was about 8 a.m. There was Natalina, in her old working clothes, down in the garden wheeling her fourth load of weeds out into the wood! Before she departed, she collected cuttings of all the plants that she didn't have in Tuscany and smuggled them back in her suitcase to thrive in their glory the following summer.

CHAPTER 59

Barga

When we first arrived in Fosciandora, the newly appointed *sindaco* (mayor) of Barga was Professor Umberto Sereni, professor of Modern History at the University of Udine in the north of the country. Umberto was born in Barga. His father, Bruno Sereni, had led a heroic life joining the International Brigade in the Spanish Civil War, enduring imprisonment back in Italy for his principles but returning eventually to live in Barga, whereupon he set up *Il Giornale di Barga*, the monthly newspaper that is still today sent out to many parts of the world, keeping alive the links of the emigrants to their homeland. In his book, *They Took the High Road*, he gave an account of the emigration from Barga of which he had first-hand knowledge, having been among those who had left to find work in Scotland in the thirties. It is a story of hardship and courage and it explains in significant detail the historical basis for the enduring Scottish factor in the life of Barga. Bruno was an inspirational figure, a socialist and humanist for whom this historic link with Scotland was a part of his own story and a source of great pride.

All of this was readily embraced by his son, Umberto, and shaped the enthusiasm with which he determined to honour his father's memory and the memory of all the remarkable men and women who had played their part in such a heroic struggle for the homeland and the challenge of diaspora. He wanted to make the historic medieval town of Barga worthy of their memory.

Along with improved living conditions and services, it was through the arts and literature that a place would truly grow and flourish. It was the life of the mind and spirit, through its poetry, music, visual art and written word, that opened up new and more fulfilling dimensions in day-to-day life and that was the culture that greeted us in our first months in the area.

John was welcomed with enthusiasm as someone who could and would contribute to the cultural life of the town and would be claimed by Barga as one of their own. It was an honour to which he readily responded.

Most of the Italians who had arrived in Scotland in the thirties and forties had made their homes in the west of the country, particularly in and around Glasgow, and so, in order to celebrate and honour this Scottish dimension of Barga, an event was planned for the summer of 2002 combining a major exhibition of John's work with a visit to Barga of the then Lord Provost of Glasgow, Alex Mosson. The commemorative photograph shows the long procession of the mayors and representatives of all the neighbouring councils, including that of Lucca, and representatives from Florence, wending its way through the ancient streets of the old town. Led by Umberto, John and Alex Mosson and their entourage and accompanied by the major civic dignitaries, police escorts, the company was also accorded the privilege of the guard of honour of the Alpini soldiers attired in their green uniforms and feathered hats. The whole procession walked to the music of the various brass bands of the area. On reaching the destination of the historic Teatro dei Differenti the ceremony took place in which both John and Alex were awarded San Cristoforo honours underlining the importance of the roles they played in promoting Barga and its Scottish connection.

John's retrospective exhibition was held in the impressive Villa Ricci. It was opened by Lord Provost Mosson and was the first real opportunity for the people of Barga to get to know about John and his work. He, of course, had painted his major tribute to Barga and the surrounding area in his own vision of the great and solemn candlelit San Cristoforo procession that, every year on 24 July, slowly wound its way up through the stone walls of the ancient town towards the Duomo for the Mass in celebration of the patron saint of Barga. He presented this large painting to the *comune* and it hangs today within its offices in Palazzo Pancrazi, in the centre of the medieval town.

It was soon after this event that we were escorted to Florence by Umberto Sereni and members of the *comune* of Barga for John to be presented with the prestigious Pegasus medal, awarded for his contribution to the arts. This is one of the highest honours in the gift of the civic authorities of Tuscany. Subsequently we attended a similar ceremony in the Palazzo Ducale in Lucca, where he was awarded a second medal in recognition of his place in the art world of Scotland and now as a resident of Tuscany.

Later in 2002, after having lived in Fosciandora for two years, we were invited to attend a very special occasion at the nearby Santuario della Santissima delle Stelle. Il Santuario had its origins in the twelfth century. It had been rebuilt and altered over the centuries and had sheltered the vulnerable, the elderly and the children during the years of the Second World War. Now it was in regular use as a church once more and on this occasion we were invited to attend a special Mass, after which the ceremony to honour John's residence in Fosciandora took place outside. The Fosciandora Filarmonia were present in their navy uniforms and military hats to play and a few Scottish airs had crept into the repertoire as he was awarded the Freedom of Fosciandora. Just being part of that community was enriching for us both, and the generosity underlying all those gestures of fraternity was something that we would always cherish.

John's state of health meant that he had need of regular medical supervision and we were fortunate in having two of the best hospitals nearby, one in Barga and the other in Castelnuovo di Garfagnana. It was mainly the latter that he attended for the necessary blood tests required by his prescription of warfarin, or 'rat poison' as he called it. This is where Dott. Rino Simonetti played a crucial role in our lives. Apart from becoming one of our closest friends he was also our doctor and oversaw all John's medical care, which, as the years went on, became an increasingly demanding task. Rino came quickly to deal with crises of varying degrees of severity. His professional skill and attentiveness gave us the confidence to enjoy life in the Garfagnana to the fullest extent possible. Rino was called on to tackle many different symptoms and did his best to try to help. One thing defeated him though: a problem with John's Achilles tendons. John always made light of his ailments and generally, on good days, joked about them, resigning himself to the things that could not be cured. He would have to go slower, he told us, and now used sticks as he walked 'the Nelson Mandela walk!'

After dealing promptly with specific ailments, being an enthusiastic adherent of *la dolce vita* in true Barga style, Rino was always ready to turn our attention to the really important matter in life – social enjoyment – and he made plans to encourage John's speedy return to his optimum health. This distraction from his physical frailty was always effective. John never failed to rise above his own pain and discomfort if there was a prospect of some fun and frolics. Rino and his wife, Beatrice, would collect us to take us to join a gathering of his friends, now our friends also, at one of the local restaurants, or we would all go far up into one of the rocky valleys in the heart of the mountains to a place that was renowned for its trout or its fungi. Sometimes other friends in our circle, Agostino and his wife Anna, invited us all the way to Viareggio to have seafood in the renowned restaurant owned by friends. Wherever we went it was sure to be a good time. Nowhere was too far to travel for the best food with the best company. An hour to the Mediterranean and an hour back at dead of night was more than worth it. The food was talked about with relish for days afterwards and the fun and games and camaraderie lit up our days and consolidated the deep and special bond that would be there among us all for the rest of our lives. There were so many escapades full of *joie de vivre*, most notably one December when our friends Leonardo and Daniela Mordini and Andrea and Marianna Marcucci flew sixty of us from Barga to Gallivare, in Lapland, Sweden and entertained us for five days to celebrate the grand opening of their new hotel. Inside the Arctic Circle, the strenuous dog sledging, the sleigh rides, the visit to the Ice Hotel, the concert at the Church of Santa Lucia where the girls walked in procession wearing crowns of lit candles, the massive elks that, without warning, jumped out of the forest and crossed our path, the almost continuous darkness lit up by the luminosity of the deep snow among the pines, were all quite unforgettable.

On his retirement from his profession, Rino was elected *sindaco* of Molazzana, the mountainous area that he had served as doctor. He knew everyone and was a very popular choice. The boundaries of his *comune* included some of the wildest and most scenic reaches of the Apuane Alps. Soon we were off on evening trips up the mountains, swaying round the precipitous hairpin bends towards the restaurant in the village of Sassi, perched on the dizzy ridges far above the valley. Sometimes, at sunset and on foot, we would climb even higher to the gently illuminated campanile standing alone on a rocky outcrop. This overlooked the winding road far below through the marble mountains that separated us from the Mediterranean coast which we could just glimpse. On journeys back from the sea along that road in the valley below, the sight of the campanile of Sassi, the beacon of its tower high above us, told us that we were nearly through the mountains and home again in Garfagnana.

CHAPTER 60

Reforming the Circle

It was now several years since our family situation had slowly turned around as both our sons dramatically moved away from all of their previous acquaintances and began new lives. One evening Paul turned up with a new girlfriend on the back of his Vespa for us to meet. Blonde, Dr. Martens boots, complete skinhead gear and a lovely face. We were bowled over – skinhead or not we immediately liked her!

This was Angela, who was to become Paul's wife. In years to come her natural ability, enhanced by her training in accountancy, attained such competence and professionalism that she took over the burden of all our administration in tax and fiscal affairs. That was not all that came with Angie. Gradually she was drawn into the mysteries of John's work and studied it with growing enthusiasm. She learned not just about his art, but, just as vital, about the temperamental artist himself and how to deal with him in all his moods. She eventually became John's PA and a tower of strength to me too.

At tricky times I asked Angie how she could cope with John. She had mastered a technique, she said, which generally worked. Bad days, leave well alone but always watch for the opportune moment. Yes, it could be difficult dealing with him but, she said generously, he was worth it!

Then we became grandparents, and Sammy came into our lives, bringing all the joy a little girl can. Several years later her brother Richard was born. Paul eventually funded his course at the National Film School, gaining prizes for his work in special effects. He worked on such films as *Harry Potter and the Order of the Phoenix*, *The Bourne Ultimatum* and *Stardust*. He also, in time, made the acclaimed biographical film about John, *Fire in the Blood*, for television.

Cottbus had been the turning point for Jonathan. For the past few years he had made a new life for himself and had formed his own decorating business. He met the beautiful Chantal Parmentier from Marche en Famenne in Belgium and brought her to live with him in Saffron Walden. Although her English was excellent, her first language was French, and she always retained the inflection. She called me Hélène making me feel instantly more exotic. She had graduated, like me, in psychology, at the University of Liege and was the epitome of the chic, effortlessly elegant European woman. She immediately found her place in our family and no sooner had they been married than twin boys, Scotty and Jamie, were on their way to join the family firm. Jonathan worked hard and long hours, unafraid of the challenges involved in building up and keeping a small business afloat and loving the family life he had established for himself.

He's had another, particular, challenge to deal with. To anyone who has no experience of such a problem it seems trivial. There is little understanding in the general population of the severe disability a speech impediment can be. Out of the blue, at the age of sixteen, at the time when our family life was in ruins, Jonathan developed a stammer. At first I believed it must be a temporary response to the chaos around him but it proved more enduring. Everyone who suffers in this way knows this will be a struggle throughout life and that some scenarios are extremely difficult to deal with. Speaking to strangers, making speeches, telephone conversations are but a few. Talking on the telephone is a major part of how one conducts business. He has over the years struggled and sought help in all sorts of ways. Many times it defeated him but he carried on trying to help himself. Today the stammer is largely undetectable. His hard work and discipline have won through. It is an achievement that anyone could be proud of and it is a source of great pride and admiration to all our family.

It takes courage to pick up the pieces and it takes even more to accept the responsibility of a wrong path taken and to live down history by honest, open and steady labour. It takes special people to do such a thing. A mother's love always sees the special in her children but beyond that, I recognise what warm and worthwhile people my boys are.

Anya, having gained her first-class degree at Liverpool University, had begun to study for a PhD on the subject of Stanley Spencer. This was a lonely and formidable undertaking and in the end not for her. She left Liverpool and returned home. Soon she met a local boy, Steven Sparks, and they were married in Saffron Walden with the reception at the Clock House. It was no time at all before a troop of four little Sparkies hurtled into our lives: Luke, Ollie, Arabella and Joe. Our beautiful daughter, once so troubled and unsettled, now spends her time bringing up her four children and working in the Saffron Walden County High School helping children with special needs to find ways of learning and coping in a difficult world. Many years ago someone helped her to do just that. It is a job for which she is well qualified, one that she loves and finds immensely satisfying.

About ten years after my father died, my mother moved to live for the first time in her life in a city. In Aberdeen she enjoyed living near to Joan and Roger and their three girls, Sally, Anna and Jenny. During the first two years of the new century, however, her health had begun to deteriorate quite markedly. This had necessitated a move from her spacious ground-floor flat to a sheltered apartment in the same area, near my sister. Being now less mobile she began to feel a sense of isolation. Phone calls were a lifeline and our regular evening calls were vital links when she would tell me about her day.

Latterly Mum was admitted to a geriatric hospital, where she stayed for a few months. For part of that time we were in Italy and I had the guilt of knowing that we should have been there for her so much more in those last years. When one moves away, as most of the young people did in my part of Scotland, one enters different worlds from one's parents, geographically and experientially, bringing about an inevitable gulf of some kind. What I am describing is no more than the generational shift encountered in most families. However, Mum and I were good friends and fortunate in retaining much that we enjoyed sharing. We both loved reading and drama, and we talked about our current interests. We also had a great love of the family history, of our relations near and far-flung. News of them and stories of the old days and talk about Golspie brightened our conversations and left us warmed up and laughing. But with the decline in her concentration, this too began to fade away and I could tell that she was preparing to take her leave.

Although I knew that while we were all in Italy she was well looked after, I suddenly had an overwhelming need to see her. I found a flight to Edinburgh from Pisa and from there I hired a car to take me to Aberdeen. I will always be glad of the two days I stayed there. I decided I would take her out of the hospital to have afternoon tea with her close friends in a local hotel and it was a joyful event where Mum took centre stage reciting some of her favourite poems.

The next day I took her for a drive down the coast to the fishing village of Stonehaven, nestling in the cliffs to the south of Aberdeen. Several months previously she had had cataracts removed from both eyes and she was elated at the improvement in her sight. We stopped at the harbour and had ice creams and watched the children playing on the sand. I chose that moment to call some of the family in Saffron Walden so she could speak to them. It was then that Paul was able to tell her the special news that their long-awaited baby boy, and Sam's longed-for baby brother, Richard, had been born. She was also happy to know that in a few weeks' time Jonathan and Chantal were going to be married in Belgium.

Those were her last days out and she enjoyed them. For me they were a special time we spent together, just the two of us, a last goodbye for which I will always be thankful.

We were no sooner back in Italy than I had to return to

Aberdeen. Mum was being taken into a residential home for the elderly. It was not a pleasant task to visit and choose the one we considered best for her and it was not a good day when she moved there. After this, Mum went into dramatic decline and the vigil began for Joan and me, to watch over her till the end came. One late September evening sitting beside her at twilight I watched a skein of graylag geese calling out as they made their way south over the city and it was in those moments that a change took place. Suddenly, it was all over. My mother had gone.

She had been born Helen Wiseman (but always called Ella) in the fishing community of Macduff on the Banffshire coast. Her father was a fish curer and she was the second youngest of a family of nine. The family had spent a number of years following the herring fishing moving between two places that on the clearest of days were faintly visible to each other across the North Sea horizon, Macduff in Banffshire and Golspie. Finally they settled in Golspie where they lived for the rest of their lives. Ella met Harold in her first class at primary school in Golspie and both of them later on, in married life, entered into the community activities with enthusiasm, my father writing scripts for social events and Ella taking part in the amateur drama performances. At the age of eighteen she had been part of the team that had won first for Scotland in the Scottish Amateur Dramatic Festival of that year. This had been adjudicated by the celebrated actor and producer Charles Laughton and the play was broadcast on BBC Radio, causing great excitement in the village.

She had been much loved by John, had been the subject of several portraits, and she had loved him every bit as much in return. She enjoyed visiting us at the Clock House and from time to time her friends would ask her about some of the well-known personalities she might have met while she was with us. She loved meeting people but was singularly underwhelmed by whoever they were. Only if they were kind and convivial were they memorable to her. Fame did not impress her. Nobody could match up to John and if domestic decisions had to be made she was always in his team rather than mine. No maternal loyalty whatsoever! When at the age of fifty-five I began to learn to play the clarinet, far from applauding the worthiness of my belated ambition and offering the encouragement it might be reasonable to expect from a proud mother, she would say to him, 'Oh, listen to her squawking away there! Shut the door, John, will you, for goodness' sake?'

We took her home to Golspie and buried her with my father under the watch of the Mannie, within the sound of the sea, among all their childhood friends in the place where they had played out their lives and where they belonged.

CHAPTER 61

China

Nicolette and Frederick Kwok offered to take us to China to
see for ourselves what the country was like and we jumped at
the chance. With regard to John's uncertain health there were
many concerns over us travelling so far away. To my shock,
out of the blue with no warning, I too had recently had a minor
heart attack. This alarmed us all, especially John. I had had
no warning of such a thing and no medical conditions could
be found to explain it. The day it occurred I had been feeling
exhausted but it was a mystery. After a short period of recovery
and after acknowledging the advice of doctors, I was keen to
put it behind me. 'Live for the day' was always our mantra so,
courtesy of our friends' generosity, we set off to Shanghai. As
with Chris Armero in Mexico, what Fred and Nicolette gave us
was a feast for the imagination.

The trip to China had been planned well before Mum had
become ill and so it was only a couple of weeks after her funeral
in October 2003 that we flew out from Heathrow. As I was
still suffering the impact of her death, my thoughts and also
many of John's throughout the long flight revolved around my
mother, what she had meant to us, to me, what she had given
me through her personality and spirit.

As we flew over what we realized was a stretch of the Great
Wall of China and entered Chinese airspace, I remember notic-
ing that the roofs of buildings throughout the countryside were

cerulean blue, an observation of no importance, but all I could glean of the Chinese countryside, until we were above the polluted mass of Beijing and travelling on south to Shanghai, our journey's end.

Skyscrapers that grew overnight, slowly revolving cranes always on the move, impenetrable walls of shiny glass and concrete, acres of it: this was the modern city of Shanghai, the spirit of present-day China. It was fast-moving and brash, all neon messages clamouring for attention high above the multi-lane highways that sliced through the city. This was our view from our sky-high hotel room. But down there you could still catch sight of the huddle of the *hutongs*, the basic dwellings of the very poor, the ones that still survived to house working Chinese families. The days of the *hutong* were numbered, as they were being swept away in the race to build more and more shiny new office blocks promoting all that the Western world could promise. The *hutongs* would be gone the next time we looked. The inhabitants were being swiftly decanted into soulless blocks of cramped concrete accommodation on the outskirts of the city, modern and instantly dilapidated battle lines of high-rise chicken coops plastered on the outsides with clumsy air conditioning boxes.

As usual when we went travelling, a large portfolio of watercolour paper and paints accompanied us. John was always at the ready to get to work. It was a force that could not be contained. He saw, he experienced, he breathed, so he created.

Soon he was busy and I could leave him in our room and take myself off to explore. I went to the leafy boulevards of the French Concession with its elegant buildings that must have been there during the Japanese occupation of Shanghai. Now its sophisticated designer stores and restaurants were in stark contrast to the old Chinese department shops, notably the Friendship Store with its mix of traditional Chinese garments and others in cheap, dated Western style. I went to the markets away across the city where I saw the live chickens and ducks waiting to be bought. After money had changed hands, they had their necks wrung and were handed over the counter. Fish and eels would be swimming, rabbits cowering in hutches, birds in cages chirping their last. There was also everything that markets everywhere have: fruit and flowers and vegetables and clothing and shoes and shoddy tat of all kinds – hundreds of plastic nodding Chairmen Maos. The noise and the clamour and the action were intoxicating.

Strolling in the parks we could see t'ai chi being performed. It was generally an early morning activity but there was a steady stream of people practising the art all day long. Dancing too: women and men, women and women, young and the elderly – especially the elderly – were always dancing and exercising in any public space throughout the day. Everywhere we saw the single child accompanied by its parents. Seldom could a group of children be seen in the city. It was a lonely sight to Western eyes but for the Chinese there was no other option.

In the dreary cafés of the department stores, we saw the workers taking their lunch breaks, people bent forward over the tables, sleeping with their heads resting on their folded arms. We saw a funeral in one of the more run-down streets where, after the funeral rites had been completed and the body had been removed, all the possessions of the deceased were publicly burnt in a bonfire outside the door of his newly vacated dwelling. We were informed that this was so that the spirit of the departed would not linger and cause distress or trouble. We saw vendors with their modest paraffin stoves doing sporadically brisk trade in hot food, often with their personal washing hanging above and around them to dry. Then there were the mah-jong players. There was always a game being played somewhere.

John was always in need of canvas. There were few places we visited that he did not manage to obtain some. Before we left home he was muttering about getting some in China. We were going on quite an adventure as it was and I considered that if he managed to travel to China and see the country and use his watercolours to take some impression of all that inspired him, from which he could work on once he had returned home, he would be doing well. The complication of oils and canvas was, for me, a headache too great to contemplate. I was therefore relieved when we boarded our flight at Heathrow with no more having been said about it.

One morning six days after we had arrived in Shanghai, the telephone in our hotel room rang.

'Mrs Bellany, I am calling to inform you that your consignment has arrived and is down at reception.'

'Thank you,' I said, 'but what consignment might this be?'

'Four large packages have arrived for you, Mrs Bellany. Very large packages!' Heavy packages? Her excited voice continued, 'And we just wanted to know where you would like us to bring them?'

My heart sank. Here we go again!

'I think I'll pass you on to speak to my husband. Just a moment.'

As I glared at him, John, who was not yet properly awake at the time, attempted to squirm his way out of the uncomfortable spot in which he suddenly found himself. Oh, yes, certainly, he would come down to reception immediately! I wanted to know nothing about it; I would leave him to sort it all out himself.

We were living in a normal hotel room, millions of floors up in the Shanghai Hilton. The following day we were going by train to Beijing, where we were to spend another week before returning to Shanghai for our last week. The problem was, you might say, not inconsiderable. Four large packages of around twenty-four canvases measuring approximately 8ft x 6ft each. Oh, and a heavy box of oil paints and brushes too.

Not only did I not anticipate this happening (why, I do not know because I surely knew his ways by now) but neither Nicolette nor Fred knew anything about it either. As they had arranged our travel details, they unfortunately had to be brought in on the problem-solving, and messages went to and fro all day from their Hong Kong offices to the Hilton managers. John was shown different locations in the hotel that could accommodate his canvases and where it was suggested he might be able to work. A conference hall. The ballroom. A windowless storage area.

I heard about all of this later but while it was going on I was sitting trying to pretend it was not happening. Then John eventually arrived back in our room to tell me that we had to get ready and go somewhere immediately. Seemingly we were being taken to see two other hotels that might have suitable accommodation for his canvases and also for us, in that order. I was not at my most cooperative, it must be said, but off we went in the taxi across the city to be shown round other newly built flashy hotels that had, in desperation, been brought in to try to solve the problem. Finally, the solution was found at the end of a long day. John was shown one of the penthouse suites on the top floor of the Hilton. It was an executive suite fully equipped for business meetings. Large sitting room, dining room, bedroom, other bedroom, bathrooms, kitchen and so on. The panorama from the windows was dizzy.

Yes, this would suit the artist very nicely. Thank you. The huge packages would (almost) fit into one of the bathrooms if the door was left open for us to be able to squeeze round them to get in and out of the apartment. He would move one of the desks in the sitting room, put protective sheets down on the carpet on which he would lay out his paints and brushes, turps and oil and so on, and he could then paint to his heart's delight. Not only that but the manager assured him that the apartment would be locked while we were in Beijing and everything would be safe until we returned.

This was John at his most typical. A thread of unpredictable single-mindedness ran through his life from the very start. His health was uncertain but we were able to take risks up to a point and mind over matter worked wonders for many years after his transplant. But even in the last years of his life, as he deteriorated, this determination and drive never left him. Painting was everything to him. He needed to paint and nothing was permitted to stand in his way.

When we arrived in Beijing on the overnight train that had carried us across the country, other delights awaited us. We met the director of Beijing Central Academy of Art and were shown round the schools and studios. It was encouraging to see classes in drawing taking place where students were very concentrated on learning. The method of instruction was strictly academic and there was a strong sense, among the students, of having to get it right. At that time in China there seemed to be two approaches to visual art. On the one hand, there was the supreme emphasis on the skill or craft as an entity in itself. On the other, there was the encroaching lure of Western style. It seemed to be either all discipline with no creative input or no structure with an arbitrary stab at superficial sensation. From what we saw, neither end product appealed but our ability to have a wider view of the Chinese art world was limited, so perhaps that affected our assessment.

John was kindly offered a space at the Academy in which to work and he readily accepted. Canvas was not a problem this time. He travelled to the Academy in the mornings from our hotel in the centre of the city. We were generously entertained by the staff of the Academy, by members of the British Council in Beijing and by the British Ambassador and his wife who invited us to lunch at the Embassy.

While John was attending the Academy, I was off to visit the Great Wall on the northern outskirts of Beijing. Such historical wonders and places of outstanding beauty have to be seen to live on in the imagination. Most of what I saw in China, sometimes a remarkable building, often individuals I met, remained to be revisited in my memory long after we had returned home. The same was true for John, who made sure that a lot of it lived on in his work.

One day I was strolling round the old-fashioned Friendship store of Beijing, having left John in the men's department. In a short time, from somewhere out of sight in the massive open-plan store, I heard a commotion and sounds of squealing and laughter. I found him surrounded by a bevy of giggling female shop assistants. He had tried on a rather eye-catching, retro style suit and had been encouraged to appear at a mirror to assess its aesthetic value. There he was being pinned up at the hem and adjusted here and there, collar up, collar down, this way and that. Several other assistants had immediately spotted a lucrative sale potential and had hastened to come running out with various alternatives for him to try. In an effort to keep the momentum going they were giggling and repeating excitedly the only English words they knew.

'DAV ID BECK HAM! DAV ID BECK HAM!' Clapping their hands in time, carried away by the thrill of the whole pantomime.

Now it was time to return to the Beijing railway station to catch our train back to Shanghai. Amid the confusion of the masses thronging the terminal, flustered as he always was on embarking on a journey, John set about paying the man who had helped with our luggage. Out came the wad of 'Sidneys' he always carried with him and he fumbled for a note to offer in payment. All of a sudden a cascade of coins and notes of all size and denomination fluttered out and rolled away underneath the feet of the crowds around us – British, Turkish, Israeli, old Italian lire, Euros, US dollars, currency of the world that had remained, like everything else, in his pockets, transferred from one jacket to the next, long after they could be called into use.

Back we went to Shanghai and to the canvases and paints that awaited. For that last week John worked. Every day the Chinese chambermaids shyly came to service the apartment, after which they tiptoed out, bowing and giggling. They must have seen every facet of human behaviour in their job but this was obviously something new to them. We carefully avoided discussing what would happen to all those wet paintings when we had to catch our flight home. Needless to say, it was due to the magnanimity of Nicolette and Fred that they were all collected and stored in Shanghai for the next time we came to China.

And there was a next time. A couple of years later, in 2005, we returned with a deputation of Royal Academicians to stage a joint exhibition in the halls of the National Gallery in Beijing in which John's Shanghai paintings would feature. That exhibition later transferred to the Royal Academy in London.

On our second trip we not only returned to Shanghai and Beijing but visited the south of the country, another tourist destination but one of the most scenic parts of the world we had yet seen – Guilin and the astonishing mountains of Yangshuo. Floating above them in a hot air balloon was a truly exciting experience only rivalled, in a quite different way, by travelling down the river by raft, meandering through their extraordinary rock formations. The profound silence of that river trip in such a landscape induced a calm we savoured for long afterwards.

It was down in this part of China that John earned a new title. After being pestered once too often by a gang of children begging for money, he relented and put coins into a few small hands with the instant result that hordes more children suddenly flocked around him asking for some money too. After he shouted at them to 'go away' they continued to follow us, hands outstretched, chanting

'Mista Buggel Off! Mista Buggel Off! Mista Buggle Off!'

CHAPTER 62

Honour and Delight

The year 2005 brought John enormous happiness in the honour bestowed upon him by his own community. In a convivial ceremony at Winton Hall he was awarded the Freedom of East Lothian, a gesture of affection and pride shown to him by Provost Pat O'Brien and East Lothian council in answer to those sentiments he carried with him of his birthplace and of which he spoke so eloquently all his life. If you have been fortunate to have been brought up in a caring and nurturing environment, be proud of where you come from, love your origins and remember them always. That was his message and he sang it loudly. There could have been no one in the world whom we met who was not made aware of what he cherished in the special character and charm of Port Seton and his home county. Many of them, including Billy Connolly and David Bowie, felt bidden to make the journey to see the place for themselves.

About that time, we were filming in Edinburgh for a BBC programme, some of which referred to John's early life. Part of the script involved returning to Rose Street and to some of those early student haunts. We were with the well-known art critic, our close friend John McEwen. He is the author of the much celebrated monograph on John's work and he was doing the interview. The first place on the schedule to visit was 150 Rose Street South Lane, our first love nest. An extraordinary thing happened as the filming began just outside Ma Scott's Bar.

The street door of the stairs to our former flat had been locked but when we met one of the previous residents who had actually lived in the building back in the sixties when we were there, he offered to open the door for us, and I couldn't resist the temptation to climb up the old stair. It now was no longer dark and dilapidated. It was freshly painted white and lights had been installed. Everything looked renovated and clean and respectable. As I reached the top and the last bend in the stairway, there were the two doors to the flats, ours on the right.

Propped outside our door there was something that looked like a piece of hardboard. An oil painting? Perhaps other artists now lived there. I couldn't resist looking closer. It was a life painting, a bit scuffed and neglected looking but a half-decent academic attempt. It looked like a student painting of the kind of model we painted in our day. I turned it over and there was my own name.

This was one of my own paintings!

Incredible! What was it doing here? Now? Today?

Although I had often passed by on my way along Rose Street and had always given a glance in its direction, I had not returned to this stair in forty years. No one knew we were visiting that day and, furthermore, the door had been locked.

In my excitement at the strange coincidence, I ran with the painting down the stairs to tell the others. It stopped us all dead in our tracks for a while. As the filming resumed and we moved on along Rose Street, I didn't think twice about taking the painting away with me. It didn't occur to me that I shouldn't. It surely had been waiting for me, for all those forty years, to come back to reclaim it. On the other hand, perhaps I should have left it for the spirits, our own included, that inhabited that blessed place.

Subsequently we discovered that the lady who lived in our previous flat had found several paintings and fragments of work left by John and me, and that day she had left my painting out as she was going to store it in her attic. According to her, it did not belong to me now, but to her. But the whole bizarre happening was too much for me and she very kindly let finders be keepers.

All the many honours he received delighted John, including the honorary degrees from many of the Scottish universities, the Edinburgh College of Art and the Royal College of Art in London who made him a Senior Fellow and member of the Council. The major museum exhibitions celebrating his work thrilled and encouraged him too but there was one event that meant a great deal in a personal and emotional respect. In Port Seton a new purpose-built day centre for the elderly was opened bearing his name: The John Bellany Day Centre. It was to cater for the contemporaries of his parents, many of whom had known him from childhood and were close friends and well-loved personalities from the town. It would go on to provide social support for future generations of the elderly in the place in which he had been brought up. Of all the causes with which to be associated it was the one that filled him with greatest pride and contentment. Transport was speedily arranged, a group of paintings, mostly of the fishing, was chosen and installed before the opening ceremony. It was John's gift to his own people with the hope that they would provide pleasure for many years to come.

Similarly, in his honour, Barga was twinned with Port Seton and the towns of East Lothian. To mark this occasion John was delighted to gift some of the work he had carried out since he arrived in Italy to form a permanent exhibition in the Villa di Reposo Giovanni Pascoli, a residential facility for the elderly in the Barga area.

CHAPTER 63

Days of Disbelief

Several years back, in 1997, John was attending a meeting at the Royal Academy during which he suffered what we would learn was a TIA, a mini stroke. He wasn't able to explain exactly what he had experienced but had driven home from London to the Clock House on his own afterwards. Subsequently we were given a diagnosis. An impenetrable depression followed when for the only time in his life he stopped painting. For three months, through Christmas and beyond, he lay in bed, day in, day out, and on the few days he managed to get himself to the studio he just sat motionless in his chair with his work in total disorder around him. He could not rouse himself from the deepest despair. Sometimes he felt unable to form words and when he did, finding the appropriate word was a challenge. It was the first time that I had ever seen him unable to put on a performance of well-being for visitors.

The mini strokes, once begun, were to continue, sometimes silently, bringing a fragility to the workings of his brain.

One of the great pleasures of our last few years was to spend time at the Girnal, an old stone granary owned by the Sutherland estates situated at Littleferry on the shore of a tidal inlet from the Dornoch Firth, a designated wildlife area inhabited by all sorts of seabirds, seals and other wild creatures. Just outside Golspie, it meant that all our old haunts were accessible and from there we could roam to our favourite places on the west coast of Sutherland and Caithness too. It seemed like a refuge from the encroaching darkness and there we experienced an illusory and all-encompassing peace.

Watching the changing weather of the passing hours and the busy activity of the natural world around us, hearing only the wind in the pines and the occasional cry of the curlew, we saw the sunset fill the sky with cerulean blue, lemon yellow and cadmium scarlet or the mist approaching far across the sea bringing rain. At night, darkness was dispelled by bright moonlight reflected in the seawater lapping on the sand-worn stones just outside our door. In June, darkness might never really arrive and the evening light never die away but in times of true darkness the lighthouse of Tarbat Ness sent rhythmic beams of light over the water from across the firth to comfort and reassure as it had done all throughout my childhood.

To say John loved being there was an understatement. He had always loved Golspie and the far north. Some of my parents' friends still lived there and so did some of my cousins and school friends and we always knew that there was still a place for us.

The car was packed with canvas and paint in Edinburgh and as soon as we arrived at the Girnal it was offloaded. John turned the writing room at the far end of the long building into his studio and I covered it with newspaper and dust sheets before he began. I don't know how he had done it but through all of his life he never made any mark when he was painting, totally out of line with anything else he did! Now, though, paint went everywhere, usually on the soles of his shoes, and thus was tramped all through the house. Not the best recommendation for renting distinguished properties. Much rubbing and scrubbing preceded our departure before we could happily hand the house on to the next tenants.

One evening before dinner I called him to the door of the Girnal. The water was still and glassy, lapping quietly on the shore, and the hills were silhouetted black against the evening sky. Across the water came the sound of music and the leaping flames of a campfire. It was a travellers' encampment. Not a gathering of the great tinker families of my childhood where the sound would have been the fiddle and mouth music. That noble generation had passed and now the music came from electronic sources, but there was, nevertheless, an echo of traveller days gone by that brought back the past and I wanted John to see it.

He slowly made it to the door. As he got there he began to stumble and a frightening emptiness came into his eyes as if life was draining from him. He was caught by my brother Michael just before he fell and somehow the moment passed and, after a rest, he regained his equilibrium.

The City of Glasgow had, through the direction of Julian Spalding, the charismatic director of Glasgow Museums, been prominent in its support of John's work, notably in the great exhibition *A Long Night's Journey into Day* at Kelvingrove, held on the occasion of his fiftieth birthday. Now, in 2005, there was to be a celebration of work he had completed during the last decade, including much that was inspired by our life in Italy. The exhibition was to be held in the galleries of the Mitchell Library and the opening fixed for an evening in June.

We were staying overnight at a nearby hotel and decided we would walk to the Mitchell. This meant that we would have to cross over the major motorway that dissected the city but it would only be a short walk. No walk was ever short enough for John but he reluctantly agreed and we set off. He was relaxed and in good form as the photograph Paul had taken of him minutes before we left the hotel testifies.

A large crowd had already assembled at the Mitchell and were waiting for us to arrive. John Lindsay, senior executive of East Lothian Council, and John's old school friend Provost Pat O'Brien were walking with us along with some of the family. We had reached the first traffic island at a busy junction that fed on to the motorway when I saw John, who was walking with Paul, sink silently to the ground. Everyone ran to help him and getting near enough I caught sight of his face. It was grey. His eyes were open but there was no sign of life. The light had gone from his eyes.

The light had gone from his eyes.

John Lindsay just happened to have recently completed a first aid course so he set to giving cardiac massage and resuscitation. The rush-hour traffic was hurtling around us, huge container lorries and buses and car horns blaring, all adding to the frenzy of what was taking place on the tiny traffic island in the middle of multiple lanes of moving vehicles. Scared to watch the efforts being made to help John, I was frozen to the spot. A young boy with a hood had stopped to offer help and advice and then a car drew up and stopped in the middle of the stream of traffic. A nurse on her way home from work had seen what was happening on the traffic island and despite the suspicion that it could be just some poor drunk that had collapsed, her better instincts told her she was needed.

It seemed ages before the ambulance arrived. I was allowed to go with him as he lay unconscious and being closely monitored. The paramedics had instantly administered defibrillation but on the way to the hospital a second shock was required. On arrival at Glasgow Western General John was whisked away and I was shown to a small waiting room, accompanied, for some reason, by two police officers.

My mind was a blank. Something was reverberating in my head, like a gong striking and echoing over and over again.

John is dead. John is dead. John is dead.

How long had it been since we had been reunited, something like twenty years? How many times during those years had I been at his hospital bed when he was in a serious condition and I was advised to prepare for the worst?

Well, now it really had happened. He had been taken from me, suddenly and violently. The likelihood of this happening had been well established in my mind ever since our second life together had begun and it could be said that, in one sense, no one was more prepared than I. In the event, however, I had not been prepared at all. Perhaps it is not possible to embrace a full-blown optimistic life while keeping watch for the sudden approach of death. Well, it has to be impossible, hasn't it?

All I remember was the long wait. Paul and Angie were with me by then. Cups of tea were brought and left to go cold. A television droned on, mindlessly irritating. After about an hour, a nurse appeared and handed me a plastic bag containing John's ripped-up clothes, his favourite black Nehru jacket and red and white striped tie he had chosen for the private view. It didn't make sense to me why I would be given these things. Somehow it just confirmed and accentuated the horror of the event. I asked the nurse what was happening and she said that she would be back soon.

Another wait.

I did not know what I was waiting for. I assumed that someone would come to talk to me and give me forms to complete. My mind would not take me further than that.

The nurse eventually returned and I asked her to tell me something ... anything.

'Well,' she said, 'you can go in and see him now.'

'Is he ...?'

'Oh,' she said jauntily, 'he's sitting up in bed telling us he's a famous artist!'

Times like these, and there had been not a few of them, prompted me to consider my own mysterious heart attack and all I could think was, is it any wonder?

Living as we did was to dance to a frenzied tune, you have to be agile, to have the ability to turn in opposing directions simultaneously, and turn again and turn again, without warning, somehow keeping a sense of balance at the same time. You have to look fearlessly and without flinching towards the promised outcome, on the path your life is heading and then, all of a sudden, without a second's notice and without missing a breath, spin on your toes to look with a steady gaze in a totally different direction.

Death? Life? Death?

Once again I was speechless with shock.

Opening the door to his room, there he was propped up on pillows, all wired up, complete with oxygen mask, high on analgesic and whatever, regaling the nurses with irrepressible repartee. A scene of insane hilarity which, once I had regained my breath, I was more than happy to join, delirious with joy.

CHAPTER 64

Winding Down

John spent two weeks in Glasgow, first recuperating and having tests at the Western before he was transferred to the Royal, where he was fitted with a state-of-the-art cardiac defibrillator that promised to jolt start his heart automatically if such an event were to happen again.

Not only was there drama in the medical sphere of his life, there was also variety. Many were the hospitals that had to offer him respite, in England and Scotland, and few hospital departments that he did not call into action. While he grew increasingly tired and dismayed at having to stay in hospital, it was there that he felt safe. Once installed and each time beginning to feel better, he was a keen observer of the insular world that is hospital life. He had names (not always flattering) for everyone. He liked all the nurses and doctors and loved delaying them on their rounds with his banter. And he loved hospital food. He told everyone who was interested that it was the veritable Ritz Hotel. He liked to boast about how fine a cook I was but now he urged me on to greater things, suggesting it would be a good idea to get the hospital recipes!

Never having needed spectacles, he was surprised when cataract operations were recommended and in the autumn of 2005 both cataracts were removed. Remembering the dramatic improvement in my mother's eyesight, which was what I understood to be the usual outcome of the operation, I waited for the same response from him. It did not come. Eventually we returned to see the consultant who referred him to another specialist. Within six weeks of his second cataract being removed he was informed that far from benefiting from vastly improved eyesight, he was now suffering from macular degeneration, in which central vision is progressively destroyed. He would now be classified as partially sighted. Oh, and it was wet macular for which nothing can be done, not the dry form that can be treated. The guaranteed development would certainly be for the worse, stopping just short of complete blindness.

Everyone lives through their eyes and their mind, so how does one adjust to such news? Especially someone who lives so completely in the visual and cerebral senses? Both faculties had begun to deteriorate and nothing would stop the decline. Twenty years previously he had received with gratitude the gift of a second life and had fought valiantly to honour the humanitarian action of someone else's family whose personal tragedy had brought about that extraordinary turn of events for him. He had courageously and decisively changed his habits of a lifetime. Every treatment and advice he had been given by the medical profession had been assiduously followed and respected and he had won through. The battering that he had given his body in his drinking days, however, had been severe and payback had come with a vengeance.

Now it was the world of visual aids. Glasses to keep out the sun, glasses for reading and for painting and special beer-bottle, mad-professor ones for watching television. Magnifying glasses to wear. Special glaring daylight lamps to help him. He gave them all a try but his patience was tried too. The quality of light was, of course, key to the quality of his vision but sometimes even good light failed him. Some days he would tell me that even though he was close up beside me, he could not see my face or that of a visitor. Sometimes the television screen was just a blurred glow. Some days he felt able to paint as he wanted to and other days he would give up in frustration and go to bed.

His painting was affected in that it was possible to detect good days from bad but he largely lived the life of the mind and his long-term memory was full and rich. He could conjure up images embedded in his visual field with a skill that defied failing sight and during those years of deteriorating eyesight he still managed on good days to produce a fair number of paintings of which he could be proud and satisfied. To me those works have an honesty and directness and a special poignancy. At other times it was also true that he was compelled to paint in the same way as W.G. Sebald relates in his book *A Place in the Country*, where the copying out of musical notation by Jean Jacques Rousseau was purely his effort to keep at bay the thoughts constantly brewing in his head like storm clouds. Counteracting the disease of thought. But then this was a lifelong inner need for John and, I would guess, probably for many other creative people.

John's internal dialogue could be alarming. He was haunted, and in the last few years he would describe the extent of his phantasmagoria. His brain would be constantly 'swirling'. He could never still the motion. He lived day-to-day in ongoing internal 'dramas' in which he would have a major role. He was powerless to halt them. Visual hallucinations were made more real by the silent dialogue that he conducted with these apparitions, sometimes human, sometimes animal. Paranoia troubled him even more and this spilled over into our day-to-day life. He became obsessed with the idea that I was going to leave him for someone else. His dreams were vivid in the extreme and some mornings as we awoke and for much of the day afterwards, he glared at me furiously so I could tell that in his dream the night before I had been up to no good.

This was very difficult to deal with at times and wore me out. He could find no relief from the torture and I found it hard to see him suffer in this way. His paranoia, coupled with the violent mood swings that afflicted him, also caused several verbal outbursts that came out of the blue. This alarmed everyone, himself most of all. He was at a loss to know what was happening to him.

When John got angry, he went over the top. It was always hot air and I knew an apology would follow almost immediately, so I could never take his blustering seriously. Sometimes, however, it frightened people out of their wits, though it was never intended to have that effect. His outbursts became a regular feature of his last declining years and the alarm he caused could be startling. He hated this lack of control in his behaviour and suffered such pangs of guilt as a result. Many were the apologies made to those who had unfortunately found themselves in the firing line. He would dwell on these occasions and they revisited him unrelentingly until the end.

For twenty-five years, since his transplant, his health had depended on long-term use of extremely powerful drugs, each of which had their side effects. The immunosuppressant cyclosporin, which was vital in combating rejection of the new liver, caused him to suffer gout, a painful condition that went on plaguing him for the rest of his life. But even worse were the effects of the steroids, widely known to cause mental disturbance including severe depression, psychosis, paranoia and even suicidal thoughts. The ability to enjoy our way of life as we did came at an increasingly high cost in terms of his psychological stability, particularly in the last eight years of his life. Of the list of symptoms associated with steroid use, all of them, excepting suicidal thoughts, were familiar to him, especially in the watches of the night.

As his body failed in the final years, the wheelchair years, powerful opiates were needed to deal with the severe pain that had him in its grasp. Hallucinations kept him company day and night, and I often had to reassure and comfort him. It was extremely difficult to calm him after he had seen and heard so clearly such disturbingly real visions and presences. He was often terrified of those apparitions and I would have to search the house to reassure him that they were gone. It would not have helped to tell him they had not existed and were merely a product of his troubled mind.

In those last years it was mostly towards me that the power of his black moods was aimed. I was a reliable target, as he knew I understood that there was no substance to his outbursts, only frustration and frailty which he was helpless to deal with. The spontaneity of his outbursts was more than matched by his declarations of love to me. Every day and all the time he made them, and I to him too. He described the 'bursts of happiness' he had when he thought of me. Although he suffered tumult and psychological torment as his mind and body failed him, the loving was deep and indestructible.

He often left me notes, sorrowful and contrite. One such sums up what we were to each other over all the years:

Dear Helen

I'm profoundly sorry if I upset you this afternoon. I was at the end of my tether with fatigue when ...arrived with ...

Helen, surely you know in your heart that there is nobody who understands the depth of my work and there is nobody who knows it better than you.

My whole *raison d'etre* is entangled with you, and without your help, depth of intuitive thought of my work ...

I trust you more than any other human being with my soul. You are my lifeline and guiding light.

All my love
John

Such was his mental distress that eventually we called on psychiatric services for help, and a degree of respite was achieved. Superficial calm set in for moments at a time. The notion of being exposed to the 'meddling' of psychiatrists was something that he would have previously rejected in the most vigorous terms. His creativity and his mental processes were one and the same thing and they should never be interfered with. He was in a bad way though and he knew it, so he went, in trepidation but in the hope of some help.

At his first appointment he was introduced to Kathy Walsh, an Irish psychiatrist with whose professional skill and visual attractiveness he was more than willing to cooperate. When, after a few years, it was decided that a different department of psychiatric care should deal with him, he was blessed with a second psychiatrist of equally favourable attributes. Attractive, intelligent women who, for a whole hour at a time, would listen to his every word. What was there not to love about that? Halfway sorted before he began!

He engaged with them and enjoyed the interchange. He concurred with all of their advice but then proceeded to put into practice absolutely nothing whatsoever of the changes in behaviour which they had agreed in their sessions. Slow down, fewer hours in the studio painting, not so many large canvases, less stress, a little gentle exercise, '*con calma*', etc., etc. – it all made sense but that kind of effort was not for him. His morale, however, was boosted by the care and time they gave him. The psychological input of the medical profession to vulnerable patients is something that is rarely taken into account but must have a significant effect on well-being. This aspect of the treatment he received from all his medics – doctors, nurses and associated personnel – was something to which he responded readily and positively. They meant something to him and, while their paths crossed, he wanted to mean something to them too.

Then pain in his leg and back began to nag and bother him. This agony was quite quickly and simply diagnosed as being due to his spine calcifying and beginning to crumble. Add this to the frequent spells of gout and he had a remarkable level of pain that had set in and was here to stay. It was as if he had been selected as a recipient for any and every affliction. They now came fast and furious, one after another.

John's poor health did not deter us from going to Italy. Bearing in mind hospital appointments, we could be there for all of the summer, return in the autumn and winter and spring. It was our home just as much as the Clock House was. We were fortunate in having excellent medical attention from Rino and Dr. Maurizio Lunardi, the cardiac specialist in Castelnuovo, and being with our friends there always brought us comfort and reassurance. It was as if in the Garfagnana we could close the door on John's encroaching frailty and feel as if we could arrest its development. Only in the last couple of years when his mental distress became severe did the visits necessarily become less but it still remains our home.

In 2009 we made a last trip to Varangeville on the Normandy coast, that most special place to us. John was now in a wheelchair. He could only walk with great difficulty and for short distances. He still had to climb stairs where we lived and it was a slow and tortuous procedure. Not only was it painful but now he also lacked the energy to pull himself up from one step to the next. This was becoming a serious problem that we would obviously have to address. In the meantime we could only soldier on, continuing to reach out for the best that life could offer.

I regret that last visit to Varangeville. Someone who has never lived with long-term searing pain can only imagine how it must fill the days in monochrome misery. It demands a strength of will and a sense of purpose just to cope with the day-to-day but even so, while the mind urges you on to go and see and do, the destruction of the body exercises a crushing power over the striving spirit.

Our hotel did not have a lift and although we were offered a ground-floor room, it came without a view of the sea which would never do, so he wanted to take on the stairs to the upper floor where we could look out over the water, watch the great tankers appearing and disappearing in the mists of the Channel and see the sunset if there was one. John's vision was at best blurred now but he still seemed to be able to see to some extent, to draw, watch football and appreciate the world around him.

We spent time in Dieppe and, as usual, he couldn't get enough of the harbour. He had drawn and painted it so often over the years. Although there were not many fishing boats left there, there were enough to inspire him. The scene had not changed that much since our honeymoon of 1964. We went along the quays taking it all in, watching everyone and catching it all in our eyes. We gazed up to our personal icon of youthful dreams, the small church that guarded the entrance to the harbour of Dieppe.

But it was a struggle. I was fairly new to pushing him in the wheelchair and found it difficult to negotiate the cobbled streets and narrow pavements of the town. I would get stuck, unable to move forward or back until eventually someone helped me. There was a biting wind and John was getting tired and I was fighting back tears of disappointment and regret – in myself. This was not how I wanted what would be our last visit to Dieppe and the Normandy coast to be. I wanted it to revive our memories of happiness reclaimed, as it usually did, but this time, while there was pleasure, there was a new weariness in him, in spirit as well as in body.

It was October and the skies were grey and misty. Rain was never far away. There was the dying away of the year in the air. John, who always had a nap in the afternoons, began to sleep on into the evening, finding it difficult to waken up, and this added to my deepening sadness.

While he was sleeping I sometimes took myself off down through the narrow, steeply descending gorge that led to the shore. If the tide was out I walked far along the sands, the mighty cliffs with the just visible roof of the church bathed in the blue and gold of a restless evening sky and reflected in the rock pools that, as I retraced my steps, were beginning to flood with the incoming tide. I was walking with Braque, Monet, Seurat, Delacroix and all the many other painters and writers of the past who had known that way too and had seen what I was seeing. But in my mind was John. We had returned to this place that had, against all odds, given us back the life on which we had started out in our student days. The years that followed had been overflowing with the good and true feeling of being back in the places we belonged, with each other. We could never have foreseen the unimaginable miracle of reclaiming such extraordinary happiness. But it had come to us and been ours for almost thirty astonishing years.

Now I was being made aware that the circle of our second life together was beginning to close. The intimation was sounding on the chilly sea air.

We would never come back here again.

CHAPTER 65

The End of Days

John loved driving and being in the car. It was his favourite form of travel. It suited his lazy attitude to anything that wasn't the physicality of painting and while in the car we could see and talk to our hearts' content. They were special times of sharing.

Latterly, when he could no longer drive, I took him out again. As we left the house I would ask him where we should go. 'Scotland' was often the reply. He wasn't joking. I had only to agree and we would instantly have been off on the long journey, without a care in the world. No car journey was ever too long for him and no time of day was the wrong time to go and there was never a day that was not a good day to go back home to Scotland. Every time when we crossed the border without fail he would shout out: 'Bonnie Scotland! We're home!'

For our next stay at the Girnal I began to plan a special surprise for him. A mystery tour, if you like, in the spirit of Blaikie's Mystery Tours of his childhood. I would take him by the west coast, making two stops en route. Crossing the border after the Lake District, I planned to follow the old familiar scenic route by Loch Lomond, Moor of Rannoch, Glencoe and up the banks of Loch Ness to Inverness and then on to Golspie. This was the way, as children, we had been taken by my parents when we visited my Auntie Jessie and Uncle Cedric in Gourock. It was a stunningly beautiful route and held so many memories. I had taken John that way before, but rarely, and I knew he found it inspiring, as I did – especially the drama of Glencoe. It would be something that he would enjoy and so would I.

It was on the second day when we stopped for tea at a place in the middle of the moors that I began to realize he was in more pain than usual. He wasn't one for complaining but on this occasion he was writhing about and could not find a comfortable way of sitting. Bumps in the road made him groan. We stopped overnight at Ballachulish, where we had a spectacular view across the loch from our window and reminisced about Michael's second marriage that had taken place at the hotel we could see across the water, a happy occasion, only a few years ago, which had reunited our families and all the young cousins.

We were preparing to have dinner at one of the local restaurants and the evening promised everything that we enjoyed, but he was distraught with pain. As always, he tried to reassure me that he would feel better in the morning and once he arrived in Golspie he would be fine. If not, he would see the doctor there.

The glory of Loch Ness, the mountains, the first sighting of the symbol for home, the Mannie on Ben Bhraggie, came and went in a haze of agony, robbing him of the excitement and sense of anticipation he would normally have felt. This was the onset of shingles, diagnosed when we arrived in Golspie.

'What's shingles?' he asked. The explanation was given to him. It could last for a few weeks. Or months. Rarely for years.

It lasted for almost four years. Until the day he died.

How can so many afflictions hit one person? He had no immune system to talk of and hadn't had one since his transplant almost twenty-five years ago. Did that lay the way open to so much disease? He depended on more and more medication. Were the side effects of so many drugs causing Armageddon within his body? It seemed it had become a vicious circle and I was aware that the doctors were now at a loss as to how to improve matters. All they could do was tweak the prescription in minuscule ways. John had found himself in a cul-de-sac from which, with the best will that the medical profession had shown him throughout all those years, it would be impossible to escape.

This final infection was intolerable and relief impossible

to find. We tried everything on the market. American friends who had been inoculated against shingles sent suggestions of treatment but nothing worked. He decided to try one type of medicated cream and although what it achieved was minimal, it became the one thing he decided he could not do without. Biofreeze froze the area of the greatest agony.

With the worst spasms and constant nagging of the pain he would cry out for this cream. He was always adept, throughout his life, at conjuring up his own idiosyncratic names for people and things. Now on top of his inventiveness, mini strokes often robbed him of the ability to find the correct word when he needed it but he never failed to find his own word for things. The result was often hilarious. It was not meant to be. He was being deadly serious.

He was calling for the cream.

'Helen! Where's the marmalade? Bring me the marmalade for f**** sake! This is agony!'

Sometimes without warning the 'marmalade' would turn into something else.

'I need the Irn Bru! Quickly! I can't find it!'

Shingles was usually 'Shambles' and consultations with the medics would be strewn with references to 'shambles' and the agonies thereof. Intimate parts of his body would be similarly named, bringing hoots of laughter from his nurses. His conversations were strewn with words such as 'frillies', details of the ongoing trouble he was having with his 'rockies' and as for his 'Harry Lauders' ...

At the end of 2011 the Scottish National Galleries informed me that they were planning a large retrospective of his work to be opened in the RSA building on Princes Street in Edinburgh that was now in their possession. Delighted that another such tribute as had been given him in 1986 was forthcoming, I suggested that, with regard to John's health, sooner would be better than later.

This news was a tremendous boost to his flagging energies and carried him aloft through the last months of his life. I drove him along to George Street to look down Hanover Street at the great neoclassical building that for a couple of months would have his name emblazoned in huge lettering over the whole of the façade:

BELLANY

In his student days he had exhibited his paintings around the outside of that building in protest against the prevailing state of Scottish painting at that time – and here he was all those years later, invited to show a comprehensive exhibition of his life's work inside the great building purely on his own terms. It was a sight that pleased him very much. No matter how much loved and respected someone is, the need for a vote of confidence is always there. The well-being of the creative spirit depends on such gestures. Especially, therefore, in the knowledge that time really was running out for John by now, I bless all those who were involved in bringing about the exhibition *A Passion for Life* and for making it such a rewarding, triumphal and warmly affectionate farewell to John.

He was in his wheelchair on the occasion of the opening night but he was as usual a striking figure in his dark velvet jacket, flamboyant tie and, of course, his lucky scarf. He was a frail figure compared to what he had been in the past but few would have been aware of the extent of his fragility – his excruciating pain, his struggle with depression, his 'swirling brain', his confusion, his clouded eyesight, his diminished hearing, his painful 'rockies' or his depleted energies. For his last appearance it would be a virtuoso performance. It was no more than was expected of him and he was not going to let himself down.

He had asked me to give the speech of thanks. He was too unsteady on his feet and he no longer had confidence that he would be able to deliver all that he would like to express. He couldn't do it, he said, when I asked him again just before I started to speak.

I was coming to the end of the speech when I noticed out of the corner of my eye that he was moving the footrests of his chair out of the way and I could tell that he was going to make the effort. I had hoped this would happen. He was not going to let this occasion go by; he was going to have his say after all. He never did like me to have the last word anyway!

He brought the house down with a tale of pure invention. He lived up to all expectations and he was himself to the last.

Three days after the opening of *A Passion for Life* he had to be admitted to the Western General Hospital in Edinburgh with another serious bout of pneumonia that kept him there, on oxygen and antibiotics yet again, for nearly two weeks. He had almost recovered when I was suddenly struck by a particularly intense and debilitating bug that prevented my visiting him for a couple of days.

On being told that he could be discharged, he decided that he wanted to get home to our Edinburgh flat immediately. I was out of action, with the vomiting at its worst, so I asked if he could wait until the following day when I was bound to feel better and the risk of contracting, what could be for him a dangerous infection, would be diminished. Understandably, after a long hospital stay, he was not very happy with this idea, even though I had spoken to him on the phone and explained. As I was never ill I don't think he believed me.

A few hours later he rang again to tell me that he had found someone to bring him home. An ambulance at this hour of the night? And will they help you to get up all the stairs? The answer was yes to everything and I wasn't to worry. I sighed and resigned myself to the mysterious workings of the NHS. I had informed the hospital of my bug and they agreed about the timing of his discharge. But it was all different these days. The main preoccupation was to get people out of badly needed beds, regardless.

The downstairs bell rang. I got out of bed and pressed the buzzer to open the door. I opened our own door and waited. All I heard was a bit of scuffling and people's voices. It was ages before I heard them on the floor below, by which time I had tumbled to what was going on.

Margaret had gone in to visit John. He had harangued her about wanting home and demanded that she take him there. Margaret, eternally kind and loving was, all her life long, putty in the hands of the brother she idolized and adored. She did as she had always done. What he told her to do. He never understood why what he wanted to do might have associated difficulties to be negotiated. In this instance, he wanted to go home, late though it was, and his sister would take him there. What's the problem?

The night shift would have come on duty in his ward and, in the middle of their urgent tasks, discharge letters had to be written, medicine obtained from the pharmacy and it all took time. He would never have caused any rumpus. He never did in hospital. He was always far too grateful for anything like that. This delay, however, must have tried his patience. His short fuse, always aimed in the direction of his nearest and dearest, was fired up to exploding level as Margaret found herself negotiating lifts and struggling with him in one of the unwieldy hospital chairs making for the exit, himself bawling like a madman, 'You're going the wrong way! Not that door! Watch out, you're going into the wall! Look where you are going!' and the like.

Margaret deposited him by the door while she went to bring her car round as near to the entrance as possible. It was nearly eleven o'clock at night and the hospital was deserted. No one was about, as visiting hour had finished ages ago. It was a freezing winter night with a bitter wind, pitch dark with remnants of snow still lying in corners of the icy walkways where it had been blown. There he was, for no one except the CCTV to witness, attired in nothing more than thin pyjamas and some kind of hospital slippers. When she mentioned the fact that he had no warm clothing Margaret was curtly informed that he was not in the slightest interested in any of that. He just wanted home!

Looking around in a vain effort for something to shield him from the cold, in the boot of her car she was relieved to find a pair of old curtains she had acquired from a charity shop. This would have to do. She wound them round his shivering body and mercifully having also found a couple of football scarves in the back of her car she was able to equip him for the short journey to Great Stuart Street and the final touches were made to his ensemble. With one of the Hibs scarves draped round his head and tied in a knot under his chin, the like of which Maw Broon would have worn when she had a gum boil, the other round his waist to keep the curtains in place, they set off. The trip from the hospital was short but ascending the stairs to our flat was another matter entirely. For the fit and healthy it was a challenge but for someone like him who was extremely weak and fragile, on top of which he was recovering from a dangerous respiratory infection, getting to our second floor took almost three times longer than the journey from the hospital.

After this heroic climb he was completely done in but triumphant. Defiance and a rhetorical 'What?' glinted fiercely out of eyes all but submerged in the Maw Broon headgear as his tragically wasted frame collapsed on the sofa, bare ankles blue with cold protruding from entanglements of dusty curtain fabric, gasping for breath.

He had, by then, only another six or seven months left to live but this is what he would be to the end of his days. He would be himself. That had been his life's lodestar – to be himself and to make it worth being. Hadn't MacDiarmid's words been inscribed indelibly around the walls of our home all those years ago at the very beginning? 'Tae be yersel, and tae mak' that worth bein,' nae harder task tae mortals has been gi'en.'

Assuredly the most difficult task. But he had been himself, sometimes in spite of himself. He had been true to himself when at times he had no sense of self-recognition. He had tried to run away and hide from what he saw of himself, to mask what was within, in the anxiety to make his being worthwhile. He had at times been fooled by his own self, that elusive will o' the wisp that leapt and cavorted, ducking and diving and dancing through all the rapids and troughs of his life. Many times there had been other more duplicitous selves that he had caught glimpses of but they had proved to be, like Eederadder, my childhood companion, no more than imaginary friends.

He had never confused me. Not once over the stormy years. I had certainly been a trusting victim of his duplicity and I had been hurt, wounded, exasperated, embarrassed and out of my mind with fury and distress, but about the deep core of his being

I was never fooled. He had never been more himself than on our very first encounter in the art college studio fifty years before. He had been openly and innocently himself in the days and years of our first life together and it had never been possible for me to lose sight of what I had seen then. Throughout all my years apart from him I had carried the knowledge of that self that was his and no slogans or sweet talk were needed to convince me of how truly worth being it was.

CHAPTER 66

The Dying of the Light

It is now a few months further on, summer 2013. John's seventy-first birthday has just passed.

Must be morning. Feels like it. The whole room fills with light. The four tall windows of the Clock House studio can't keep it out without the help of blinds or curtains of which there are neither. The midsummer sun is already flooding away the darkness of the mind that will bide its time until the shadows of the evening fall again. The coming of the new day brings a flare of elation that flickers and immediately dies.

Quick!

The eye darts across to the other bed. Yes. The chest rises and falls – with effort.

The only noise is the steady 'Oom Pa-a-a-a-h ... Oom Pa-a-a-a-h ... Oom Pa-a-a-a-h ... Oom Pa-a-a-a-h ...' of the oxygen machine faithfully carrying out its life-giving task.

The morning sun has brought a benign warmth to the studio. This has always been the perfect place to be. It is where dreams are spun and nightmares exorcised, where identities are fixed, places revisited and worlds are made to last, forever. The past is here and the future awaits in the blank canvas. Plans and possibilities are entangled in tumbled thought while in the shadows, in the unvisited and unseen corners, there has always been the lurking fear.

There has been a big clear-out to make way for the hospital

bed but large canvases are still stacked over on one side of the room below the high windows and along the balcony. Drawings, prints, watercolours – the constant stream abruptly brought to a sudden halt. Perched on a box there is a canvas drawn in by the familiar hand – Eyemouth yet again – and waiting all those weeks to feel the weight of pigment. The brushes, heavy with the remains of last gestures, uncleaned as usual in anticipation of speedy resumption of activity, lie where they were left on the paint rag along the floor beneath, ready and willing. They will be taken in hand when the good days come again.

Catalogues, books, framed drawings, great portfolios crammed full with the work of years, letters, photographs, old shoes, 'I love Granddad' cups, children's drawings, poems in frames, poets in frames, his old friend George Bruce, football regalia, a 'Scotland Forever' banner, stacks of CDs spilling out over the paint-splattered carpet, lamps leaning and lamps broken, a large photograph of Jonathan, Paul and John at the World Cup in Paris, a cap proclaiming 'Barga' out of its sunshine yellowness, tables that through no fault of their own found themselves turned into pallets groaning with teetering towers of oil pigment, the whole wriggling spectrum of colour whose urgent and frenzied purpose has been abruptly arrested and now abandoned – statements formed in the mind but never now to be proclaimed to the world. Half-empty screwed-up tubes of paint in knee-deep heaps, paint brushes of every size lying in their thousands, fossilized in clarts of colour, some daubed only once, others worn away to a frizzy stubble, metal supermarket baskets carrying brand-new ones for the work to come, white stacks of canvases and mountains of tubes of Artist's Oils newly ordered for the 'beezers' that lay ahead, model boats, masks of Mexico and mementos from China, favoured landscapes of the Garfagnana elbowing up against Eyemouth, St Abbs, Port Seton, the black paint-spattered revolving chair, a helpless casualty in the crossfire of creation, bottles, jugs, dead flowers, more boats and old biscuits, old biscuit tins and black ink and empty boxes, boxes unopened, a hefty dose of morning medicine forgotten, now never to be administered, CD players broken and unusable but never to be thrown away, a trio of accordions long since sacrificed to declining strength. In an unseen corner shelters a perfectly preserved, long dead and dried-up bat and on unreachable window heights, wasps and butterflies, moths and bees in all stages of decay among the cobwebs keep their timeless vigil.

But now there is the hospital bed with the ever-rippling mattress that can arrange itself in any position, in brash promise of ultimate comfort that, even with its extension for long legs, is defeated by the undulating slope of the bed.

'One, two, three.' We would hoist him up to an easier place, his bony frame resistant to our efforts, his need for oxygen the priority.

More oxygen! Urgent! Desperate! Gasping for breath, his eyes full of wild alarm.

'*Con calma! Con calma!*'

'Say it, Helen!'

'*Con calma! Con calma!*'

'Keep saying it, Helen!'

'*Con calma!*

Con calma! ...

Con calma ...

Con calma ... con calma' ... until Natalina's words had soothed him once more and the crisis had passed.

'That was a near thing. I was almost away ... I felt I was going.'

Community nurses now come every morning and every evening, administering medication and care. Their equipment has found a place among the confusion of the large studio, the yellow emergency box lying sealed out of sight of children. At night the Ross Nurses come to wash him and make him comfortable. He likes all of them that come, whatever their mission, and looks on their visits as social occasions, on good days preferring to chat about their lives and joke rather than to be 'mucked around with' but patient and grateful for their efforts to help him all the same, and forever singing their praises for the warm kindness shown to him and the good humour of their repartee. He also likes nothing better than a visit from his GP who happens to be Scottish and so knows the lingo.

By the bed table stands the large oxygen machine on which he depends. Many times I have found him fast asleep with the tubes displaced but, more and more often now, his respiratory distress alerts him. On his table, among his drinks and CDs and sweets, the appeal of which now rarely calls, there is a small jar of sweet peas from the garden squeezing in beside the watercolour box and brushes and water jar. There must always be pencils and a knife to sharpen them. Sheets of watercolour paper and sketch-books lie at the side of the bed – all at hand for when the energy will flow again.

Paul has set up a TV positioned by the pallet and close to his bed to cater for his failing vision and to provide his favourite pastime, watching football with his boys – his sons and grandsons.

Beyond the paraphernalia of frailty, the nurses' equipment, the Zimmer frames, the wheelchair, a bed settee has been made up for me. Sunny, the adored Labrador, has his bed on the floor between ours. We all sleep there together in the studio, watching over each other throughout the night, the door always fully open at John's request in order to banish the lurking feeling of claustrophobia that now seems to be coming over him.

Lying in my bed I look over to his sleeping shape. The morning light streams in with the glow of a new dawn. Its promise holds nothing for him now.

Across the hall, through the open door of the studio I see into the dining room. On the wall behind the music stand and the old piano, there is John's small self-portrait from 1962, the year our lives together began. From my bed I see him there, in this little portrait, as I first knew him – eager, virile, shining with life. Twenty years old, he is only beginning his journey and has no fear or apprehension about what it will bring. He is hungry, ravenous, eager for it all to begin. He is still the boy who, around the age of eight, on the first day of the summer holidays from school was up early, eager to get into his new Sloppy Joe and out on his bike cycling around Port Seton looking for someone to play with – no time to lose. Ten minutes later he would be

back home, deflated. No one was yet up and about. His urgency was not everybody's. That moment he would replay over and over in many guises throughout his years.

He wanted life today, not tomorrow, and that is what he got. He called out and beckoned to it and wrapped his arms about it. It sang for him and wherever he was he danced to its tune, urging everyone around him to do the same. He thrilled to its rhythm and sucked the sweetness out of it. The mysteries of it teased him and tantalized. He was not to know that eventually they would, however, also begin to haunt him and taunt him in the dark hours. They would interrogate and accuse and intimidate him. They would scare the daylights out of him. He would turn from the terror of it all and close his eyes to it, swimming against its currents, but ever find himself drawn back again into the whirlpool of its power. He would sink and suffocate but somehow catching on to the merest strand he would manage to surface again and survive. And the music would play on, sometimes discordant, sometimes benevolent, often crazy and many times sorrowful, but on it would go seeking an elusive harmony until the fading out began.

The fading out had begun and had now brought us to these summer days and they were going to be his last.

'If I die before I wake, please oh lord, my soul do take.' The terror of the prayer implanted in the young child had never left him. He had carried it with him his whole life long. He was as afraid now as he had been as a little boy.

'It's the last lap, John,' his doctor had said.

'How long is the last lap?'

'No one knows the answer to that, I'm afraid.'

Out of his lifelong fear and denial, he was tentatively now coming forward to confront his own approaching mortality. He knew it was coming for him and that there was no escape this time. Gradually, the realization had dawned on him that this time he was beaten and that he could devise no final resurrection. Sadly, but without a struggle, he was conceding defeat. The mighty tempests were being becalmed and the fight was being abandoned.

He had to go and he would go, quietly now.

Just when one could have wished for a merciful blurring of the lines, he emerged from his confusion and paranoia and hallucination to take charge of an unexpected clarity of mind. The terror remained, however, and the nights were still not for the faint-hearted. Often he would call out to me, seeking company in the quiet hours. Fighting veils of sleep I heard him calling me from across the studio, wanting to share whatever was crowding his thoughts.

'Do you mind your Uncle Willie's draper's shop in Macduff, Helen?'

'Yes, I do.'

'Do you mind his naked plaster shop models with the bald heads that he would put in his windows? And the corsets and things they wore!'

'Yes, John, but can we talk about it in the morning?'

'OK.'

Sigh.

Silence.

Ten minutes later: 'Helen? I'm frightened. Will you talk to me for a while?'

Though awash with sleep, this brought my instant surrender and so, then, fully awake, we would see in the morning hours reminiscing about days and times gone by, crazy, hilarious, romantic, magical – only the happy spectrum of the brightest colours of our road.

But the regrets. He was obsessed with his regrets.

Much as I wanted to, I could not dismiss this preoccupation, as he needed to talk about those things that bothered him. He was not a churchgoer and had not been for most of his adult life, but he had never become disentangled from the torments of his religious upbringing or from the well-developed sense of superstition of his own fisher folk. He wanted forgiveness. Absolution. He needed to cleanse himself in preparation for what he imagined lay ahead. It had to be granted to him before he could leave this world in peace. It was no good trying to reassure him that everyone had regrets, and I had more than enough of my own too. But all that we had buried in the torrent of joy and happiness we had had the great good fortune to reclaim in the almost thirty years we had shared in our second life together. I tried to divert him back to the good times with friends and family, all his kindness, good humour and generosity and all the great times he had created simply by being himself.

'You are the most loved person I know, John. Just think of all the people with whom you have had such great times. They all loved being with you. You are so much loved.'

He would then lapse into reminiscence that had us rocking with the crazy joy of it all.

'What a life we have had!'

United in that thought and with the coming of another dawn, the solace of sleep would mercifully begin to descend on him.

He had been in his hospital bed in his studio for about three months. To begin with, in the afternoons, I got him in his wheelchair and took him to the car outside. We went for drives round some of our favourite country roads. A short time was enough to tire him out, though, and after a few weeks this too had to be abandoned. Too exhausting. He never left his bed again.

One evening he was becoming agitated. He was looking at the blank canvas that we had set up at his place of painting in readiness for his return to work, and he announced that he had had enough of this 'f***ing around, wasting all my days lying in bed'. Tomorrow he was going to get up early and do a whole day's painting.

In the morning I found him, one leg stretched out aiming for the floor, but on realizing the impossibility of such an effort he had fallen asleep, half on, half off the high bed. He had wanted so much to snap back into his everyday life, doing what he loved most – painting. But it could never happen now. The strength was gone from his body.

About his impending death there grew a resignation in him that I had not anticipated but now gladly welcomed. Was the edge of his lifelong fear being softened by a gentle acceptance that his relentless pain and sickness would be relieved by the sleep of death? That death could offer him release from all of that? Of course not! He would always choose life, however painful, over the incomprehensible annihilation of death. He never wanted his day to end. He still retained a vivid concept of Heaven and Hell, and his conviction remained strong, no matter how we tried to pacify him, that the latter would be his inevitable destination.

He began, however, to allow himself to wonder at what might lie in the immediate beyond.

'You see, I don't know what is going to happen, Helen. What do you think it will be like?'

He was looking into my eyes with all the earnestness of a child seeking answers to impossible questions.

'Will it be just a blank space with nothing in it? Or will there be a hundred pipers an' aw' an' aw?'

'My beloved John, I can't tell you that, but knowing the life we have had I wouldn't be surprised if the massed bands weren't out in force to welcome you. I do hope they will be. I would like that for you so much.'

In those last summer days, I would look across to his bed and find him looking at me. He watched me as I moved about the studio. He wanted nothing and never complained about the pain he was in. Or of his fear of what was to come. He was full of tenderness. He told me over and over again, as we had always told each other throughout our tempestuous lives, that he loved me, that we loved each other, so much. All impatience, all argument, all bluster, all fireworks and fight had now forsaken him and what was left was the great loving of the life that was now quietly ebbing away from him.

As we sat, my hand in his, one afternoon shortly before he died, he looked into my eyes and said, 'The worst thing [about dying], Helen, is that I'll never see your face again.'

Chapter 67

Taking Leave

It was early on the sunny evening of 28 August 2013, to the sounds of our grandchildren playing out in the summer garden, with some of the family, including our sisters, sitting sipping wine on the terrace, that he took his leave. Anya was in Italy, at Sepulicchia, on holiday with her family, but Jonathan and Paul were with me by his bed as the last breath left his body and we knew that it was all finally over.

I stroked his beloved face, following the familiar contours of his brow down through the hollow of his temple, the translucent skin now taut over his cheekbone, almost as smooth as it had been when he was young, when I had first known him.

The evening light was fading, and from the sudden silence, gradually there arose the first faintest murmurings of the great shingle sound of the surging tide. No travails of the Horse of Selene, no force of moon across the sky had the power to reverse the retreating motion of that wave. Nothing would be reprieved. Nothing returned. All would be carried away. All of him that I had ever known. And all of that part of me that was forever him.

He was now on his way across the mighty ocean. The boat had long been moored awaiting him, the Seacat biding her time, the anchor ropes straining from the pier. The seagulls were milling overhead, piercing everything with shards of ominous laughter and shrieking and screaming. The Seacat, who would

THE SAD PIA

Bellany

83

be his companion, had now whispered that it was time for departure. Fragments of crazy piano music were already flying on the wind. The piano player, low in the stern of the barque, intent on his uncanny task ahead was working up the jingle jangle of his repertoire. The clamour of its unearthly promise would resound and answer back as they safely rounded the Hurkurs until finally they lost sight of the last landmarks of home. Unforsaken, he would be accompanied on the journey without end, past and away from the watchful cliffs of St Abbs, the mighty Bass Rock, the islands of May, Fidra and the Lamb, all the islands of his life, and the cormorants and the puffins and the crying, screeching gannets would see him go. Out into the beyond.

Over and over I stroked him gently, trying to hold in to me the warmth of his blessed life now departing.

'*Con calma*, John.

Con calma, my beloved John.

Con calma ... Con calma ... con calma ... con calma ...'

Elegy

My beloved John,

Yesterday I left the Clock House and drove up the Great North Road listening to a recording you had made for the British Library a few years before you died. You were with me all the way north and I was with you, my heart brimming with love and longing.

You spoke beautifully and concisely in the wonderfully expressive way in which you had always excelled. Close and warm, honest and open and intelligent. Your most lovable self. The way we always spoke when we were just you and me.

On the long road from England to Scotland I always make the detour, turning off just after crossing the border, to Eyemouth, that special place, just as you did a year ago on your own very last journey home to Scotland when you were being brought to your funeral.

Since then, I never arrive or leave Scotland without going to Eyemouth. It is a pilgrimage. Love takes me there.

Since you died, many are the days when I am saddened by my inability to feel your presence around me, but there, in Eyemouth, I always know I'll find you. Grandma and Grandpa and the rest of the dear family too. I hear the voices. I feel the kindness.

When I arrived there last night, it was twilight and the last gleam of light was leaving the sky. I stopped in our usual place high up near Gunsgreen House overlooking the harbour and the lovely old town. Your beloved Eyemouth. It was glimmering in the stillness of the fading light.

I wanted to share that moment with you as we had done so often together since we were young. Last night I so wanted you there with me again. I was aching with the pain of losing you and of knowing that now I would only ever come there on my own. Never again with you.

This morning, in Edinburgh, as I write sitting at the high window of our Great Stuart Street home, looking away out over the valley of the Water of Leith, over the Firth of Forth to Burntisland sparkling in the sun on the coast of Fife, my heart is weeping for you and all that you were.

I miss you so much. There are times, like this moment, when I feel broken now that you're gone.

Mostly I am OK. I have lived alone before and so I am no stranger to solitude but this solitary life is not something I embrace willingly again. I just acknowledge it as part of the inevitable pattern that forms at the end of the day.

I still, however, have purpose and I am blessed in our family around me. I am as yet unafraid of going forward into the time I have left. But I am incomplete. There is an echoing emptiness and a yearning and sorrow.

We had, what they say in Ireland, 'the two days' – the bad and the good. We had plenty of both. But we were, the two of us, born with an innocence that was never burdened by cynicism or worldly scepticism in our recognition of what love really means and this we had recognized simultaneously when we were young. We sensed then the credibility of the idea that when you look into another's soul you see your own for the first time.

Back here in Edinburgh, where our lives first became entangled, I feel the passion and pure joy I had then of knowing what I had found in you. Way back in our student years we had instantly blended into one. We were so sure we were blessed.

We were not wrong.

It never did go away, that deep union of souls. It was always there. Later, as we went on to blunder through our lives we did

394

our best to deny and betray what we knew we shared. Not just you. Me too. And this sense of betrayal went with us throughout all the long years apart.

In the afternoon of this golden autumn day I'll walk down through the Dean Village to your grave that lies in the old cemetery by the National Galleries of Modern Art. You lie there, still and silent, beneath the marble stone I chose for you from our beloved Italian mountains and where one day I'll join you. We'll share the endless silence of eternity while your great paintings in the museums around us will go on to commune with the world in our place.

They will follow the journey of your life, the questions, the unresolved mysteries, the torment and the passion but the most resonant song will be of love. The love of family, of heritage, of place and people, the only enduring meaning in earthly existence.

In your voice will be heard strains of the sweet sadness of our lifelong bond that was ignited in our first young days, and that lived on, in spite of everything, over all the years whether together or apart. Woven through the fabric of your entire life's work will be the shining thread of that love with which we were blessed, in which we had unshakeable belief and of which we sang with such optimistic hearts at our Sutherland wedding all those years ago; the words that followed me down all the tempestuous years:

'that theirs may be the love that knows no ending
whom thou forevermore dost join in one.'

Dear Helen,

I am profoundly sorry if I upset you this afternoon. I was at the end of my tether with fatigue when ... armed ...

Helen surely you know in your heart that there is nobody who understands the depth of my work, and there is nobody who knows it better than you.

My whole raison d'être is interwoven with you and without your help, depth of instinctive thoughts of my work.

I trust you more than any other human being with my soul. You are my life and guiding light.

Lovingly John x x

ACKNOWLEDGEMENTS

This book had been on the go for a few years, on and off, left abandoned for months at a time. No one had seen it until I showed it for the first time to my lovely friend Jenny Brown of Jenny Brown Associates. I was amazed and excited when, after reading through the first draft, undaunted by the unwieldy volume of words, she decided it might be something that could be worked on and knocked into a shape suitable for publication. Not only that, she honoured me by agreeing to become my agent.

Jenny had the perfect person in mind when she set the highly skilled Ailsa Bathgate onto the formidable task of wading through the mire of bracken and brambles, wild empty glens and dense forests, waterlogged peat bogs and acres of scratchy heather and untamed grass to find the heart of the home itself. There was a ruthless hacking away, all totally essential, done with Ailsa's sickle, not without a few whimpers from me. 'Where have my lovely aunties with their flowery frocks and their home knitted lacy cardigans gone?'

Ailsa did such a sterling job that the resulting text caught the discerning eye of Robert Davidson of Sandstone Press who, to my great delight, agreed to publish it. Bob's patience and good humour were exemplary. Anxiously awaiting long promised photographs he would nudge me in the most endearingly gentle way. Emails would arrive simply saying 'Pigtails please' or something to that effect.

Then his partner and editor-in-chief, the magnificent Moira Forsyth, got her hands on the text. More mighty slashing and burning and finally everything was in digestible order. The wild duckling had been turned into a swan and was now ready to fly.

All of those people tirelessly and whole-heartedly, with enormous professional skill and good humour, showed me continual support and encouragement and I am filled with gratitude, admiration and affection for them all. To all of them and all at Sandstone Press and Jenny Brown Associates I give my thanks. I'm grateful also to Gravemaker & Scott and Iolaire Typesetting for their beautiful design for the cover and text.

There are countless people we meet in the course of our lives who, simply by being themselves, contribute elements of enduring value and beauty that we cherish in memory. There are many such people, not mentioned in this book, who played a part in my story and enriched and illuminated and inspired me and still do to this day. I remember you all with love.

My most profound thanks must go to my children. It was a daunting task for all of you, as it was for me, to revisit times we would rather forget – times, in fact, we have successfully, long ago, buried securely in the past. Thank you for allowing me speak of this. The courage and strength you each individually showed in working your way through the difficult roads you travelled to find your true place is a matter of enormous pride for me as it was for your father. It forms a major part of the great crescendo of reclaimed happiness that reunited our family. I admire and love you always.

INDEX

Index